Sixth Edition

Making Sense

A Student's Guide to
Research and Writing

Engineering and the Physical Sciences

Margot Northey
Judi Jewinski
Andrew Trivett

OXFORD
UNIVERSITY PRESS

OXFORD
UNIVERSITY PRESS

Oxford University Press is a department of the University of Oxford.
It furthers the University's objective of excellence in research, scholarship,
and education by publishing worldwide. Oxford is a registered trade mark of
Oxford University Press in the UK and in certain other countries.

Published in Canada by
Oxford University Press
8 Sampson Mews, Suite 204,
Don Mills, Ontario M3C 0H5 Canada

www.oupcanada.com

First Edition published in 2005
Second Edition published in 2007
Third Edition published in 2009
Fourth Edition published in 2012
Fifth Edition published in 2016

Library and Archives Canada Cataloguing in Publication
Title: Making sense : a student's guide to research and writing : engineering and the physical
sciences / Margot Northey, Judi Jewinski, Andrew Trivett.
Other titles: Making sense, engineering and the physical sciences | Student's guide to research and
writing : engineering and the physical sciences
Names: Northey, Margot, 1940- author. | Jewinski, Judi, 1952- author. | Trivett, Andrew, author. |
Series: Making sense series.
Description: Sixth edition. | Series statement: Making sense series | Previously published under
title: Making sense: a student's guide to research and writing : engineering and the technical
sciences. | Includes index.
Identifiers: Canadiana (print) 20200195018 | Canadiana (ebook) 20200195026 | ISBN 9780199026791
(softcover) | ISBN 9780199026722 (ebook)
Subjects: LCSH: Technical writing. | LCSH: Report writing. | LCSH: English language—Rhetoric. |
LCGFT: Textbooks.
Classification: LCC T11 .N67 2020 | DDC 808.06/662—dc23

Cover image: © Monkey Business Images/Shutterstock.com
Cover design: Laurie McGregor
Interior design: Sherill Chapman

Oxford University Press is committed to our environment.
Wherever possible, our books are printed on paper which comes from
responsible sources.

Printed and bound in Canada

1 2 3 4 — 23 22 21 20

Contents

Acknowledgements

Many colleagues have helped and encouraged me through the revision of this book. I treasure the collaboration with my coauthor Judi Jewinski, who originally encouraged me to take on this project. This new edition would not have come to fruition without help from my excellent colleagues at the University of Waterloo, including Roydon Fraser, Gordon Stubley, Andrea Prior, Mehrdad Mastali, Mary Wells, James Baleshta, Sanjeev Bedi, and Michael Collins. This book was mostly written at my home institution of the University of Prince Edward Island. I am fortunate to have support from engineering colleagues Anna Demeo, Nadja Bressan, Elizabeth Osgood, Bishnu Acharya, Andy Swingler, Truong Ngo, Ali Ahmadi, and Grant McSorley. In Physics, I am lucky to have excellent colleagues in Bill Whelan and Doug Dahn. In addition, I acknowledge the support from the team at Oxford Press, especially my ever-hopeful editor Kaitlin Thornber. Thanks to them all. Their advice has been essential to making this work better and, of course, any errors are my own. I should have listened to them.

My students at Waterloo have been tremendously inspiring, as have my students at UPEI. Many of them were wonderfully generous for providing examples of their work. Over the years, it has been my role to listen to them, and to watch their struggles in their first year. These memories always came to mind while revising this book. The book is for them. I appreciate them all and I hope it will help future students.

Of course, my family has been essential. I'm blessed with three intelligent, eloquent, and opinionated children who have made a major impact in revising this book. Emma, the academic and historian, has a critical eye for what students need. Martha, the architect, has helped me remember how it feels to be a student. Simon, the engineer, is always the crucible in which ideas get tested. I especially thank him for generously providing example work.

Finally, this book is dedicated to my patient and talented wife, Lana Beth.

1   Writing and Thinking

Chapter Objectives

- Describe the differences in writing for the three main types of audiences: yourself, your colleagues, and your clients
- Identify strategies for the three stages of writing: planning, drafting, and revising
- Formulate questions to help you understand your audience
- Incorporate drafting and organizing tools into your writing process, including idea maps and outlines

Introduction

To produce clear writing, you first need to have done some clear thinking. The best way to develop clear thinking is to write your ideas down. So, we have a motivating feedback loop: the more you write, the clearer you think, and the clearer your thinking becomes, the more readable your writing will become. This book was created to help you, the student of science or engineering, to become a better, more successful, and clearer thinking professional.

In science and engineering, clarity is crucial. Clarity comes from practice writing. That means practising daily for all sorts of reasons and writing tasks. The book is organized according to how you will typically be writing. The first section, "Writing for Yourself," describes a type of writing you will keep in draft form: rough, raw, and close to the actual observations you make from your lab tests; your design team meetings; your research conferences; and your classroom lectures. This writing holds the database of ideas upon which your career will be based.

The rough writing that you do every day—in class, in lab, in meetings, and while reading—will rarely be shown to anybody other than you, the writer. The ideas and observations that you will create, however, must eventually be extracted from the raw data and communicated to your closest colleagues. Those colleagues—your professor, your lab partners, your design teammates, your business associates—are all people who have intimate knowledge of the topics and background theories that make up the foundation of your work. You will be an effective and influential professional only if you can communicate clear ideas to these people as you go about your work. These writing tasks include meeting minutes, lab reports, exams, or design progress reports. This form of writing, that done for your close colleagues, is the type of writing we cover in the second section of the book, "Writing for Colleagues."

The smallest number of writing projects that you will undertake are those which go "over the wall" to readers that are unfamiliar with your work or with your field of expertise. This sort of writing needs to be extremely clear, well-documented, and justified in fact or theory. It often has strict formatting demands, and, even though it will represent the fewest pages you will ever write, it will consume the greatest time per page. This formal type of writing is the subject of the third section of this book, "Writing for Others."

Writing is very much the process of recording ideas, revising, revising again, and then sharing those ideas with others. At every stage, there are three steps to the process of writing: planning, drafting, and refining. The planning stage calls for you to assess the various requirements of the job at hand. When the time you take researching and preparing to write is well spent, the final two stages—drafting and refining—are a lot easier.

Planning Your Writing: Initial Strategies

With every project you undertake, from notes in class or in lab to a formal research paper or final report, a good strategy is to ask yourself a few basic questions:

- What is the purpose of this?
- Who is going to read it?
- What form will it take?

Think about the Purpose

Your first reaction to an assignment may be, "Well, I'm writing for my lab instructor to fulfill a course requirement," but that's not useful. Your first writing (for example, while you stand at the lab bench watching the temperature and pressure gauges on a tank rise) will be to clearly and honestly record what you see. The reader of this writing will be you, the student. You will need to think about content and format in order to make your next tasks, recalling and analyzing the experimental results, easier.

After the in-lab experiment is complete, your purpose has changed. Now you need to show that you have understood and tested a hypothesis, which calls for a different approach from the basic lab records. In the first, your approach is straightforward with an emphasis on the accurate recording and reporting of a process. In the second, you need to provide convincing support for your analyses, interpretations, and recommendations to people who are as well-informed as you in your field of study.

Finally, you may have an opportunity to present your work at a student conference or with your professor in their research. While your original lab records and your lab report are fundamental, once again your purpose has changed. Now you will need to spend more effort in eliminating the content and graphics that may not address the core issues, and you will need to go find background literature that supports or opposes your ideas. Because this writing will be read by people outside of your own circle of experts, you will need to spend a great deal of effort to clarify, explain, and support. Each task has a new purpose that requires different elements for the piece of writing to be successful. If you don't approach thinking about your purpose before you start writing, you're more likely to miss incorporating important elements that are essential for your audience to understand your work.

Think about the Audience

Whether you are writing for yourself as a reader, or writing for multiple readers beyond your immediate circle, it is essential to "name" the reader. WHO is the reader? Try to picture WHY they will be reading your work, what they KNOW before reading it, what you want them to KNOW after reading it, and what you want them to DO after they read it. This could be a song in your head: "WHO-WHY-NO-NO-DO." For example, perhaps you are writing an internal report to your CubeSat design team:

WHO: The other engineering team members that aren't doing mechanical design. They mostly know the electronics and radiation issues, but nothing of the structural design or materials.

WHY: To get an update of our progress and to make sure they understand our problems with volume and mass for all components.

KNOW (before): They know the electrical requirements and the system design, but they know nothing of the space limitations and the righteous circle of reducing mass.

KNOW (after): They need to understand what decisions on circuit board design, interconnection, component mass, and battery size will mean for the overall package.

DO: I want them to maintain the strict space limits that we recommend and resist the temptation to add more size here and there as the design evolves.

Keep this list at hand as you write. When you edit your writing, refer to the list to ask yourself if the writing satisfies it.

Think about the Structure

Many approaches exist for the formal presentation of written material. All are variations on the basic introduction–body–conclusion structure you've seen since grade school. Beyond that simple, universal structure there is a great deal of variability. Many engineers and scientists think of things graphically, even if we don't know we are doing so. One of the key features of writing in engineering or science is our extensive use of graphics within our narratives. How often do you work with people in your classes who talk over ideas with a team but then stand up, mid-sentence, to find somewhere to draw? Very soon, the entire team is standing around a whiteboard, pens in hand, talking while drawing cartoons or bubble-diagrams of ideas. You could start your writing project the same way. Figure 1.1 shows an example of an "idea map" of a writing project.

The idea map is a great way to get started on a project. Creating one, as the example shows in Figure 1.1, goes beyond your written work because it creates a framework of ideas that helps hone the core of what you need to do.

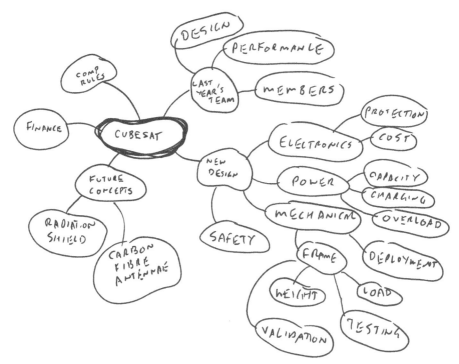

Figure 1.1 Idea map of a writing project for a team design.

The main topic starts at the centre of the map, and ideas that are offshoots of the core grow into branches from there. Through the development of the map, the most important branches become evident by virtue of the level of detail you add as you plan the project.

The example idea map shows the planning of an interim report on design for a CubeSat done by a student team. Start with the central topic at the middle of a blank sheet. In this example, the central theme was "CubeSat." From that central theme, the author of the idea map imagined all the major topics that might be interesting and related to the central topic. In this case, those were Finance, Future Concepts, Competition Rules, Last Year's Team, and New Design. It helps to be open-minded about all the sub-topics. As you carry on, you expand each sub-topic into the elements that are related and important to it. In the end, you will end up with a map like the example (Figure 1.1).

Step back and have a look at the idea map. Some of the branches (New Design) have many sub-branches. Some have no sub-branches. That gives an indication of what you may consider to be important in a report. It is okay to trim branches at this point and to expand areas that you feel need more sub-areas.

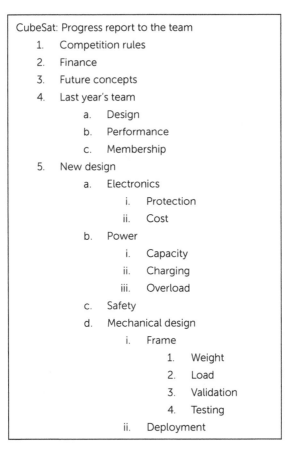

Figure 1.2 The idea map can be converted into a table of contents or outline for the work.

By trimming branches and reordering the idea map, you can generate the structure of a clear report.

Once you're happy with the idea map, it's a good time to try to convert this graphical picture into a draft list of topics or table of contents. The outline in Figure 1.2 shows a more traditional list of topics and sections that was copied directly from the idea map. As the idea map evolves, the table of contents can be refined, and then better organized for clarity and flow. In the end, this approach to planning your writing will help you refine the central ideas while also eliminating superfluous material that would detract from your more important issues. In this example, perhaps the purpose of the document would be better served by leaving out the section on finance. Perhaps the competition rules section also belongs in a different document.

Think about the Length

One of the most frequently asked questions by students when given a writing assignment is "how many pages do you want?" Students are often frustrated by the truthful answer "no longer than it needs to be." In some cases, there are standards that may apply (an abstract must be kept to fewer than 250 words, a cover letter kept to a page, and so on), but more typically there is a lot of flexibility. An excellent piece of writing may cover in four pages what another writer struggles to communicate in 15 pages. In general, a complete rough draft of a report will only be improved by editing, simplifying, and ultimately reducing the word count of the final document.

Creating a First Draft

Once you have an idea about what you want to write and what the final product should look like, the best strategy is to just write it: get all your ideas on paper. You will find specific strategies throughout this book for getting your ideas compiled in draft from your notes and other sources. Don't worry at this stage about grammar and spelling, or even if your content is in the right order—that comes later, with revising and editing. Your main goal is to get the ideas you laid out in your idea map and outline on the paper in solid paragraphs and sentences. Once you've written down all the content you both want and need to include, then you can work on editing.

Take Time for Editing

Whenever you embark on a writing project, please remember that good writing needs to be read, revised, and read again. No matter how many times you read something, you can always find better ways to say what needs saying. Give yourself time to do the editing and revising. It's genuinely part of the process. Keep the following editing questions in mind as you read your own work:

- Are your subject and your purpose clear? What is it you expect to achieve?
- Will your audience, the reader(s) of your writing, understand this?
- Have you defined the terms that are not already familiar to the readers?
- Are you accurate in all your statements, in your analysis and presentation of data, and in your documentation of sources?

- Does your material flow logically?
- Is everything truly relevant material? Or are you padding your writing to achieve a certain length?
- Are your conclusions clearly based on the evidence you have presented?
- Have you achieved an appropriate tone and level of formality throughout?
- Can you read the document out loud and hear that the wording flows naturally?

Good writers are those who take the time to revise well. The best professional writing is unobtrusive—no one notices the writing because it fits. Your reader's attention is entirely upon the topic and content, which is the ultimate goal of your writing.

Chapter Checklist

- ☐ Identify the purpose of your task and create a list of what content will need to be included for the task to be successful.
- ☐ Write a quick summary of WHO-WHY-NO-NO-DO before you start your next writing project.
- ☐ Create an idea map of your project before writing, and prune branches before converting it to a project outline.
- ☐ Draft, revise, and repeat as many times as you are able. Writing is like making bread: the more you knead it, the better it will be.

Part I
Writing for Yourself

2 Keeping Notes for Yourself

Chapter Objectives

- Describe the role of good note-taking for personal writing
- Identify strategies for taking effective notes in three academic tasks: lecture notes, lab notes, and research notes
- Compare three different note-taking formats
- Determine ways to evaluate sources when doing literature research

Introduction

One of the most daunting challenges in writing, whether for work or pleasure, is the blank page. You may have already found that sitting at your desk staring at a white sheet of paper or a blank computer screen is a sure-fire way to encourage you to put off writing. The solution is simple: always have something to start with!

If you learn to keep clear, detailed, and habitual notes as your work progresses, you will never find yourself trying to start a lab report or project proposal from a blank sheet. You can always look back in your own notes for inspiration. Carefully cross-referenced files of articles, references, data, ideas (inspired or not!), and sketches provide a record that builds throughout each stage of your work for the rest of your career. If you are working alone on a project, or even on practice problems, stop occasionally to jot down a paragraph about what you are doing, what things have been difficult, and what things you have done to overcome problems. Your personal notes, with every entry dated, help you trace the chronology of your work and, when corroborated by an independent third party, even serve as proof of authenticity in case of legal disputes. Ultimately, your notes and files establish a foundation for everything you write. It's important, therefore, that they be thorough and complete.

This chapter is entirely about writing to record things for yourself. You'll learn strategies for note-taking, as well as best practices for the three main types of notes you will be taking during your academic career: lecture notes, lab notes, and research notes. The only reader of your notes will be you—a day, a month, or even a year later. Thus, the basic style and approach to your notes can be very individual. However, if the notes are going to make sense in the future, they must have a few essential features.

What to Include in Your Notes

The key element in note-taking is the need for accuracy and completeness of detail. If we simply proceed to collect data and take notes without knowing what kind of information we are looking for, the amount of content could become very unwieldy and confusing. Your notes will be populated with all kinds of irrelevant trivia. What kind of information should you be collecting? Consider the 5W's of old-fashioned newspaper reporting: Who, What, When, Where, and Why. These are the same elements you should keep in mind when you're taking notes.

WHO: Write down each of the names of the people with you, and some indication of their roles. For instance, if the event was a project meeting, you might want to record some cues to the work each attendee promised to do and what work they had completed.

WHAT: What happened? Record data, sketch physical configurations, draw graphs of concepts presented, cite references that you found, and summarize main points. This will probably be the bulk of your notes, and it will most likely contain the most concrete ideas and information. Make sure that you write it down in a format that allows you to understand it later. If you sketch a graph that was part of a topic explanation, remember to include labels. If you are measuring an object or space, make sure that you include units and dimensions clearly.

WHEN: Record the date that you are writing this material down. If you are taking notes throughout the day on different topics, projects, or courses, then you should include the time as well as date.

WHERE: Make sure that you note, in detail, where this activity was taking place. Just simply reading back to yourself the location where an event occurred weeks later will help you to recall details about what happened, so give yourself this spatial memory aid.

WHY: Perhaps the most crucial part of your notes is that which most students never do. Take a few moments late in the day, or after the activity is complete, and jot down your thoughts about the activity or information.

Why did you do this? Why was it important? Why did the experiment succeed? Why did it fail? Why did the professor cover this topic in class? Even if you aren't sure why something happened, sitting to think about it for a few minutes will help you develop those answers, and will help you the next time this project or activity comes up.

Note Formatting

You will be the reader of the notes that you collect. Whatever format you choose needs to be something that makes sense to your way of thinking, and that will, once the details of the moment have faded, still be perfectly clear to you. Don't bother using a format for your notes that someone else has prescribed for you (unless required). Rather, try a few formats and see what works best. While there are many different approaches, three common formats to consider include idea maps (Figure 2.1), the Cornell method (Figure 2.2), and jot notes (Figure 2.3).

Figure 2.1 An example of an idea map.

In the centre is the purpose of the task (a class lecture) and then main ideas and sub-points branch out from the centre. This shows the way ideas connect to one another.

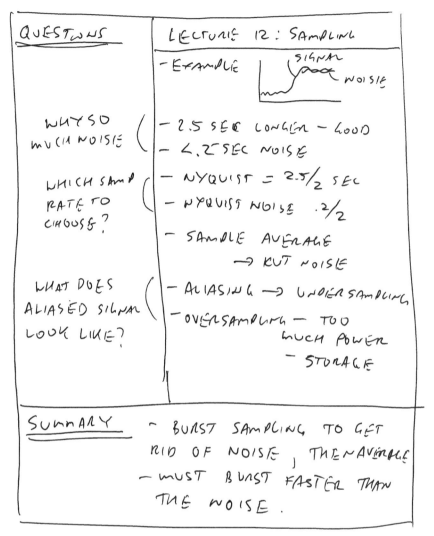

Figure 2.2 An example of note-taking using the Cornell method.

A left-hand column (cue column) is created that has the main ideas and key questions (written after notes are complete) while the right-hand column (note-taking column) includes key ideas and important information. At the bottom is a summary of the notes in your own words.

The format for your notes will depend upon the types of notes that you are taking. Your format for lecture notes will be very different from the format you prefer for lab notes or research notes. In all cases, however, you should think about the content in light of the 5W's. We will review each of the three main types of academic notes in the remainder of the chapter.

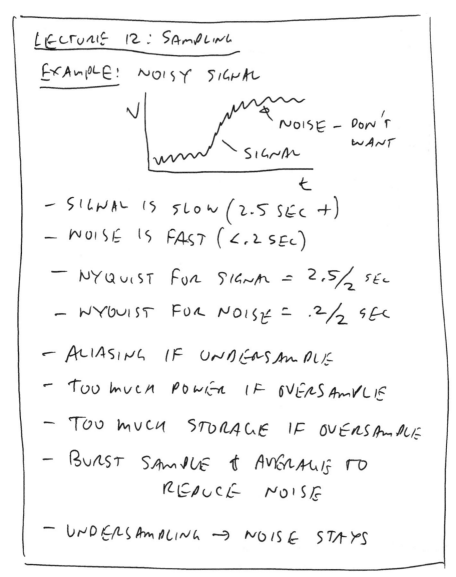

Figure 2.3 An example of jot notes.

Key points are listed down the page (usually in the chronology they were explained). This method is useful in gathering information quickly.

Lecture Notes

When you attend a presentation, meeting, or workshop, you don't get to set the pace and direction of the discussion. In a lecture, the professor has a set amount of content to communicate to the class and time is of the essence for you to capture the important points covered. You need to learn how to quickly and accurately capture the items that are worth retaining. Most commonly, people use jot notes or idea map sketches to take lecture notes, but using any of the formats listed above will be useful. It all depends on the way you learn and retain information.

Whatever your favourite note-taking format, take advantage of the following time-honoured techniques for making the most of your classes:

- For each course you take, keep a binder for handouts and create an electronic folder on your laptop or tablet to include both your own notes and copies of slides and supplemental readings. If a learning management system is attached to your course, organize your own notes to be consistent with its contents and sort your notes under each topic.
- Be prepared for class. Note-taking is much easier if you know beforehand what the topics of discussion will be. Keep track of the course outline so that you know what content to expect from class to class. Do assigned problems or readings before class and review previous notes, too.
- Define your own acronyms or short forms for common terms or topics.
- If you have software that allows you to record the lecture while you take notes, you'll soon appreciate being able to replay the sections that you want to work on. Note that you should ask your professor before recording a lecture because the content is their intellectual property.
- Highlight important points or mark them with an asterisk. Put a question mark next to points to reconsider and clarify after class—either with classmates or with the course instructor.
- Record all key terms, including names, numbers, and nomenclature. Write out all definitions.
- If you take pictures or otherwise make copies of diagrams, sketches, charts, and graphs, remember to move the saved images into a place where they are organized according to course topic. Rename image files to make them easy to find again.
- Keep a master calendar to track all assignments and due dates.
- Take time, as soon as you can after class, to review and refine your notes. Be sure to set down questions that might show up on an exam. This is the "Why" part of your note-taking. Try to explain why this

topic was covered, or why this particular lecture or example problem was given by the professor in the context of the course.

- If you have recorded references to external material (the textbook, websites, course notes, etc.), read these and add summaries as necessary.

Sharing Class Notes

You will naturally develop close relationships with your classmates. Whether or not you establish study groups for each class, make sure you find reliable colleagues in case one of you must miss a class. However, don't abuse a friend's willingness to share notes. If you must borrow notes, don't just copy them. Invest the time to work through them as if you had been to class.

In most universities and colleges, the course content comprises intellectual property that belongs to the institution, or, if the course is entirely from a published textbook, that belongs to the book publisher. In some cases your professor will add their own unique knowledge that comes from experience and research. Perhaps they don't use a textbook and they are delivering content entirely curated from other scientists' research. If this is the case, your professors will supply the reference citations for the original work in order to acknowledge its owner. The owners do not give up ownership of that material by speaking it in class or copying it on the course management site. This means that your notes are primarily a record of intellectual property owned by somebody else, not your own. Course notes are for you and for you alone.

Lab and Project Notes

When you take notes in class, you must adjust to the pace of your instructor. In the lab, however, you control both the process and the timing. This is true whether you engage in a set scientific experiment lab or a design project lab activity. You determine how much time you need to keep accurate and complete records. All the same principles apply in lab as they did in class: use whatever form or structure you are comfortable with. Your goal is to clearly capture everything that happened in lab so that you can recall it later.

Taking a few extra minutes before the lab to format your notes, make tables for data, draw sketches of apparatus, or record manufacturers' part numbers will help save you time and improve the quality of your observations. Taking the time during lab to ensure that you have captured everything important will save you aggravation when it comes time to write your lab report. Your lab experience will be the best if you come to lab fully prepared.

It is a very good practice to do the following:

- Complete all required pre-lab exercises so that you are well prepared. Review and record the context and the methodology and look up the operator's manuals for any apparatus to be used for the experiment. If you can, bookmark this material so that you can find it quickly once you are working in the lab.
- If necessary, prepare data grids, spreadsheets, or other templates to be filled in during the experiment. Whatever you can do to organize the recording of data during the lab will make the job of analyzing it easier.
- Be systematic and thorough in recording calculations and equations. Be sure to identify all terms, prepare careful sketches, label graphs, and include dimensions and units.
- Supplement your notes with video clips and photos taken throughout the experiment.
- Write down any discrepancies you observed from what was expected and note items that you would like to ask for help with understanding.
- After the lab, but before writing the report, arrange to speak to the professor or lab assistant to ask for clarification of any issues that came up during the experiment.

Finally, there is no universal format for lab records or report formats. You should follow the instructions and policy of your lab instructor or professor when preparing work that will be submitted for evaluation.

Research Notes

In addition to team projects, lab work, and course notes, your work in engineering and science will certainly lead you to researching and reading academic publications. The recording of your path through scientific literature is important. It can either be done in a way that will enable you to quickly reference good material, or it can be done in a way that will make you retrace your steps to find the perfect citation that you saw three months ago. Imagine discussing a detailed issue about thermodynamics of compressible flow with your colleagues. To add to the discussion by recalling a paper read last year on compressible flow and the design of hypersonic wings will not only impress your friends, but it will help you to design good fact-based technology. Doing good literature research, and recording it for future access, is essential.

Engineers and scientists aren't typically paid to build things and measure things. Instead, most of us are paid to communicate what we have designed or measured so others can build. The place where we communicate our work is not the newspaper or Internet chatrooms; it is in professional reports, peer-reviewed scientific papers, and government publications. These will be the main sources of learning for you while at school and beyond. Your university library holds many of these publications in physical form and many more in electronic databases. Becoming familiar with the resources, and all the ways to access them, is essential to your career. The six steps described below will help you navigate the research literature.

Step 1: Explore Internet Resources

All students are comfortable with a quick Google search. Doing so should be considered a start of your research, not the entirety. It is easy to access the huge volume of information available on the Internet from billions of different websites, but that material is not well catalogued, fact-checked, or organized. In fact, you would need to already be an experienced engineer or scientist to truly know what is valuable and what is not. As a student, you need to approach the world of online content very cautiously and with a good dose of skepticism.

You can make very effective use of online searches as a novice in some topic areas by realizing that this is your starting point. Using the online content will help you gain access to more serious sources. Suppose that you are looking to find out about "compressible flow." By googling the term "compressible flow," you will come up with general definitions from sites like Wikipedia and the Engineering toolbox. You may find some scientific papers referenced from Google Scholar, and you may find hundreds of items that have the words "compressible" or "flow" but used in unexpected contexts.

Step 2: Define Important Terms

Look through the most relevant search results and become familiar with the terms that surround those that interest you. Continuing the example of "compressible flow" above, you might find words like "adiabatic," "hypersonic,"

"Mach number," "shock wave," or "thermodynamic" close to the links that seem to be on-topic.

Once you have found a good collection of terms that are related to your original topic, search for the definitions of these extra words. You could search "Definition: shock wave" and you will find references to help clarify the meaning. You will also see the context in which this phrase is used. It is sometimes used as "shock wave" or "shockwave," for instance. It is related to supersonic, elastic media, and so on.

Write down in your notes the words that you find and the definitions that seem most relevant to you, as well as the common variants. It is also helpful to jot down those terms that frequently confuse or negate the correct use of the word in your application. For example, perhaps you found some shock wave citations that were about a "shocking wave seen on the beach." You might note to avoid items where "beach" or "surf" are also used. These keywords begin to help you understand the language and connections of the topic you are researching. The first time you use this approach, you will be surprised to find how much clarity this simple step brings to your understanding of a topic. The best part is that these words now become the keys to finding genuine credible scientific sources of information.

Step 3: Explore Library Resources

Online catalogues list all the holdings at your library, including books, videos, archived materials, and print journals. These search engines are not as intuitive as Google. A search by subject or keyword will give you a list of relevant sources, but they don't anticipate your intent in the same way that the online search engines will. The beauty of this is that these search tools will give you back materials that respond literally to what you asked, and only what you asked. If you want to know about shock waves, for example, these search tools will give you everything where the words "shock" and "wave" are found close together in certain places in the documents.

Databases simplify your search for information because they make millions of journal articles and electronic resources available in a single place. Libraries subscribe to online services like e-books, e-journals, e-data, and electronic encyclopedias. A single search gives you access to original research papers and reports written by the scientists and engineers who stood in the lab and collected the data.

To conduct a database search, simply go to your library website and follow the link to resources for research. You can then search by keyword, subject, author, or title. There are options for narrowing the search if you prefer; for example, by restricting it to specific databases or specific journals. Your search results will be given in the form of a list of articles on your subject, including the title, author, publication information, and an abstract. You will likely be given the option of downloading a file of the full text of the article, which allows you to read the material online as well as print, save, or e-mail it.

Ultimately, the articles and content that you will find have very different stories than the websites and discussion forums you have seen online. Even though you have found this content through a computer interface, this material is not from "the web." You are looking at an electronic form of a physical publication, whether it is an academic journal, a newspaper, a government report, or a data transcript.

Step 4: Evaluate Sources

It is always up to you to sift through the sources of information and decide which is credible and which is not. It is crucial to distinguish between academic websites, which are peer reviewed and tend to be reliable sources of information, and websites or discussion forums which do not have editorial boards and publish material that has not undergone any review process. Anyone can upload material to the Internet or answer a question on Quora, regardless of his or her credentials (or lack thereof). The best published books or academic journals, on the other hand, go through a rigorous editing and review process. Before trusting any material, make sure that the author or publisher has the necessary authority to lend credibility to the work.

Here are some tips for evaluating material you find, regardless of its source:

- Look for a statement identifying the author's qualifications and contact information. Academic articles always include contact information for the authors, including their institution affiliation. Many websites are affiliated with an educational or professional organization, and sites hosted by an individual should provide you with specifics about that person's qualifications. It's often possible to identify domain and IP owner information behind any website by performing a search at www.who.is.
- If the material is privately published on a website, check the URL. Pay special attention to the domain name, which may help you assess the

objectivity of the site. Be aware of the differences between and the motivation of sales-oriented enterprises (ending in *.com* in North America and *co.uk* in the UK, also *.biz* and *.net*) and not-for-profit or public-service organizations (ending in *.org*). Any one of them may still provide reliable information and valuable links to other sources, but you want to be sure that the source is credible.

- Genuine academic websites rarely have advertisements, except for their own services and programs.
- Recognize that not all commercial websites have obvious domain names. Because every country has its own two letter abbreviation (for example, *.ca* is for Canada, *.de* is for Germany, and *.mx* is for Mexico), you may link to information sponsored by businesses anywhere in the world. Note also the domain names for government sites (*gc.ca* in Canada and *.gov* in the United States) and academic institutions (*.edu* in the United States). Just because the website is that of a college or university doesn't guarantee the quality of the material you find. When in doubt, ask an instructor or your school librarian. Your increasing good judgment and experience will help you decide whether material on any site is trustworthy.
- Check the publication date. There should be a clear indication of the date when the material was written, the date when it was published, and the date when it was last revised. Be skeptical if the date is not recent or is missing altogether. There should be a contact e-mail address for questions. If not, be suspicious. If there are links to other sites, confirm that they work. A site with broken links is not current. Check thoroughly before basing research on information that is either outdated or simply wrong.
- Evaluate the accuracy of the information by checking facts and figures with other sources. Data published on the website should be documented in citations or a bibliography, and research methods should be explained. If there are obvious errors, do not trust the source.
- Take special care with *wiki* sites, where information is revised frequently and anyone can contribute or edit. The most popular of these, by far, is Wikipedia (wikipedia.org), which has versions in all the major world languages. Its professional look can be deceptive, and errors are always being discovered, corrected, and re-corrected. Still, there's no denying the instant convenience of Wikipedia's extensive discussions. Before you include them, however, it makes sense to check their acceptability

with your instructor. Remember that the references in Wikipedia are simply a good starting point for expanded research.

- Be wary of blogs and discussion forums. There are millions—from personal online diaries to corporate and organizational blogs, like those on college or university websites that give visitors a glimpse of student life. There is value in the networking possibilities of such social sites as Twitter, Facebook, and LinkedIn, but often there is just a lot of noise, and even the most respected expert's comments get drowned out.

Step 5: Systemize Your Research

More important, perhaps, than finding research material is taking notes from it that are comprehensive, dependable, and easy to use. One simple method would be to use a table format with two columns. Reserve the left-hand column for a citation of the source material so that you can easily find it again or turn it into a proper academic citation. On the right-hand side, jot down your thoughts, questions, and observations that occurred to you while you looked through the citation. Jot down how useful you thought it was, how reliable, what you might want to use it for, and what pages and points were especially helpful. This right-hand column is the note to yourself that will help guide you to find the best evidence and support material for your work in the future. Try to make these notes to yourself as valuable as possible.

The following are some guidelines for taking good notes while you review the results of your literature research:

- For every source, start with an entry that includes all bibliographical details eventually required for your reference list:
  - the name of the author(s)
  - the full title of the source
  - the place and date of publication
  - the journal volume and issue numbers
  - the relevant page numbers
- Record the DOI (digital object identifier) for electronic journals, the ISBN number if it is a print book or journal, or the complete URL for a website, and the date the website was last updated. You will want this accurate information so you can find the reference again.

If you are studying at a college or university, your library likely includes a free link to RefWorks, a time-saving web-based tool for managing citations and bibliographies. You can easily establish a personal account (or a joint account if you are working on a group project) and create your own database of bibliographic information for a project, importing citations and references from electronic sources anywhere. RefWorks is not the only web-based citation manager available (others include Bibus, EndNote, and Zotero), but it's the one to which most Canadian schools subscribe. It does not replace the value of writing the reference citation by hand, and it certainly does not automate your personal jot notes on each source that you have read. Be sure to check with your instructor about their preferred citation style (for example: IEEE, Chicago, or APA). Knowing the basic information needed for your instructor's preferred style will ensure you take down the right information when doing research. (See Appendix A, Documentation, for styles.)

Step 6: Seek Expert Help

If you are having trouble finding just what you want, don't hesitate to ask for help from a librarian. These professionals can give you guidance or walk you through a search. They will almost always turn up materials that you couldn't find on your own. Most college and university libraries offer information services with names like *Ask a Librarian*. If you take advantage of such help while preparing a major project, don't forget to thank your librarian in your acknowledgements.

Chapter Checklist

- [ ] For one week, record everything that goes on in your academic life. At the end of the week, go over your notes to see how the week has progressed and what you have learned.
- [ ] Practise using each of the three different note-taking strategies for a week. Evaluate each method to decide which works best for you or create your own hybrid approach.
- [ ] Before your next class or lab, create a set of pages that anticipate the material you will want to record in the activity or class.
- [ ] Create an account with the web-based citation manager provided by your school (RefWorks or other) to organize all your sources for projects.

3 Graphics in Your Notes

Chapter Objectives

- Apply strategies to find the right level of detail to include in personal notes
- Explain the value of including graphics and text in notes
- Identify essential elements to include when creating physical and schematic sketches
- Differentiate between three types of graphics: physical sketches, drawings, and photographs

Introduction

Among the writing skills invaluable to an engineer is the ability to distill something to its essence—to reduce something quite complicated to a few lines, either on a sketch or in a document. Whether you are writing a business plan or taking data for an experiment, your ability to show your observations or concepts in a very compact form helps you bring people into your vision and, ultimately, to achieve your goals. In order to explain complex things effectively to others, concise graphics are tremendously effective.

In this chapter, we will show an example for distilling instructions and information into both written notes and graphic notes. In engineering and science, the graphical component of note taking is extremely useful, and this chapter will emphasize graphics. We show where sketches and schematics are helpful tools in capturing the essence of information. These skills will not only help you to accomplish tasks and create robust notes, they will also come in handy when you are creating more complex graphics for your formal reports and papers.

Summarizing Instructions

Knowing what you need to record is a skill that takes years to develop. Consider the following scenario involving two co-op students, Josie and Miles, arriving at their placements:

> We got to the hybrid team bay at 10:17 this morning. Neil and Sam were there already working on the brake cylinders, while Jake was also there checking the dimensions for the battery box. Rishi came in to provide instructions for the task he wanted us to work on that day. He led us over to the sanding bay where the mold was on a stand for the battery box. He told us that we were supposed to finish sanding the mold, then we could wax it and proceed with a layup of the carbon fiber on the mold. As he explained, he sketched some notes in a lab book. He showed us where the sandpaper was, and then gave us these instructions: "The best way to sand the mold is by 'going through the numbers' ... that's the grits. Start with 80-grit, then 120, then 180, then 220. Each time wipe down the mold with IPA, and use a clean shop towel. They are stored over on the shelves by the corner. After you've finished with one grit, which will get rid of the coarse dust, you can then move to the finer level. It should be about 20 minutes per grit if you work hard. By the time you are done, you won't see any swirls of the previous grit. You can check each grit level by ensuring you sand in only one general direction, 90 degrees from the previous grit. When you are done, you should vacuum up the shop, then blow the mold all over with compressed air to really get rid of the dust. Finish off by wiping it down with IPA. When you are done that, then you can start waxing it. If you have any questions, just text me, my number is on the wall by the door."

Josie used only the 5W's and took these notes:

Who: Neil, Sam, working on brakes, Jake checking battery dimensions; Rishi providing instructions

What: Sand mold, then wax, then layup carbon fiber

When: Arrived 10:17

Where: the hybrid team bay

Why: My job from Rishi: sand and wax battery box mold

Miles took these notes:

Sand battery box starting at 80-grit, then 120, 180, and 220. Should be 20 min per grit. Go in one direction only per grit, alternate directions, 90 degrees different

Wipe down mold between sanding grits with IPA (IsoPropyl Alcohol) using clean shop towels (shelves in corner)

Check for swirls of coarser grit before moving to next step

Vacuum shop before finished

Blow down mold with compressed air

Wipe down with clean towel and IPA after shop is clean

Start waxing

Questions: text Rishi . . . number on wall by door.

Josie, despite using the 5W's, erred on the side of too little detail. From her notes, how would she know to work through the grits or to alternate directions at 90-degree angles between grit levels? Josie might have started with 1,000 grit paper, making her task more challenging and wasting everyone's time. While knowing precisely what time the students arrived to work and who was there at the time might be useful in some cases, for example if the brakes failed and someone wanted to know who did the work, or if tools went missing from the bay and people wondered who was present, but these cases are the extreme. A more productive use of her notes would have been to provide more detail in the "What" section. The 5W's are an excellent starting point when thinking about taking notes, but they should always be treated as a starting point that may require more detail down the road.

Miles on the other hand focused on taking down information related to the task. He wrote down each of the steps, ensuring that he'd be able to work through the job and refer back to his notes if needed. By focusing on the tasks, he would also be in a better position to ask questions if he was confused by a step or if he felt something was missing. His notes were also incomplete in some of the basic details that were captured by using the 5W's. More useful notes would have combined both Josie and Miles' records.

The most common mistakes in taking notes are errors of extremes:

1. Too little detail. In the example, Josie did not include enough detail to do the task effectively. By providing so little detail, she made it hard to follow the instructions and to know what was important, and ultimately made the task harder to complete properly.
2. Too much detail of superfluous things. In some cases, too much detail detracts from the important issues, but the danger in including too much is less devastating than the danger of not writing enough.

Over time, note-taking skills become second nature, and with practice you will learn the right level of detail to include, and you will hone your ability to ignore the superfluous. When you think about what details need to be included in recording events, think about how you would instruct another person to copy what happened. Some detail can be left out, but only those which you are sure are really not relevant. Start with the 5W's, but then use careful judgment to consider how much you need to dig into each "W."

Integrating Words and Graphics in your Notes

In the example above, Rishi had been sketching his thoughts while giving his instructions to the students, creating something like Figure 3.1. As he sketched the instructions, the sketching helped to remind him of several important

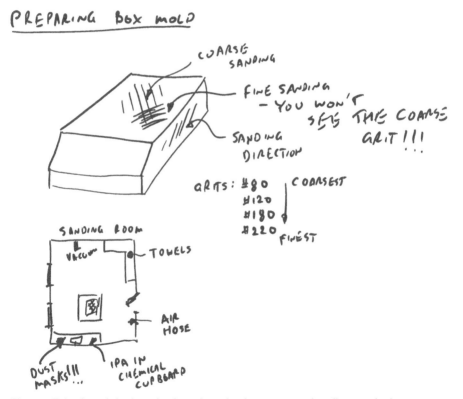

Figure 3.1 A quick sketch showing the important details needed to complete the example task of sanding a battery box mold.

The example shows the sort of quick hand-drawn sketch that you might do on a dusty shop table in conversation.

points: details such as where the shop towels are stored, where the vacuum is located, and how to use the compressed air. On sketching the layout of the room, it also occurred to him that he didn't remind the students to use a dust mask. In the sketch, he indicated the cupboard in the shop where the masks are stored and reminded them that their use is mandatory.

Rishi gave a simple graphical sketch to show what he meant by sanding in directions that were 90 degrees compared to the previous grit. Combined

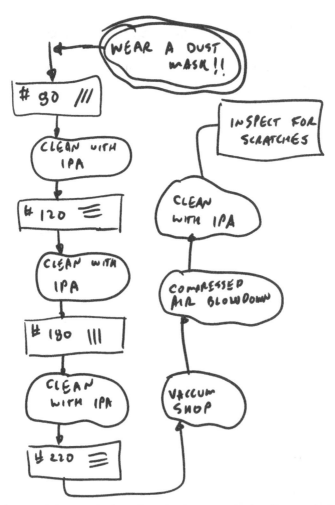

Figure 3.2 A quick sketch showing the important details needed to complete the example task of sanding a battery box mold.

The example shows the sort of quick hand-drawn sketch that you might do on a dusty shop table in conversation.

with the verbal instructions, the graphical notes made the task much easier to complete properly and even helped to remind about an essential safety policy.

The sketch shows some helpful physical configuration, but it wasn't a very clear set of task instructions. Think about what questions might come up as Josie and Miles start the task. The faces on top and side of the mold clearly are meant to be sanded because there are sanding marks sketched in the figure. Were the front and angled face also meant to be sanded? There were no marks sketched there. With the explanation and the sketch proceeding simultaneously, the listener might have asked questions and helped to clarify issues that would not have come up otherwise.

Before he was finished giving the instructions, Rishi summarized the task using the sketch in Figure 3.2 to clarify what steps were required. This sketch is a very different type than Figure 3.1. The new sketch shows the process of sanding and prepping, not the physical appearance of either the workshop or the battery box. After the instructor leaves, it will serve as a good reminder for the tasks. The first sketch is fundamentally a physical, or geometrical, representation of the parts. Each of the items looks somewhat similar to the shape and orientation of the physical object. The second sketch is an example of a process sketch or "schematic." The remainder of this chapter will focus on creating physical sketches and schematic sketches.

Physical Sketches

Sometimes the physical dimensions and spatial relationships are of primary importance when recording lab observations, design concepts, or physical examples. There are some essential ways to create useful sketches, and there are some that merely add to your confusion. This is not a book on technical drawing. There are a wide range of resources to help with drafting and drawing. This section aims to address WHAT to sketch.

The two terms "sketch" and "draw" are often used interchangeably. In this book, the words "draw" or "drawing" are used to describe a formal technical drawing. These would be the classic "blueprint" or shop-drawings that might accompany an order to a machine shop for parts to be manufactured. A simple example of a technical drawing is given in Figure 3.3. Making technical drawings is a skill that takes years to develop, and skilled draftspeople deserve a great deal of respect as accurate and conscientious detailers of the world.

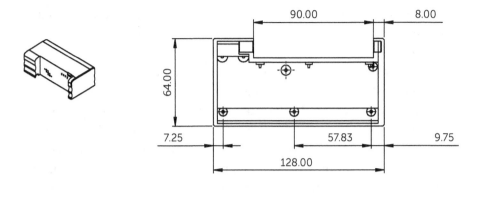

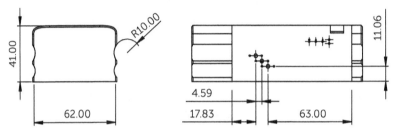

Figure 3.3 This is a small example of a technical drawing.

For a drawing, we expect to see a scale and dimensions. Multi-view drawings are needed for complex objects. As opposed to sketches, a technical drawing is not always helpful in explaining the function of a device.

What we describe as a "sketch" is something different altogether. Sketching is more informal. Sketching helps quickly and succinctly capture the data we need for scientific and technical record-keeping. It is not a work of art, although some excellent design or technical sketches are indeed artistic and beautiful to observe. The purpose of a sketch is not to show beauty; it is for information and understanding. Whether hand-sketched or computer-sketched, the characteristics are the same. The resulting graphic need not be completely detailed, and it need not follow a rigid drawing format. It should, however, contain certain essential elements of information.

1. **Measurement units.** As a physical record, the units must be explicitly stated. This can be done in a note or caption that makes clear the standard used, or it can be done specific to every dimension noted.
2. **Scale.** The scale of a sketch is not typically important. A good sketch will, however, show clear and correct relationship between the sizes of different elements in the graphic. For instance, a sketch of the layout

of a lab setup would be misleading if one flask is shown much larger on the sketch than another flask that was intended to be the same volume. Thus, overall scale is not important, but maintaining proportional **relative scale** is essential.

3. **Detail.** A sketch can eliminate unnecessary details so as not to confuse the information. Unlike artistic works, the information conveyed is the priority.

4. **Style, shading, and colour.** Elements of style all must be focused on improving the communication. If a component is shaded, then it must be for a reason, rather than just style.

5. **Annotation.** Whatever text that is needed can be neatly written on the sketch, so long as it does not obscure or confuse the sketch's clarity.

6. **Speed.** The sketches done by scientists and engineers as part of our work are meant to help our memory and understanding, and to be a record of an event or object. To be useful, they must, with practice, be completed quickly in less than ideal settings.

The physical sketch is truly a powerful tool for a scientist or an engineer. Quickly creating a sketch of an existing artefact not only helps to record the details of the item, but it also helps the sketcher to pay attention to the details, how parts fit together, which parts are essential, and subtle differences in components, dimensions, textures, and any other detail. Imagining a new design, and then translating that to a sketch of the physical item is one of the most effective methods for testing concepts because it forces the designer to build the item in their head, and make it work on the page. Parts that don't fit, or would be misaligned, show up quickly, as do components not yet imagined that will be required for a working device.

Whether in the form of a CAD rendering, or a 2D line drawing, sketches are typically far superior to photographs for communicating your ideas. A sketch allows you to highlight the important aspects and eliminate any distracting details. Figure 3.4 shows a sketch used in a simple statics problem with three masses and three pulleys. The simple graphic, while merely a cartoon, conveys sufficient information to grasp the test problem that might have been asked. The basic dimensions and labels would be related to the test question. A more elaborate image, or a photograph of a real apparatus, might have been far too complicated or too full of extraneous details to suit a test question such as this.

In another example, a three-axis robot manipulator is shown moving a water glass in Figure 3.5. The analysis of dynamics for this device can be

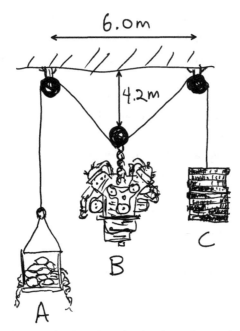

Figure 3.4 A simple sketch showing the basics of a statics problem.

In the written problem, we would expect to see the masses of A, B, or C to be defined and something about the cables attaching them.

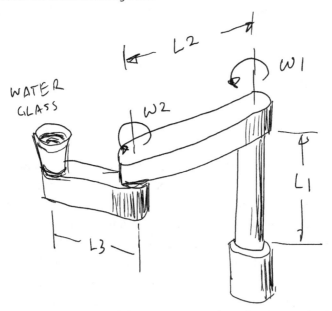

Figure 3.5 A simple sketch of the geometry of a robotic manipulator moving a water glass.

This sketch might be used to help define coordinate systems for doing the dynamics and control model for the robot.

done using only the dimensional variables shown in the figure. More detail, such as a photograph or dimensioned drawing of the robot might not increase the clarity.

In recording the steps of a design, or the stages of a scientific research project, simple sketches are invaluable. They are fast to create, can provide nearly an unlimited amount of information, and can be made to be exceptionally clear. More than any other documentation tool, your ability to sketch in science will help your work. It's a habit that is worth developing through practice.

Photographs

It is tempting to include photographs in your notes because "a picture is worth a thousand words." However, the detail in a photograph may obscure labels or important details, unless it is a remarkably well-framed photo. Use photographs to provide a visual record at defined points of time (e.g., photographs of a project site during its development) but use sketches instead to highlight layouts, structures, or models.

If you must include photographs in your log of your work or research, black and white is best, especially if the image is to be scanned or photocopied. If you must use colour, label the colours on the diagram to avoid any confusion. In making choices about illustrating your work, always make drawings or diagrams as clean and simple as possible. In the interests of maintaining your notes and the ability to return to the source material later, document the sources of all visuals unless you've created them yourself.

CAD Images: Renderings versus Line Drawings

Computer Aided Design (CAD) renderings are similar in a report to drawings. While it is fun to create these virtual images, they are expensive in time and resources to produce and can obscure the image. In Figure 3.6, a handheld sensor device is shown. The image was produced as a render from a CAD assembly file.

Details like colour, material finish, and texture are evident in Figure 3.6, but compare this with the line drawing of the same device shown in Figure 3.7. The line drawing is more appropriate if we were to try to explain the parts of the device or its features. Many students prefer to use the rendered images in reports, particularly design projects. The renders, if well done, make it appear that the device exists. This can be misleading by projecting that a design project is further along than reality. Rendered images have their place, but for

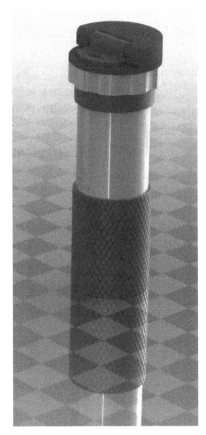

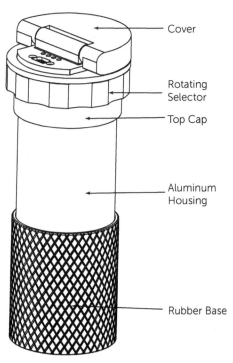

Cover

Rotating Selector

Top Cap

Aluminum Housing

Rubber Base

Figure 3.6 A rendered photograph-quality CAD model.

The image is extremely hardware-intensive to produce and space-intensive to store for the information contained.

Figure 3.7 A line drawing from CAD software for the same device shown in Figure 3.6.

This line drawing is more effective at communicating design details and is much faster to create.

most of your records of design and research, a good sketch or line drawing is much more useful.

Schematics

In many applications in science and engineering, the clear, careful development of a schematic helps to make concepts clear and aids your understanding of the world. Whether you are recording the setup of a lab experiment or showing a concept for the operation of a medical device, good hand-drawn schematics in your own logbook or notes will help a great deal. The act of creating the schematic will not only help you to capture those relationships between components or states that you imagined initially, but also will help you to consider alternative ones.

In contrast to a physical sketch which shows the geometry of an object, a schematic sketch shows relationships between tasks or concepts. Figure 3.2 shows this sort of schematic instruction. In it, the elements do not resemble the physical world, but it does a better job of capturing the relationships between activities or processes. The same set of instructions is represented by a flow of arrows from one task to another. It is evident that we start by putting on a dust mask, then proceed through the different sanding grits. The same sketch could have been oriented horizontally, diagonally, or anything else. The important information is the relationship between the tasks.

The schematic sketch of sanding the mold in Figure 3.2 helps to clarify the relationships between steps in the process, showing what steps must occur in what order. It physically looks nothing like the room or the object being sanded; however, it can capture important aspects of a task or design much more clearly. In this case, the requirement for safety ("wear a dust mask") is not just a final thing to remember. Instead, it is a key step before starting the tasks.

Making Schematic Sketches

An essential concept in understanding schematics and process sketches is something we will refer to as "state." This is a concept akin to the snapshot of a device under a specific set of conditions. In the chemical or the thermodynamic sense, a "state" of a system of material is represented by the set of properties that describe the matter under specific independent conditions. An ideal gas is ideal only under a specific set of pressure and temperature conditions. Its "state" can be fully defined in all its properties by those two properties. More generally, if we look at a device, its state is the result of the history it has undergone and the various independent conditions that have determined its behaviour or action. A cup of coffee could be described as being in either of the two states shown below. That state might be full, fresh, hot, and ready to be consumed. Likewise, another state might be empty. Which state we find depends upon the processes it has undergone.

In order to develop a process sketch or schematic, you must first define the important states of the system you are describing. Then you can look at the processes it undergoes to change from one state to another. Figure 3.8 illustrates two states of a coffee cup, one full and one empty. This sketch shows no hint of how the cup was filled or how it was emptied. The schematic representation shows the states, and it shows how they relate to each other through processes connecting the states. In the example, the full cup of "State 1" must be followed by the user drinking the coffee for the cup to be empty. It must be refilled, and sugar added in order to reach "State 1" again. Figure 3.9 shows a process schematic of the cup and its various states.

In sketching the schematic of Figure 3.9, you might realize that there are other process pathways. There is an initialization process shown starting from the empty state. Likewise, the figure could be expanded to show alternative paths to go from a full cup to an empty one. The cup could be spilled. The cup could be poured into a drain. The cup could be shared with a friend. Only a schematic representation sketching the processes between the states helps capture these options.

Figure 3.8 This sketch shows a cup in different states.

They are identical except that one state is full and the other state is empty.

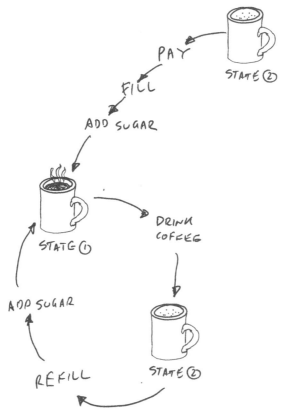

Figure 3.9 The example process schematic shows states of a coffee cup and how they can be transformed from one state to another via the processes.

In most complex tasks or designs, both physical and schematic sketches are required to explain work. Figure 3.10 shows the electrical schematic for a simple sensor device created for a first-year engineering course. The schematic indicates which pins are connected to other devices and shows the interconnections. The discrete components shown in the schematic do not resemble the devices they represent, but it is possible from the figure to know how each is interconnected. In contrast, the same electronics design was ported to a circuit board layout shown in Figure 3.11. The circuit board layout is precisely the geometry that was manufactured. It is certainly possible to trace connections on the circuit board layout to find the interconnections, but the physical routing of the wires is much more difficult to follow than the schematic. In this example, the schematic does a better job of clearly indicating the interrelationships, while the circuit board layout shows the physical shape, size, and location of the components.

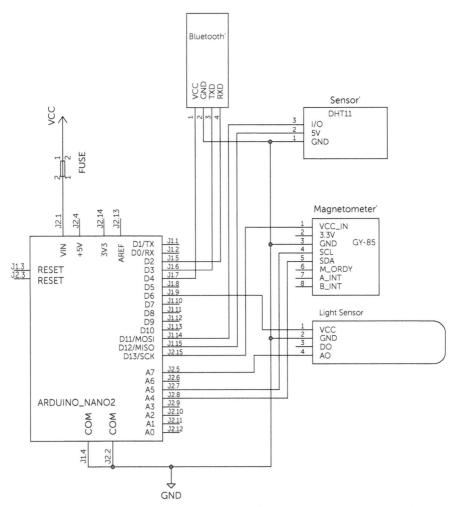

Figure 3.10 A schematic of an electronic device.

The blocks represent specific integrated circuit components and the lines connecting them represent electrical flow between the devices.

The steps for creating a simple or complex schematic can be summarized as follows:

1. List each of the separate components or states that compose the device. These should be either discrete parts that have different functions, or clear and distinct states of the device. Schematic components can resemble the physical devices, depending upon your intent. In the coffee cup example, the state of each cup is sketched to look like the

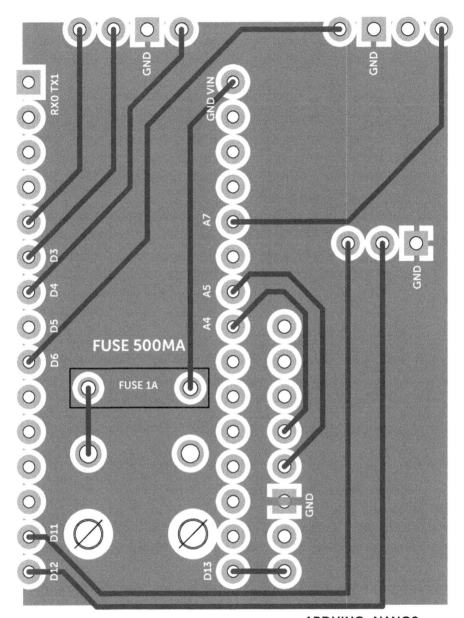

ARDUINO_NANO2

Figure 3.11 The same electronic instrument shown in Figure 3.10 represented by a mechanical drawing showing the actual physical layout of components on a circuit board.

This drawing is the result of the schematic, and typically produced in software after the schematic is verified.

actual cup. The electronics examples, in contrast, show components in the schematic that do not resemble the actual components, but the connections represent those functional connections which actually exist in the physical device.

2. Show the pathways and interconnections between each state or component. It is acceptable in early-stage design to show these connections in fairly simplistic form, as in the coffee cup example. As design or experimental observations evolve, the level of detail and the fidelity of those connections must increase to adequately represent the system being explained.

3. A text explanation of the process should accompany a process schematic. While the pictorial representation of a full coffee cup shows the liquid level, it takes more detailed text to note that the temperature of the contents is an important property of the state, as is the fact that the state of the cup includes both hot coffee and sugar. Words of annotation on the sketch can be a help, as seen in the preceding examples, and so can explanatory prose.

Following these guidelines, and adding sketches and schematics to your personal notes, will help you to retain and explain concepts better down the road, and will help you to create more complex graphics later.

Chapter Checklist

☐ Record simple instructions for a task using notes first without graphics, then augmented with simple quick sketches. Test which method yields more accurate recall.

☐ Examine a complex set of operations and create a set of simple schematic sketches to show the states involved, as well as the discrete processes required to change states.

☐ Sketch a few simple physical objects around you and create labels of their features.

4 Recording Data

Chapter Objectives

- Describe the value of incorporating tables and graphs in your notes to record data
- Identify six basic guidelines for recording data in your notes with tables and graphs
- Define when to use tables and when to use graphs in your notes
- Characterize three types of simple graphs and when they are used

Introduction

In your work as an engineer or a scientist you will need to collect data and find ways to interpret it to bring to light some useful conclusions or new understanding. You can't make sense of data unless you have somehow stored it. Your notes in the lab and at your computer will become your core data upon which your further work is based. The most basic data collection will use tables and graphics to store information, which will later allow you to communicate detailed and complex concepts. The language of graphics and tables, like any language, has its common syntax and expectations that need to be followed if you want it to be easy to recall. This chapter will highlight some of the basic standards to help get you started.

When we think of graphics in this chapter, consider that tables of numbers are graphical constructs just as line graphs and other ways of plotting numerical data are graphical. The examples we have chosen throughout this chapter are the most basic ones we can produce. The intent is to focus on the core elements that every graphical figure must include. If you can capture those basics, then the more complex forms of images will be much clearer when you need to represent very complicated ideas, or many layers of inter-related data.

General Guidelines for Including Graphics in Your Notes

All graphics in your notes will be easier to read later if you follow a few simple guidelines.

An illustration should complement your notes. Never include plots or tables in your notes without written explanation of the context for the data. What were the experimental conditions? What were the model parameters used in the simulation? You need to explain the context of your data in order to extract meaning from it later. You need to define variables, explain methods of measurement, and sketch geometries that explain the data context. Images cannot stand silently alone.

- Simple illustrations are always better than cluttered ones. The easier it is for you to grasp the information quickly and accurately, the better will be the quality of your results.
- If you plan to record data in the lab, or in front of the computer while you carry out experiments or run simulations, create the axes and table columns beforehand. Think about the units of each column and include them in the headings and axes. Whether or not your data is being recorded on a computer or by hand, take the time to think about and construct the data recording format before you sit down to do experiments.
- Your data needs captions to explain the graphic in your notes, so don't just label your figures with a title or the time. Place the caption above for tables and below for figures. There is always room in your captions for a sentence or two of explanation, as well as a reference to the source of the data if it is derived from secondary-source measurements or calculations.
- With all tables, graphs, and figures, be sure to include the reference to the source directly below the graphic. If the data was collected by you, be sure to include dates, locations, and who helped. If the data came from a secondary source, such as a database or published paper, be sure to include all the reference details needed to find that source again.
- In all your raw notes, neatness counts. A neat format for data or observations is less likely to lead to data collection mistakes or to misinterpretation of the results afterwards.

Tables or Graphs?

The simplest way to record observations is with a table. Tables help you to avoid repetitive text and long lists of numbers in your notes while also enhancing your ability to represent and interpret the information. Tables have the advantage of being more exact than charts or graphs because they provide precise numerical information. On the other hand, large tables can be overwhelming and confusing if there isn't enough explanation of each of the variables. In the end, graphs created from data tables can give a more compelling impression of the overall pattern of results.

Suppose we collect numerical data such as that presented in Table 4.1:

Table 4.1 The table shows a simple record of two parameters.

GRADE	# OF STUDENTS
< 5	1
5	3
6	4
7	4
8	6
9	5
10	2

However, what if we also had data to present on the average height of students in each of the grade categories? In this example (Table 4.2), we can see from the table that, while the results might be interpreted to conclude that tall people in this class perform better, the table makes it clear that some of the numbers are the result of an average of only one or two people—not at all a statistically significant population. It would be challenging to show this caution regarding the interpretation through the use of a graph of the same data plotted in a number of ways.

Compare Table 4.2 with the graph shown in Figure 4.1 (below). The graph is neater, and it has been done using software, but the data is the same as that used in the table. The bars showing the number of students are clearly indicated on the left scale, and the average height is shown on the right. The plot of average height is very misleading. It obscures the fact that the data is calculated with too few samples to give it meaning. In addition, the selection of the range for the plot is misleading. Why did we choose 1.4 metres as a minimum and 2.0 metres maximum? Would the message from the plot have been different if we had chosen a different range?

In general, tables are necessary tools for collecting data, but graphs enable you to interpret results with more insight.

Table 4.2 The table shows a simple record of one independent parameter (grade), and two dependent parameters (# of students and their average height). In this example, we would need a caption to indicate that the height was measured in metres and the grade was out of 10.

GRADE	# OF STUDENTS	AVG HEIGHT
< 5	1	1.7
5	3	1.75
6	4	1.6
7	4	1.7
8	6	1.77
9	5	1.8
10	2	1.9

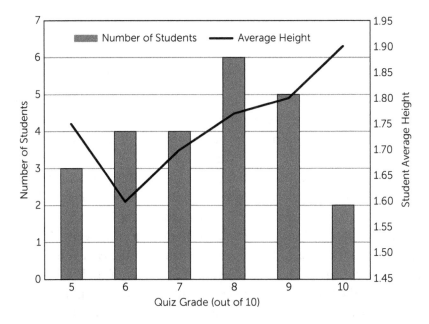

Figure 4.1

This figure shows a combined bar graph and line plot of the data from Table 4.2. It is possible in this figure to see that the distribution of grade through the class is centred on eight, while the height does not follow a similar distribution. Looking at a graph like this allows more insightful conclusions to be drawn than from just the table. Because only two or three students are included in the averages at either end of the graph, it should be evident the height results cannot be interpreted as a trend.

Regardless of your data, it pays to create a data structure for your observations or your analyses before you start an experiment or compare information. The data that you record in a clear, neat table that contains all the contextual information can then be used in more analyses.

Types of Basic Graphs

If your data would be better analyzed in graph form rather than in a table, there are several simple options to use.

X–Y Graphs

One of the most common graphical forms that you will use in your work is the simple two-dimensional (X–Y) line graph. Although you've seen these since grade school, knowing the basics of a good graph and using them in your notes will help you retain and share data. Figure 4.2 shows a simple example of the most basic graph of data. The key features should give you a checklist of what your graph needs at its most basic level.

Figure 4.2 shows two axes with labels, "independent" in the horizontal and "dependent" in the vertical. In order to make a good graph, you must include

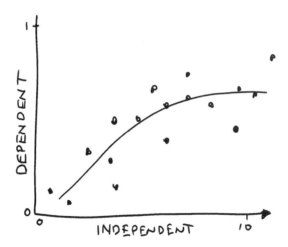

Figure 4.2

This shows a basic X–Y graph of data. The independent variable is typically placed on the horizontal axis, and your resulting measurement of a dependent variable is on the vertical axis. On the scale, both minimum and maximum are shown on both axes. The units should also be indicated, otherwise, as in the example, the numbers are assumed to be dimensionless.

the clear label for each axis. It is customary to show the horizontal label below the axis, and the vertical label oriented at 90 degrees to the horizontal with the text oriented as shown in Figure 4.2. The choice of which variable to plot on the horizontal versus vertical is important. Typically, we try to place the "independent" variable on the horizontal. That could be the parameter in an experiment that you choose; for instance, you might mix up several different concentrations of a solution and measure its fluorescence. To show the data in a report, it would make the most sense to place the mixture concentration (the "independent" parameter that you determined by your own hand) on the horizontal, and then the measured parameter (the one which depends upon the mixture concentration, the "output" of your experiment if you like) on the vertical.

Each axis should clearly indicate the scale. In this case, the horizontal goes from 0 to 10, while the vertical goes from 0 to 1. In this case, units are not shown (the reader might rightly assume that the scales are dimensionless in the example), but in general you should denote the units of measure along with the axes. Typically, you do not need to show a title for a graph, but you will want to provide a clear and fully descriptive caption.

The data fills most of the coordinate axes, both in the horizontal and the vertical. The data scales are adjusted to allow this to be the case.

The origin is very important. A graph can take on a different meaning if the data shows change from 0 to 1,000 versus 980 to 1,000, so suppressed zeros are considered something to avoid, even in notes. If it is common to inflate the scale, then you would want to clearly highlight that in your notes to avoid confusing yourself later.

The data shown on this graph clearly has some individual measured points. These are shown large enough and dark enough to be clear to a reader. Using colours or unusual shapes for the simple data points is not necessary because this shows only one set of data. If there were several different experimental sets, then you could try different colours and/or symbols.

The data represents experimental results, and so you should expect your data to have some noise. Showing the raw data points as well as your predicted trend line through the data helps to point to what is important in your results.

The trend line that you apply to data can change the way that you interpret the data. In Figure 4.2, we have drawn a curved line through the points. Presumably, this shape of curve has some significance to the theoretical model that you have for your results. Figure 4.3 shows exactly the same data points with a linear trend line. The eye is easily fooled to believe either of these plots as "true." In fact, you are correct whichever trend line you choose because they

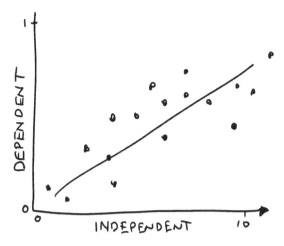

Figure 4.3

This shows another basic X–Y graph of the same data as in Figure 4.2. The only difference between the figures is that a linear trend line is shown in Figure 4.3. The form of the trend line can influence how you interpret your data.

both shoot through data which has a very high scatter. The difference between them is in the implication of which model explains your data. By choosing one sketch or the other, you are implicitly limiting your perception of the results.

Perhaps the data is not represented by a model. It is possible to simply connect the dots, as shown in Figure 4.4. This presentation, again of exactly the same data points, gives an entirely different perception of the same data. In this case, the points might be time-series measurements in which we might not expect a straight-line relation, or in which we are unsure of the errors in our data.

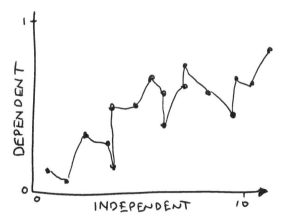

Figure 4.4

This also shows the same data as Figure 4.1 and Figure 4.2. In this example, we have chosen to just join the dots. Notice how this changes your perception of the data points and their relationship.

Finally, notice that all three of these figures (Figures 4.2, Figure 4.3, and Figure 4.4) are sparse on clutter. There is no background grid and there are minimal tick marks on the axes. There is no separate title on the figure, other than the caption below. Adding clutter can make your records harder to interpret.

Multi-variable Plots

Your data is rarely one set of data from one series of tests. If you are serious about experiments, or models, you will vary parameters and try again. While it may be tempting to record the data found in separate graphs (Figure 4.5), it will create a series of uninteresting and incoherent plots where the data is in isolation and almost meaningless. Even if the scale of the axes is the same from plot to plot, it is hard to see the relationships. If you return to your notes later, you'll have a harder time deciphering the information you gathered in your experiment.

The correct way to show difference between a series of trials or a series of simulations under different conditions is shown in Figure 4.6. In this figure, the three traces are shown on the same coordinate axes. The fact that temperature T2 rises sooner than T1 is clear. It is also clear from the graph that the rise rate of T1 and T2 are very similar, while the rise rate of T3 is much slower. Judiciously using the choice of axes to help present data improves your ability to clearly interpret results.

If your data consists of time-series of several electronic measurements, then we frequently look at a plot of the variables versus time. Figure 4.7 shows a plot that might have been the x and y channels of an accelerometer. The data is collected many times per second, and the device this is mounted upon is moved or rolled over. Whether your notes include a computer-generated plot, or one you have sketched by hand, the relative changes of the two components is important for interpreting the results. One channel (A) goes from a low value to a high value and stays that way. Meanwhile, the other channel (B) experiences a brief change while the movement occurs, then goes back to its original value. The relative behaviours of these two traces is fundamental to understanding the physics, and the common axes time-series shown is a good way to see the relationship. Note that, even in this graph, the same elements of the earlier figures are consistent.

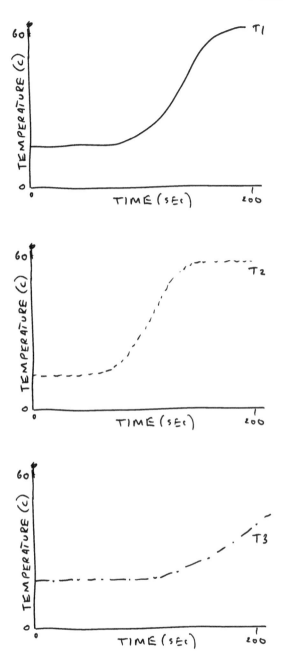

Figure 4.5

Three plots are shown, and each one is a single-variable time-series of data from three different experimental trials. It is not easy to see from this set of plots how the varied parameters
of the tests differ.

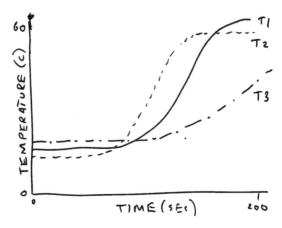

Figure 4.6

This also shows the same data as Figure 4.5. The three traces are plotted on the same axes so that the temperature magnitude and time scales are the same for all, enabling your ability to make sense of the results.

Bar Graphs

We rely very heavily on numerical data of one series versus another. Sometimes, however, the information that you are expressing is the form of some measure versus a category, rather than two numerical series. Presenting the data as a series of bars highlights the fact that the categories are not continuous scales. Figure 4.8 shows the grade on a test on the horizontal axis and the number of students having that grade on the vertical. The standards for such a graph still follow those described for X–Y plots, the axes must be labelled, and the data should fill the space.

This data could have been presented in a simple X–Y graph with a continuous line, but doing so would have led you to believe that there were 3 students with a grade of 5, 4 students with a grade of 6, and 3.5 students with a grade of 5.5. Clearly that is not the correct interpretation. A bar graph makes it clear in its structure that the grades can only be 5 or 6, not 5.5. The bars can be

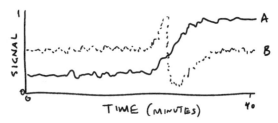

Figure 4.7

Logging of data from separate channels of an electronic instrument are easier to interpret on a time-series if you can highlight the comparisons on a single plot.

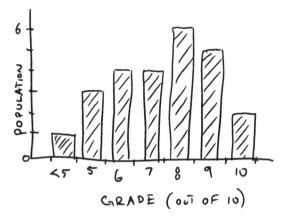

Figure 4.8

This shows the same data as Table 4.1. The data is shown as bars where the resulting number of students with a grade of 6 is clear, and the number of students with a grade of 7 is clear, but the graph implies that there is no such thing as the population of students with a grade between those two integers.

horizontal or vertical, depending on the range of data, and they can be segmented to show different parts of the whole.

Other Forms of Graphs

There are many, many more ways to present data in graphs: pie charts, waterfall plots, stacked spectra, spectragrams—the list could be endless. You might choose to develop a complicated or multi-variable plot for a final report. For the purpose of your research notes and data collection, you will do best by keeping the data presentation to yourself simple and clear. Feel free to experiment with more complex or artistic forms for your data but do so within the context of your discipline. Remember, these graphical forms are intended to allow you to quickly and clearly understand your observations.

Chapter Checklist

- ☐ Before collecting data, recording literature research results, or carrying out simulations, plan the data tables in advance.
- ☐ Explain each of your data tables and graphs in text. Do not let the data standalone without contextual information.
- ☐ Use simple plots of data in different ways to try to present the observations and comparisons of your data within your own notes. This aids your task of understanding the results.

Part II
Writing for Colleagues

5 Strategies for Successful Writing

Chapter Objectives
- Summarize the four key goals in professional writing: be concise, clear, objective, and precise
- Exchange flowery words for plain ones
- Distinguish between connotative and denotative language
- Integrate strategies to make your writing more concise

Introduction

Technical writing demands both objectivity and professionalism. Your professional success depends on your ability to communicate your ideas clearly. Whether you are reporting a straightforward result from testing or making recommendations for a new project, your writing must always be easy to read and understand, and it must stand up to the scrutiny of your peers. Luckily, you already have a foundation on which to start writing: your notes. Transforming those notes into communications for others takes a lot of work and some new strategies: be concise, clear, objective, and precise.

Writing for Your Audience

Your approach to writing depends upon your audience. Your personal notes will be material that you will write quickly and, while you must always aim for completeness and accuracy, you won't revisit it to make it nice or to improve its form or clarity. Per word, this writing will be the fastest, easiest, and most detailed writing you do. The writing that you create for others—your colleagues, the public, and non-specialist audiences—will be smaller in total

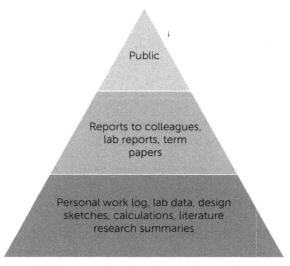

Figure 5.1 Pyramid diagram showing the volume of material that you will generate for different reader groups in your work.

word count, or page count, but every page will take much more time to generate, revise, and revise again. Figure 5.1 illustrates the actual volume of material that you'll produce. However, if we were to map the time per page produced, this pyramid would be flipped on its head. Your work for others will take longer because of revisions. Each time you revise your writing, there are certain goals you should work towards in order to improve your work.

Be Concise

At one time or another, you will probably be tempted to pad your writing. Whatever the reason—because you need to write 2,000–3,000 words and you only have 1,000, or just because you think length is strength and hope to get a better mark for the extra words—padding is a mistake. Readers suspect, quite reasonably, that you are only pretending to have something important to say.

Strong writing is always concise. It leaves out anything that does not serve some communicative or stylistic purpose. Concise writing conveys a better impression in both assignments and exams because you never look as though you are babbling helplessly. Practise editing for economy by counting the words in your sentences and reducing that number whenever possible.

Use Adverbs and Adjectives Sparingly

Don't use combinations of modifiers like adverbs and adjectives unless you are sure they refine your meaning. One well-chosen word is always better than a series of synonyms:

orig.   As well as being costly and financially extravagant, the venture is reckless and foolhardy. (14 words)

rev.   The venture is both costly and foolhardy. (7 words)

Watch for Ineffective or Accidental Repetition

Although your word processor will point out where you've inadvertently typed the same word twice, you'll need your eyes to catch most redundancies. This is another good reason to proofread carefully:

orig.   The terrain slopes to the south with slopes of up to 6.0%.

rev.   The terrain slopes to the south at angles of up to 6.0%.

Sometimes the repetition comes in a different part of speech. It still calls for a revision:

orig.   The architects will issue a certificate of compliance showing that construction complies with building codes. (15 words)

rev.   The architects will certify that construction complies with building codes. (10 words)

Eliminate Wordy Constructions

Sometimes, we use four or five words when one or two will do. Eliminating these wordy constructions will make your writing stronger.

Because they are so common, clichéd phrases can quickly come to mind when you're writing. Unfortunately, readers find them stale and unoriginal. Unnecessary words are deadwood. To keep your writing vital, chop ruthlessly:

Wordy	Revised
due to the fact that	because
at this point in time	now

despite the fact that	although
in the eventuality that	if
in all likelihood	likely
it could be said that	possibly, maybe
in all probability	probably

Similarly, verbs like *have*, *do*, and *make* often introduce wordy phrases that you can reduce by choosing an appropriate strong verb instead:

Wordy	*Strong*
come to a conclusion	conclude
have a tendency to	tend to
do an analysis of	analyze
do research on	study, investigate
make a discovery	discover
make an effort to	try

Choose Active over Passive Verbs

Active sentences are usually livelier and shorter than passive ones:

active She presented the findings. (4 words)

passive The findings were presented by her. (6 words)

Moreover, passive constructions tend to produce awkward, convoluted sentences. Writers of bureaucratic documents are among the worst offenders:

orig. It had been decided that the utilization of small rivers in the province for purposes of hydroelectric power generation should be studied by the department and that a report to the deputy minister should be made by the director as soon as possible. (43 words)

The passive verbs in this mouthful detract from the issue and leave the sentence looking as though there's something to hide. If a passive construction buries the "doer" of an action in a phrase beginning with "by," you should rewrite to save words and emphasize the subject:

rev.   Once the department has investigated using small rivers to generate hydroelectric power in the province, the director will immediately report to the deputy minister. (24 words)

To focus on results rather than on the people producing those results, scientific writing often relies on passive constructions—quite appropriately. In fact, there are a few situations that call for the passive rather than the active wording:

1. When you want to emphasize the results of actions rather than the person performing the action or achieving the results. This is generally the situation in lab reports:

   As a result, the concentration of radon was reduced by 40 per cent.

2. When the subject is the passive recipient of some action:

   The university was founded in 1959.

3. When you want to avoid assigning responsibility or blame:

   Several errors were made in the calculations.

When passive verbs produce wordy or convoluted constructions, however, be sure to rewrite the sentence:

orig.   If the fan is located in a remote space, noise will be minimized, and the fan will thus be able to be operated throughout the night. (26 words)

rev.   Locating the fan away from bedrooms will minimize noise and permit its operation throughout the night. (16 words)

If there are concise alternatives to passives, use them:

orig.   Software reengineering is concerned with the redesign or reconstruction of a software system. (13 words)

rev.   Software reengineering involves the redesign or reconstruction of a software system. (11 words)

Be Clear

Great professional writing is simple and to the point. Sentence length and style influence a reader's response to writing. The language you use to express your ideas shouldn't take attention away from those ideas. Short words and short sentences are generally easier on readers, even sophisticated readers. People who do a lot of reading like it to be easy.

Because of its technical content, scientific writing is characterized by a specialized vocabulary and academic tone that can seem intimidating. Novice writers often feel that they need to adopt an elaborate style. Not true. To convince your reader that you are in control of your subject, make your sentences precise, not convoluted. The most effective and readable style is one that is clear and concise, confident and consistent. When editing, you should always look for ways to make it easy for the reader to understand exactly what you mean.

Use Plain English

Plain words rather than flowery ones almost always make your sentences more readable. Many of our most common words—the ones that sound most natural and direct—are short. By contrast, most words derived from other languages (like French or Latin or Greek) are longer and more complicated. Given the number of synonyms and choices, you should be wary of words loaded down with prefixes (*pre-*, *post-*, *anti-*, *pro-*, *sub-*, *maxi-*, etc.) and suffixes (*-ate*, *-ize*, *-tion*, etc.). Too much dependence on big words makes your writing hard to read. If you can substitute a short word for a longer one, do so:

Flowery	Plain	Flowery	Plain
accomplish	do	efficacious	effective
cognizant	aware	fabricate	build, create
conclusion	end	finalize	finish, complete
concur	agree	modification	change

Suggesting that you write in plain English does not mean that you should never pick an unfamiliar, a long, or a foreign word, especially if it is the only one that expresses a complicated concept concisely. For example, there is no simpler way to refer to *bioremediation* or *turbulent intensity*. But do not clutter your sentence with longer words or phrases when shorter alternatives exist. Note how big words and long phrases cloud, rather than clarify, meaning in the following example:

orig. The addition of the acid and the subsequent agitation of the solution resulted in the formation of crystals. (18 words)

rev. Crystals formed when the acid was added and the solution shaken. (11 words)

If you find yourself selecting words or phrases only because they look impressive, you may find your writing criticized for sounding awkward instead.

Choose Correct Wording

Count on the dictionary to help you understand unfamiliar words or technical senses of common words. A good dictionary will also help you develop your vocabulary by offering example sentences that show how a word is typically used. The dictionary helps with questions of spelling and usage as well. If you wonder whether a particular word is too informal for your writing, or if you have concerns that a word might be offensive, the dictionary will give you this information too.

You should be aware that Canadian usage and spelling may follow either British or American practice, but usually combines aspects of both. There are several Canadian usage manuals available today that help you remain consistent in your approach. It's also a good idea to make sure that the language option in your word processing program is set to *English (Canada)*. However, when you are a professional engineer writing for American clients, you will want to use American spelling.

A thesaurus lists words that are closely related in meaning. It can help when you want to avoid repeating yourself. Your word processor makes it easy to look up synonyms and antonyms. Be careful, though: you need to distinguish between denotative and connotative meanings. While a word's denotation is its primary or "dictionary" meaning, its connotations are any associations that it may suggest. They may not be as exact as denotations, but they are part of the impression a word conveys. If you examine a list of proposed synonyms, you will see that even words with similar meanings can have quite different connotations. For example, for the word *uncertain* your thesaurus may suggest the following: *unsure, vague, doubtful, hesitant, undecided, indecisive, ambiguous, ambivalent,* and *unclear.* Imagine the different impressions you create in choosing one or the other of those words to complete this sentence: "He was _____ about the experiment's chance of success." To write effectively, you must remember that a reader may react to the suggestive meaning of a word as much as to its "dictionary" meaning.

Avoid Jargon

All fields have their own terminology, or *occupational dialect*, also known as jargon. It may be unfamiliar to outsiders, but it helps specialists explain things to each other. As a student, you are generally writing for experts, so there's no need to define standard technical terms or explain a methodology that's familiar to anyone with scientific training. In fact, by using the vocabulary of your discipline appropriately and correctly, you confirm that you are a serious student and a credible writer.

The trouble is that people sometimes try to use technical language to make themselves look more professional. Too often the result is not clarity but confusion, especially if the words aren't used correctly. The guideline is easy: use specialized terminology only when it's called for to explain something more precisely and efficiently. If plain language will do just as well, use it, especially if your reader is not an expert. In particular, avoid using scientific-sounding words in contexts that are not scientific:

orig. Consultation with managerial personnel furnished input for determining the viable parameters of the project. (14 words)

rev. The manager helped define the scope of the project. (9 words)

Keep a Clear Point of View

Where writers might once have referred to themselves, awkwardly, in the third person (as "the investigators" or "the authors"), now scientific writing generally permits the use of *we* and a first-person point of view, especially when it makes sentences more readable. The level of formality is essentially your choice, but remember that shifts from personal to impersonal are awkward in writing:

orig. We note the deformation of the surface, and it is recommended that cryogenic treatment be attempted. (16 words)

rev. We note the deformation of the surface and recommend cryogenic treatment. (11 words)

Notice that the revised sentence not only offers a consistent point of view but also features an active rather than a passive verb and is shorter, thus stronger.

Keep a Consistent Tone

Like keeping a clear point of view, keeping a consistent tone will bring clarity to your writing because a shift in tone from impersonal to personal often coincides with a shift from formal to informal:

> *orig.* The report discusses which recommendations should (in our opinion) get priority attention. A general plan of attack for making it past this phase will be included. (26 words)

> *rev.* The report discusses the recommendations that deserve primary attention. It includes a master plan and schedule. (16 words)

Generally, the solution is to keep to the middle ground—not too formal, not too casual.

Shifting from one pronoun to another will also affect the consistency and formality of your writing. Where *you* is often too personal and too casual (except in personal communications and instructions), *one* is unnaturally formal. In your writing, then, avoid generalizing with either of these choices, and be especially careful not to combine the two approaches in the same document:

> *orig.* One's resumé must look professional, and you should always include a cover letter.

> *rev.* A resumé must look professional, and it should be accompanied by a cover letter.

Be Objective

Your writing must be free of biases and subjective opinions. Your reader will be more likely to accept your findings if you follow these suggestions:

- Avoid unsubstantiated judgments. Be sure that any suggestions you make or conclusions you reach follow from the information you have provided. Never imply anything that you cannot prove. If your findings aren't foolproof, add credibility by showing where the uncertainty lies.

- Avoid subjective language. Words such as *terrible* or *excellent* detract from the objective tone you want. Instead of saying "quarterly figures show an incredible increase," give the exact percentage of the increase and let the facts speak for themselves.

The overall tone to aim for depends on the circumstances—and particularly on the intended reader. If you are writing a short, informal report to someone you see often, familiar terms such as *I* or *you* do work well. On the other hand, many formal reports try to avoid the subjectivity of personal pronouns.

If you are writing on behalf of a group or a team, you can use the pronoun *we*, which avoids awkward passive constructions. If you are writing as an individual, you don't have that option. In such a case, try to recast the sentence to keep an active verb while avoiding *I*:

✘   The purchasing system has been found to increase the duplication of forms. (12 words)

✘   I found that the purchasing system increases the duplication of forms. (11 words)

✔   The purchasing system increases the duplication of forms. (8 words)

If you can't make this sort of revision, you would do better to write the occasional *I* than to use convoluted passive constructions that strangle your meaning or substitutes like *the writer* or *the researcher* that make your writing seem old-fashioned.

Use Inclusive Language

For the sake of credibility, make sure your language is free of bias. The potential for bias is far-reaching, involving gender, race, culture, age, disability, occupation, religion, and socio-economic status. In the end, your goal in communicating is to focus on the ideas and not to alienate any of the readers.

Gender

At one time, it was common to use *he* as a generic singular pronoun. Indeed, you will still encounter this usage in books published before 1975:

If an employee discovers a way to cut costs, he receives a bonus.

Informally, we've solved the problem by replacing *he* with *they*, but this solution is not universally accepted in formal writing. Rather than use an awkward combination of singular and plural, try these options for avoiding the problem:

- Pluralize the word and the pronouns that refer to it:

  If employees discover a way to cut costs, they receive a bonus.

- Use the passive voice:

  A bonus is given to an employee who discovers a way to cut costs.

- Restructure the sentence:

  An employee who discovers a way to cut costs receives a bonus.

Use *he* or *she* only if it refers to a specific person described by that gender pronoun. If you are referring to a person whom you know prefers a different pronoun, it is most respectful to use that word which they prefer, regardless of your own personal choices (e.g. they, zie, sie, ey, vey, tey).

Race and Culture

Words attached to racial or cultural identity sometimes carry negative connotations, for example, the term *Negro*. The search for neutral language has produced alternatives such as *black*, *brown*, or *person of colour*, but these have not been universally accepted. There are similar problems with the term *Indian*, with alternatives such as *Aboriginal*, *Native*, *Indigenous*, and *First Nations* each having its share of critics. The best solution is often to find out what the group in question prefers. In scientific and technical writing, bias is just as present as it is in every other field. It makes good sense to use the most objective language so that readers focus on your message, not your language.

Be Precise

As a scientist, you already know the importance of precision and accuracy. Carry this habit into your writing. Avoid all-purpose adjectives like *major*, *significant*, and *relevant*, abstract general nouns like *situation* and *factor*, and vague verbs such as *involve*, *entail*, and *exist*, when you can be more specific:

orig. Ensuring immediate access to emergency water supplies is a major element in effective seismic disaster management. (16 words)

rev.	After an earthquake, rescuers must first ensure access to emergency water supplies. (12 words)

Avoid generalizing with such qualifiers as *fairly, rather, somewhat,* and *quite.* Indeed, saying that something is *very* important carries less weight than saying simply that it is important. For example, compare these sentences:

This is an important decision.

This is a really important decision.

The shorter sentence has more impact. When you think that a word needs qualifying—and sometimes it will—first see if there's a more precise way of phrasing it. For example, the word *critical* conveys a greater degree of urgency than *important* and is more precise than something like *really important*; using *critical* will give a recommendation more weight:

This is a critical decision.

To say that something is *very unique* makes as little sense as describing something as *rather rectangular.* The following are other redundant descriptions to avoid. In each case, you can safely delete the underlined word.

in close proximity	revert back to
many different types	future plans
sudden crisis	personal opinion
this particular context	successful achievements
each individual participant	true facts

If you are making qualitative judgments, you must be sure to back them up with specifics. If citing numerical results, error ranges can be either explicitly stated or understood from standard scientific conventions. The first example below is less trustworthy than either alternative:

The beam was approximately 12.5 m in length.

The beam was 12.5 m in length.

The beam was 12.5 m ±.1 m in length.

Use Concrete Details

Concrete details are easier to understand than abstract ideas—and more meaningful. If you are writing about abstract concepts for readers who are not experts in your field, be sure to provide specific examples and illustrations:

> ***orig.*** The following are scientists who are dealing with problems associated with stochastic process: physicists, meteorologists, economists, and so on.

> ***rev.*** The physicist measuring frequencies in the lab, the meteorologist forecasting rain, the economist verifying price fluctuations—all these scientists are dealing with stochastic processes.

See how a few specific details can bring the facts to life? Adding concrete details and examples is another way to improve the readability of your writing.

Write before You Revise

Writing is not something that comes easily to most of us, and it is never perfect in one try. Expect to write and then rewrite in order to make your work clear. Editing is an essential element of your job as an author.

Once you are ready to edit, look carefully for ways to make your sentences shorter and more manageable. Note how the revision of the following paragraphs makes its point in fewer words than the first.

> ***orig.*** The benefits of the project will include an understanding of the groundwater resources of the areas, their location, magnitude, and recharge characteristics. This understanding will be refined in the immediate well field area to produce a definition of the capture zones that will provide the basis for delineating well head protection areas around each well or well field. Groundwater protection measures in these areas will therefore be recommended or required by policies and programs currently being developed.

The three sentences that make up this passage contain 77 words. The average sentence is 25.6 words long, and 50 per cent of the verbs are in the passive voice. This text is hard to read.

rev.	The project identifies the groundwater resources of the area, as well as their location, magnitude, and recharge characteristics. These data help define the capture zones in the immediate well field area and delineate protection areas around each well head or field. Future policies and programs will recommend or require groundwater protection measures in these areas.

The number of words has been reduced to 55 from 77, leaving an average sentence length of 18.3 words with only 20 per cent passive verbs. The revision is much easier to read than the original. The shorter example does not sacrifice accuracy or detail; rather, it makes those details stand out more clearly by reducing the clutter of ineffective words.

The best advice is to take advantage of your situation as a student to try things out, to discover what your readers like or dislike, and to practise editing with the goal of reducing the average number of words in your sentences. By working on the readability of your writing, you will be well prepared for a career where your writing skills go hand in hand with your success.

Chapter Checklist

☐ Look at samples of your own writing and pick out complex words where simpler ones would serve better.

☐ Compare samples of professional writing, scientific papers, and commercial advertisements, and notice the difference in claims of performance or effectiveness.

☐ Edit a sample of your own recent writing and cut the number of words while retaining the clarity and appropriate details.

☐ Develop a list of words you use often and then use a thesaurus or dictionary to come up with a list of synonyms. Be sure to pay attention to the connotation of each word.

6 Writing without Plagiarism

Chapter Objectives

- Describe plagiarism
- Identify the three main kinds of plagiarism
- Integrate strategies to avoid plagiarism

Introduction

When you present something as your own work, you guarantee that you are its author, except for material you have specifically identified as coming from somewhere else. If you haven't cited your sources fully and completely, or if you have inadvertently cut and pasted someone else's words into your own text without quotation marks or acknowledgement, you could be accused of plagiarism. Your closest colleagues are the ones who know your field the best and will notice work that you improperly claim as your own, whether through intent or not.

If your colleagues notice that you have claimed something that doesn't belong to you, it won't much matter why. The harm to your reputation will be done. In their eyes, you could be seen as a colleague who can't be trusted to give credit where it is due, or as someone who is not a careful and conscientious researcher or designer. Either way, it's not good for your career. It will take you a long time to recover their esteem. The best thing is to be careful to avoid any hint of plagiarism.

What Is Plagiarism?

Plagiarism is theft of someone else's intellectual property. As with other offences, ignorance is no excuse. Within academic institutions, penalties for plagiarism range from a grade of zero to expulsion, so it makes sense to familiarize yourself with your school's academic integrity policy. It is not worth jeopardizing a career just because you have neglected to provide appropriate credit.

It's considered plagiarism if you:

- borrow from someone else's material without acknowledgement, especially when you don't use quotation marks;
- paraphrase someone else's material without acknowledgement; or
- present someone else's ideas, structure, or examples as if they were your own.

Because research papers and projects depend on support from materials created by various sources and experts, you add to your own credibility and reputation for thoroughness when you provide support from experts in the field. A thoroughly documented paper that includes accurately cited material shows skill, selectivity, and thoroughness. It makes sense to be complete and specific about material used to back up and document ideas, arguments, proposals, and conclusions.

Types of Plagiarism

Plagiarism is an easy mistake to make but being able to recognize the main types will help you avoid the error in your writing.

Quoting without Citation

The most obvious type of plagiarism is using someone else's words as your own. Consider the following excerpt (with underlining added for emphasis):

> In designing, the two processes that must be understood are *system analysis* and *system synthesis*. Designing is a process by which new systems are made; these new systems may incorporate many components and subsystems, and it is the object of the designer to produce the best system for certain missions. Therefore, he or she must be able to analyze the operation of the components and the overall system; he or she must also be able to devise or synthesize systems of given components. *Analysis* is the process of breaking down the system into parts

and discovering whether or not it will fulfill a mission. *Synthesis*, on the other hand, is the <u>process of building up parts into an organized whole</u> that can fulfill a mission.

One student's summary of design process includes the following passage. The underlined formatting indicates the parts that are plagiarized—exact phrasing is taken from the original with no acknowledgement given.

> <u>In designing</u>, new systems are made by incorporating <u>many components and subsystems</u> relying on *analysis* or *synthesis*, or both. <u>The object of every designer</u> is <u>to produce the best system</u>. Therefore, <u>he or she must be able to analyze</u> the workings of the parts in relation to the whole. At the same time, <u>he or she must also be able</u> to put them together. By relying on *analysis*, <u>the process of breaking down the system into parts</u>, and *synthesis*, <u>the process of building up parts into an organized whole</u>, the designer can produce something functional.

Obviously, it is plagiarism to take selections, whether sentences or simple phrases, from a source and include them in your own text pretending that they are your own. But it is also plagiarism if you use only a phrase of the original without proper documentation. In the sample passage above, the scrupulous distinction between *analysis*, "the breaking down [of] the system into parts," and *synthesis*, "the building up of parts into an organized whole," should be appropriately acknowledged by quotation marks. If you left them out, even if you credited the original source in an endnote, you would still be faulted for plagiarism. The rule is simple: if the words or the points aren't yours, identify them with quotation marks and a citation note.

And it's not just words. If you present figures or statistics in a table or in the body of your work, you must document the source. Documentation is also required for any graphics in a format that you did not create yourself.

Paraphrasing without Citation

Restating or paraphrasing ideas in your own words and phrases without acknowledgement is not a solution to plagiarism either. You might think, for example, that you could generalize about the design process cited above by saying the following: *Analysis is easily distinguished from synthesis because the former concentrates on breaking down a system while the latter builds it up.*

After all, you haven't actually copied phrases from the original, and the design concept is one that is universally recognized in your field. It's vital, however, that you accept responsibility for taking material from a specific source.

Do not deliberately rewrite something in your own words to avoid being accused of outright plagiarism. It is still plagiarism and it would be considered cheating and fraud. Instead, a simple revision can turn the evil plagiarism into a very professional review of the background in your subject, which is good and honest scholarship. Consider the difference in how knowledgeable the writer appears after adding a footnote or signal statement like this:

> Roe, Soulis, and Handa emphasize that the fundamental distinction between analysis and synthesis depends on the distinction between separating a system into sections and unifying it into a whole [1].

Here you give the authors full credit as the source of the comparison, and you receive full credit for concisely summarizing the key distinctions.

Taking Ideas without Citation

Even when you represent an excerpt entirely in your own words, it is still plagiarism if you do not include a reference to the source. Consider the following paragraphs from *Reality Is Broken* [2]:

> When we're playing a good game—when we're tackling unnecessary obstacles—we are actively motivating ourselves towards the positive end of the emotional spectrum. We are intensely engaged, and this puts us in precisely the right frame of mind and physical condition to generate all kinds of positive emotions and experiences. All the neurological and physiological systems that underlie happiness—our attention systems, our reward systems, our motivation systems, our emotion and memory centers—are fully activated by gameplay.
>
> This extreme emotional activation is the primary reason why today's most successful computer and video games are so addictive and mood-boosting. When we're in a concentrated state of optimistic engagement it suddenly becomes biologically more possible for us to think positive thoughts, to make social connections, and to build personal strengths. We are actively conditioning our minds and bodies to be happier.

Now compare it with the following summary:

> There is a good reason why people become obsessed with gaming: physically and emotionally, they are completely engaged in a challenging and satisfying activity that makes them happier, stronger, and more positive.

This summary does not copy the language or point of view of the original, but the student writer is still presenting ideas that are not his or her own. Without a reference to the source in a note, including a link to bibliographical information, such writing is nothing but plagiarism. Add a signal phrase (author's name and credentials) to introduce the source fairly and then provide your summary followed by the citation, and this example becomes an excellent review of the idea, showing its author has become familiar with the subject area.

> According to Jane McGonigal, well-known creator of alternative reality games, there is a good reason why people become obsessed with gaming: physically and emotionally, they are completely engaged in a challenging and satisfying activity that makes them happier, stronger, and more positive [2].

Stealing someone's ideas is not limited to intellectual concepts, but can also include general organization or formats, or even presentation styles. If it was created, thought of, or designed by someone else, then it is their intellectual property and you need to include an acknowledgement of their work in your own. While it might feel like there are no original thoughts left in the world and you must cite everything, you'll soon realize that building your ideas upon a foundation of other people's work makes your own stronger.

Avoiding Plagiarism

In science and engineering, we often make measurements or carry out analyses to improve the understanding of an applied principle. It can give confidence to put new results in context of what has gone before. For example, you might have made flow drag measurements on a body in a wind-tunnel. This is not a new area of research, and there are many tabulated drag coefficient results. You might choose to look up the results for drag coefficients of a sphere, and other bodies, and create a table of comparison. Citing the sources for the comparative data shows that you are an attentive and conscientious researcher. Not citing sources for the same data makes it appear that you are inappropriately claiming that you independently did the drag measurements for these other objects.

Plagiarism sometimes occurs by accident, but more often it is the result of unfair, unethical borrowing. With so much material available on the Internet and in libraries, dishonest people think no one will suspect that their work is not their own. They are usually mistaken. The writer who borrows indiscriminately is usually caught because the style of some sections is clearly inconsistent with the rest of the writing—a sure indicator that there is more than one writer at work. Experienced readers instantly recognize such discrepancies, to the detriment of the devious copier. To avoid any such suspicion, always do the following:

- Acknowledge any and all sources in notes and/or a bibliography.
- Use quotation marks around all direct quotations of words or phrases. If the words or phrases are standard terminology, keywords, or nomenclature, you won't need quotation marks to include them in your discussion, but you will need to identify the original source in a note.
- Acknowledge in notes all figures and statistics cited, even though you do not put them in quotation marks.

If you are using anyone else's ideas to support your own, acknowledge that fact. Whether or not you name the author directly in the text ("As Porter confirms, . . ."), be sure to include the reference number and cite the source fully in your list of references. Never be afraid that your work will seem weaker if you acknowledge the ideas of others. On the contrary, it will be all the more convincing: serious academic treatises are almost always built on the work of preceding scholars, with credit suitably given to the earlier work.

For students in a hurry, it is tempting to copy material from electronic sources on the assumption that it is in the public domain. Even though websites are instantly accessible, the material is the property of the individual or organization that published it, and it is protected just like printed material. Remember, then, that you must properly acknowledge the information you find on any website just as you would for anything from a book or journal. With search engines that easily detect plagiarism, you must never put yourself in a position that leaves you open to charges of wrongdoing.

Whether at school or on the job, you often collaborate on projects or assignments. Always list every contributor's name on the title page and give credit for special help in acknowledgements at the front of the paper. But bear in mind that when an academic situation calls for independent work, it is considered plagiarism to copy another person's assignment and present it under your own name, even if you worked on it together. Collaborating with classmates is acceptable, and may even be encouraged, but be sure to produce your own independent write-ups. Given the penalties, letting someone copy your work is asking for trouble, too.

In any situation, your careful selection and documentation of material confirms your ability to take advantage of, while fully acknowledging, someone else's research. Above all, remember that anything you put in writing is there to convince your reader—especially someone who is going to give you a grade or a promotion—that you are methodical, precise, and professional.

Chapter Checklist

- ☐ Review a passage you've read (in a textbook or journal article) and practise quoting, paraphrasing, and interpreting the ideas using proper citation formats.
- ☐ Take a recent example of your writing and put it through an online plagiarism check without including references (Turnitin or Grammarly, for example). Re-submit it with references included.
- ☐ Choose one textbook in a course and try to identify which material is original to the author, versus which material comes from another source. Notice the means by which they cite the original authors.
- ☐ Review a scientific paper in your discipline to look for which of the data shown is original, and which is from another source. Note the ways in which it is cited.

References

1. P.H. Roe, G.N. Soulis, and V.K. Handa, *The Discipline of Design*. Boston: Allyn and Bacon, 1972, p. 54.
2. J. McGonigal, *Reality Is Broken: Why Games Make Us Better and How They Can Change the World*. London: Random House, 2012, p. 28.

7   Working Collaboratively

Chapter Objectives

- Characterize four personality labels to help establish individual roles in a group project
- Integrate strategies for setting the team up for success when collaborating on projects
- Construct a Gantt chart to schedule tasks and organize projects
- Explain the value of a team charter
- Generate a project log for collaborative projects

Introduction

Our work in modern engineering and science depends on collaboration. Whether it is working in a team of three or a group of a dozen people in an engineering design project, or collaborating with another scientist sharing a research question and experimental facilities, your success will depend upon your ability to work with others who are as clever and knowledgeable as you. Communication between everyone before and during a team project can make the difference between a great team experience and a very bad one.

Your instructors have many ways of evaluating team projects, but there are two which seem to be most common. In one model, your instructor assigns a grade for the completed work as a whole, with every participating student receiving the same grade. If the team is unbalanced in ability or effort, it will seem that some team members do extra work to make the project successful, and some team members receive a good grade without putting in effort. In another common evaluation model, your instructor may assign individual grades to each member according to the contribution deemed to have been done by each. In this case it's even more important to make sure your work is tracked by using effective communication strategies. Whether you have been designated to a team or you have chosen collaborators, a team that openly and fairly shares each individual effort and respects everyone's effort will develop into a positive environment where trust and freedom for passionate disagreement can thrive. These are the sorts of work environments where innovative and successful results are created. This chapter will provide some methods that might help you and your team develop a productive work relationship by using great communication with colleagues.

Roles in a Team

Several roles exist in a project, depending on how many people are assigned to a team. If this is the first time you've worked together as a team, spend time in your initial meeting getting to know the other members and discovering each person's strengths and weaknesses. Everyone on a team has different abilities, and different still are your perceptions of your abilities, so it's worth identifying these talents right from the start. You should feel neither limited by your perceived abilities nor constrained by the strengths of other members of your team.

It is common for a new team to meet and assign tasks very rigidly: Alex will get the supplies, Tanuja will do the drawings, Omar will do the calculations, and Pat will write the report. This simple breakdown of work might be one of the worst ways to divide the labour. Too often, the team will be held up because one of these siloed tasks gets delayed. When problems occur, the blame rests with the person who was solely responsible for that task, even if the delay wasn't within their control. Even in small teams, it is important to have supportive overlap.

With a team of colleagues, particularly if your team is also students, it is not appropriate to think of a team boss, leader, or supervisor. Rather, all team members are equal in rank. With a team of equals, how are decisions made? How does the organization of such a team get decided? While all members are essentially equal, each team project has some common roles that must be filled. The roles need not be tied to specific tasks like the example above, they can be more fluid and more aligned with the social role in your team. We will call these essential roles *tracker*, *communicator*, *researcher*, and *scout*.

- A *tracker* is someone who guides the way through a forest. This person enjoys coordinating tasks related to the project and wants to keep all team members fully engaged and working towards a common goal.

When you get together the tracker is naturally the person who reminds everyone of the time and the tasks that need to be completed.

- A *communicator* is comfortable sharing ideas with others verbally and in writing. This is the sort of person who listens to what others have to say, then is quickly able to distill that into a clear explanation or story. When you get together, the communicator is the person who naturally listens to a discussion, notices when two people don't understand each other's positions, and jumps in to help clarify for both sides.
- A *researcher* is someone who excels when hunting down examples and information and breaks things down to basic scientific principles. They can easily relate real-life situations to idealized theoretical examples. In team conversations, the researcher stands up at the whiteboard to explain a theory related to team ideas using scientific analogs.
- A *scout* is someone who loves to be out there on the horizon, looking for new things. They might seem naturally contrarian, and they bring up the ideas nobody else has mentioned. They are always questioning "why should we do it that way?" The scout will argue their point, ensuring everything the team does stands up to scrutiny.

These aren't the normal job titles that you may hear for teamwork. There is no "team leader"; rather, all the roles are equally essential. Notice, too, that the team roles above are not directly connected to specific tasks assigned to a teammate, such as "you write the report," rather they help define the social role that a person will fill. In fact, a specific task like writing the project report must be completed by several people on the team. These roles refer to the inclinations of each team member. In the report writing, perhaps the section of the report on testing will need to be done by the *researcher* and the *communicator* in collaboration. The design alternatives section might be completed by the *scout* and the *tracker*.

If your team recognizes and appreciates these simple role definitions, and perhaps others that might be unique to your project, then the rest of your teamwork will be easier. When you attend meetings, for example, you will find that the person who is naturally a *tracker* is comfortable with the agenda and the meeting plan. The *researcher* will shine when the team needs a complicated scientific concept explained. The *communicator* will try to restate the group's decisions in simpler terms. When the project is getting murky, the *scout* will voice the difficult questions. If your team has two personalities that lean towards the *tracker*, then you can come to some appreciation that these two people can recognize that they may not always agree on planning and schedule, but they can share the role. The roles are a simple indication of personality or inclination of the teammate in a project.

Meetings

As soon as you know who is in your group, perhaps even before you know what the project task will be, plan a get-to-know-you session with the whole team. Try to make everyone feel safe and included. Sharing food is a great way to achieve this, so plan on having a potluck, picnic, or pizza together as a group. This simple strategy will go a long way in making your team feel comfortable and enjoy working together. Although there will be food and companionship, this get-together is still a meeting and there is work to be done.

Your first team meeting should accomplish the following:

- Exchange contact information and set up an electronic home base for your group.
- Appoint someone to take notes for the meeting record book or project log; this person's job begins immediately. It need not be a permanent role; instead, it could be rotated to share the burden in future meetings. From here on, your team discussions should be captured in notes, placed in a record that is accessible to all members. The content and format of your notes will be like those taken for lecture notes.
- Discuss the nature and limits of your project. Allow each person to share with the team their aspirations for the project, and why they are involved. Try to gain an understanding of everyone's ambition and level of priority for this team. Knowing why everyone is together will help to ensure future hard times will let the group pull together rather than split apart.
- Discuss roles and responsibilities. Recognizing that everyone has a role to play is key to successful teamwork. Make sure everyone knows and feels comfortable with what is expected, and give every person in the team a chance to share their strengths and weaknesses. Ultimately, the best projects are ones where the team can build upon the individual strengths, and shared effort can help each person bolster their own weak spots.
- Discuss the rules that you want the team to live by. What are your most important policies that you feel will make the team work well together?

What do you not need to worry about? This conversation should lead to drafting a Team Charter, which will become the agreement under which everyone will work.

- Organize your project, in terms of both what must be done (the plan) and when it has to be done (the schedule). For your first project tasks, assign each task to an "owner" who will ensure it gets completed, and "supporters" who are responsible for doing parts of the work for that task. It is important to make each major task shared amongst two or more members of the team so that for every task, each team member has someone they can call upon to clarify or help with difficulties. Every team member will have several tasks they own and several that they support.

- Before you wrap up, have each member of the team summarize the activities that they own and those that they will support before the next meeting. Ensure that this is clearly written in the record of the meeting.

- Establish an agenda for the next meeting (real or virtual) that calls for each member to give a progress report.

The future meeting with your team will depend upon your success in the first session. If team members feel ignored or undervalued after the first session, then future meetings will be less effective. To ensure that your positive start continues, consider following a format for your next meetings. Henry M. Robert, a General in the Union Army of the American Civil War, was a military engineer who is best remembered for writing a rule book for meetings in 1876. Not all the formal "Roberts' rules of order" will apply to your team, so we offer a very simplified form of those rules below:

- Decide on a person to chair the next meeting. The meeting chair will simply keep people on time and make sure the discussion follows the team's agenda.

- Decide on a person to be the secretary for the next meeting. This person will keep notes of what is discussed and agreed upon at the meeting.

- Set a time for each meeting and stick to it. Start on time.

- Share an agenda for each meeting. This is simply a list of the topics to be discussed and the reason for meeting.

- Start each meeting with a brief (one or two minute) report from each person on what they have been doing since the last meeting. Focus on summarizing what has been completed, what remains to be completed, and what problems have been encountered.
- Discuss only the items that were listed in the agenda. Anything new is put on a list for any spare time at the end of the meeting or for the next meeting.
- If one topic seems to get out of hand, or take over the meeting and there is no obvious solution after five minutes or so of discussion, then propose setting it aside to be brought back, or to have a special meeting to only discuss this item. Set it aside and move to the rest of the agenda.
- Once all the agenda items have been discussed, allow team members to bring up new items that weren't included on the agenda. If the items are going to be very long, then set them aside for another meeting.
- End on time.
- Before leaving, ensure everyone has tasks to complete before the next meeting, and they are clear on what tasks are owned by which team member.
- For the secretary, share the meeting "minutes" (the record of what was discussed) with everyone on the team as soon as possible after the meeting, and definitely before the next meeting.

Project Organization

There are many books, articles, and entire university programs on how to manage team projects. We can't do it justice in this book, other than to encourage you to seek out best practices in the wide range of project management techniques. To get you started, however, it is worthwhile proposing a very simple yet commonly used management tool: the Gantt chart.

A Gantt chart is a graphical way of representing tasks and time, and the inter-relations between them. You can create a Gantt chart by first setting up a list of all the tasks that will need to be carried out for your project to reach completion. Make sure to think through the fine details. Rather than creating a task like "build it," break every large complex task into smaller steps. Ideally, each step would be a day or a week worth of a person's effort. Any longer, and the task should be broken into sub-tasks.

Consider the example project from Chapter 1: a "CubeSat" team design project. In the Chapter 1 example, we showed the initial project concept map and the topics that were important to the project success. In Chapter 1, these were each static items, such as "competition rules" or "finance." In the task list, you could start with a major item like "finance" and imagine what needs to be done to realize what was meant in that category. Perhaps the CubeSat team aims to raise $50,000 to finance the satellite project. The topic "finance" now means "raise $50,000 for the team." That task will need to be broken down to manageable work tasks. Perhaps achieving this goal will require "write a funding pitch" and "deliver pitch to investors." With these better-defined tasks, you might realize that photos of a prototype model are needed for the pitch document to really sell the concept and that meetings with investors will need to be arranged. This would entail e-mailing potential investors, booking a meeting room, and ordering coffee. At every level of a project, the more that you imagine the tasks, the more you can break the work down into even smaller tasks. At some point, each task will be assigned to specific members of the team for completion.

Figure 7.1 shows the beginnings of a Gantt chart for the example project. The task list is a first step; the next step is to add time to the picture. Draw a timeline across the top of the sheet with the starting day on the left, and the end date on the far right. In between you can divide the time into whatever divisions seem appropriate. Typically, a four-month project would be broken into weeks and days. A project with a longer timeline, two years, for example, might be broken into months and quarters. Whatever your timeline, start at the completion date, and then work backwards to draw a horizontal line to show the completion of each task and the start of each task. If, for example, you need to have secured funding from investors in the CubeSat project by a date two months from now, then you might decide that your investor pitch meetings need to be complete by the end of this month. If the meetings, collectively, will go on for a three-day period, those three days now appear as a dark line in your Gantt chart with the end date in a month. Once you start populating this chart, you will realize dependencies and identify new tasks. As the chart evolves, so will your task list and timelines.

There is certainly software for Gantt charting. Once you have the concept, and you have a rudimentary list of tasks and times, you should move your hand sketch over to a software planning tool. Once you've developed the electronic Gantt chart, you will find that it becomes a useful project tracking tool. Figure 7.2 shows an example of a segment of a much more detailed Gantt chart. You can update each task, add more details, change dates, and indicate what level of completion each task is by using the software.

The key to being successful in collaborative work is how you chronicle your team's progress and manage the schedule. The electronic Gantt chart

TASK	START	LENGTH	1	2	3	4	5	6	7	8	9	10	11	12
COMP RULES														
DOWNLOAD NEW	1	1												
PARSE	2	2												
COMPARE SAFETY	3	2												
REPORTING REG'	3	1												
PRES TO TEAM	4	1												
FINANCE														
IDENT NEEDS	1	2												
WRITE PITCH	2	1												
GET GRAPHICS	2	1												
LIST DONORS	1	3												
SCHED MTGS	1	3												
DELIVER PITCH	4	1												
TRACK PROG	4	3												
FUTURE CONCEPTS														
WHAT WORKED	4	1												
NEEDS IMPROVE	4	1												
PRODUCT NEEDS	4	2												
TEAM ORG	5	1												
PRESENT T/TEAM	7	1												
FEEDBACK	8	1												
RESEARCH	9	4												
PRESENT 2	12	1												

Figure 7.1 The figure shows a simple hand-drawn Gantt chart for a project. The task list and the time each task will take to complete are the key components. Once those are estimated, the order of tasks can be shown by the timeline and links between tasks

can really help. Be sure to allow enough time at the end for a full write-up, including plenty of time for the drafting of sections and the overall editing, proofreading, and formatting required by the formal report. If you build this schedule into your Gantt chart and designate a project editor, you prepare everyone to contribute to the writing right from the beginning of the project. If you are making a public presentation, allow time for the creation of a slide-show that showcases your work in the best light.

The Team Charter

An effective way to set a positive team environment is to write down the expectations and rules everyone agrees to follow from the very start in a *Team Charter*. Like the shareholders' agreement for a new company, the team charter acts as a contract between team members. In your professional career, the function of a team charter will be served by a start-up company's *articles of incorporation* or *shareholders' agreement*, a government committee's *terms of reference*, or the *collaboration agreement* between companies. Figure 7.3 shows a simple example of a team charter for a small team of students.

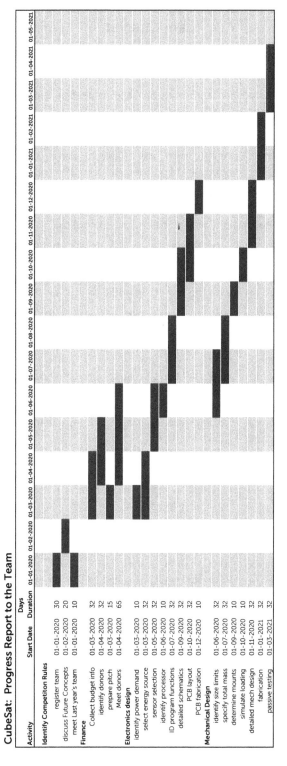

Figure 7.2 The figure shows a Gantt chart for a project created using a spreadsheet.

Team Charter

Team Members: Andi, Bob, Cara, Di, Em.

<u>**Team Objectives:**</u>

- To work towards a common goal, while respecting the value and beliefs of every team member
- To exhibit excellence in communication and collaboration with other team members
- To accept new concepts from individuals who have different opinions
- To disagree respectfully and find the best compromises

Participation: All members are subject to put in the same time and commitment to the project as everyone else. Tasks are to be split up equally and fairly. The project can't harm members' grades in other courses.

Time Commitment: Making it to class every day unless valid reason is extremely important as we don't want anyone falling behind. If you are going to miss a class, inform the other team members prior to class. We agree to 5 hours per week working on the project in addition to class time.

Team Communication Plan: All members should respect the opinions of each member of the group. For in person meetings all members must share their ideas in a respectful manner. Equal participation should be considered at all times during meetings.

For online or remote collaboration, all team members should share their opinions via the chat or discussion threads in Basecamp, and the documents section should be used to post reference documents or final document submissions. There are no dumb questions, if you don't understand your role or a particular concept, ask a group member.

Conflict Resolution: In the event that team members do not agree on a task, the team will try to find a consensus. Majority will not rule, we will always talk it out. If we still can't agree, we will ask for advice from a TA or another person outside the team.

Discipline: If one team member is consistently going against these rules the following will happen:

1. A verbal notice will be given from the team.
2. If continued, a written notice will be taken of the action.
3. If further continued, another written notice will be taken to the TA.
4. If the behaviour continues a vote will be taken to remove the member from the group (must be unanimous).

The following signatures signify that each group member agrees to the full terms of this team charter document:

Figure 7.3 The figure shows an example team charter used in a student design team.

The items listed are common ones that an undergraduate student team might consider, but your team could add many more, depending upon the concerns and wishes of the team members.

The format of a team charter does not need to be very complex: it's simply a statement of the goal for the team, the dates over which the charter will apply, and then whatever policies that you agree to follow. Signatures from all members of the team on the document show that everyone has agreed and will follow the rules. Your own personal experience working in teams will help to point to what sorts of items you want to include, but the example shows some common features seen in many student team charters that have proven to be helpful. Add whatever items your team wants; the terms in your charter should truly represent what your team believes and what is relevant to your project.

The Project Log

Your team will need to make and share a record of what work has been done, what is left to do, and what decisions have been made and agreed upon by the team. The best way to keep track of these details is to create a Project Log. It could be a physical logbook, or it could be a shared electronic drive or other platform. It must be accessible to all members of the team, and they must be able to comment on it to show that everyone agrees with what is written or to post concerns if there are any. Typically, this log should hold a copy of the minutes (record) of each team meeting; a copy of the project plan documents such as Gantt charts and budgets, and drafts of reports; and individual work contributed by all team members.

Some professors will require that this be a physical logbook. Certainly, a bound logbook is less convenient than an electronic shared drive but more secure in many ways than a simple shared Google Drive folder. Regardless of the technology used to create and maintain the team log, it should have these common features:

- The logbook should record, in chronological order, all your activities as a team—your meetings, discussions, ideas, decisions, sketches, designs, calculations, solutions. For each entry, record the date and time as well as the names and contributions of everyone in attendance. If you haven't worked on the project for a while, make an entry about the pause in activity, stating the reason and having the entry initialed by team members.
- If you want to delete something, either because it is a mistake or because it is not relevant, cross it out with a single tidy line, so that you can still read what it says. Do not tear out pages, erase entries, or use correction fluid. For electronic notes, leave the original erroneous

items in place, and add a new, updated copy clearly indicating that it replaces the earlier one. Deleting or hiding mistakes reduces the value of your project notebook, and your team loses credibility.

- Ensure that each person on the team clearly identifies their individual work, and clearly states that they have seen and agree to common items. In a paper log, this is done with signatures or initials of each member on the relevant pages. In electronic logs this is done by each team member posting a statement that clearly indicates agreement with an item.
- Be as objective and accurate as possible in recording discussions among team members. Always give reasons for decisions and use wording that cannot be misinterpreted by anyone reading the logbook.
- Keep the logbook up to date during the project and secure it for safe keeping after the project is complete.

These precautions are nothing less than standard practice in the engineering world, so it's worth getting used to following them while you are still a student. In fact, if you are working on a ground-breaking project, your logbook takes on even more importance. As a permanent chronological record of all the work your team has done, it may even be required as evidence in court. To add to its authenticity, you may decide to have it regularly corroborated by independent witnesses—especially if your work is precedent-setting.

It's important to recognize that the group project log does not replace the individual note-taking described in the first section of this book. In fact, the more personal recording that each member of the team does, the easier it will be to write the team report later. Everyone will have different but complementary personal logs, sketches, and calculations that can be incorporated in the team project log and the team report. In this way, great team writing feeds upon the complete and correct individual logs of each member of the team.

Team Writing

Often in teamwork, the report is the printed culmination of your work on a project. When you are working as a member of a team, the preparation of this document takes on new dimensions because the contributions of several people must be synthesized in a coherent document. It's a good idea to start by assigning the job of final compiler/editor to one of the team members, likely the person who has the most experience with writing.

In projects where the writing task goes badly, typically there has been one person left to do all the writing, while all the others on the team disengage. In order to prevent this from happening to your team, make it clear that the master compiler/editor is only the last person to review and fix the work. Their job is not to write all the sections, nor even to rewrite the work of others. Everyone in the team must contribute writing and graphics that reflect their own individual contributions to the team. If, for example, one person has designed a camera mount component, then that person should write the first version of the section in the report on a camera mount. In the section, the drawings of a mount would be included and the initial sketches, as well as test results and evaluation of the resulting part. Before the section is complete, another member of the team would ideally trade writing, revising, and editing the camera mount section to make it more clear, relevant, and complete, while at the same time the author of the camera mount section revises and edits their counterpart's section. Once both the original author and the reviser have come up with sections they can agree on, the sections would be added to the master document for revision by the final compiler/editor.

Working as part of a professional team is no different from most team sports, where athletes recognize the advantages of collaboration despite differences in talent and experience. The strength of a team, after all, depends on the combined power of individual contributions. The lack of timely, clear, and complete communication between team members can be the single surest way to reduce the chances of a successful team outcome.

Chapter Checklist

- ☐ Assign roles associated with group dynamic functions to keep tasks fluid and shared equitably.
- ☐ Create a team charter early in the project so that everyone understands and commits to the ground rules.
- ☐ Plan a project using a Gantt chart, making sure to break big jobs into smaller tasks.
- ☐ With your teammates, create a project log for documenting work. Establish guidelines for how the log will be updated and maintained.

8   Writing Summaries and Abstracts

Chapter Objectives

- Apply guidelines for summarizing your own work and the work of others
- Incorporate strategies for creating an annotated bibliography
- Employ two strategies for editing your summaries for brevity and clarity

Introduction

Writing as a scientist or an engineer is not the same as writing a movie script or novel. The first, most obvious difference is that you will find that the first page of a technical report or scientific paper contains a paragraph that tells the plot and the ending of the whole story. This is the abstract or executive summary. These introductory summaries are designed to save time for the reader. A good summary lets a colleague know immediately whether a document is something they need to read. A good summary or abstract enables the work to be categorized to put it in context with the field in which it is written.

As a professional, you are expected to make your summaries concise, accurate, and well-focused. Following the suggestions in this chapter will make the task of writing succinct, informative summaries easier.

Definition

Every summary is compact. Its purpose is to present, in the fewest, most precise words, the essence of a piece of writing. In an academic paper, the summary is called an *abstract*, and you write it for inclusion in a database or similar index. Its key feature is its length: almost all abstracts are typically shorter than 250 words. You already depend on abstracts to help you determine which papers, articles, or dissertations support your research. In learning to compose an abstract for an academic project or a summary for your own engineering proposals or reports, you become better prepared to join academic and professional communities.

Summarizing Your Work

A summary is not the same as the introduction to a paper. It is a composition of one or two paragraphs that can be read instead of reading the entire article. The following suggestions will help you in writing an effective summary:

1. **Prepare the summary or abstract after you have completed your document.** The summary must clearly describe the contents of the paper, so those contents must be in their final form.
2. **Identify three to four keywords.** Work these keywords into the text of your summary to make them easy for a search engine to find. They should be words familiar to other experts in your field of study.
3. **Remember to consider the needs of the reader.** Readers depend on the summary to answer two questions: *What is this?* and *Do I need to read the whole paper?* Some readers read only the summary, so it's especially important to keep it simple yet precise.
4. **Keep to the specified length.** Depending on the project, your summary or abstract may be strictly limited to a specific number of words. Most summaries for long reports should not be more than a page of double-spaced text (maximum 250 words), but an executive summary for a major project or thesis may well extend to a second page.
5. **Stress important findings.** Highlight specific discoveries or important new material covered in the report or paper. Emphasizing these innovations in your summary gives the reader a better reason to read the rest of your work.
6. **Avoid generic statements.** It's tempting to develop the summary as a roadmap for the paper, a sort of table of contents in prose. Do not, however, waste the reader's time with vague statements like "Findings are discussed extensively, and recommendations for further research are included." Readers already expect a paper to present findings and recommendations. Your summary needs to clearly report the essential factual details; it should not merely refer readers to the text.

7. **Do not include citations or references to other works.** The place for references to the work done by others is in the text of your document and in your bibliography, not in the abstract.

Structuring Your Summary

There are several approaches to structuring the summary. One of the following models and sets of questions should help you stay on track:

- the chronological summary

PAST	Where did it begin? How was it done?
PRESENT	What is the current situation?
FUTURE	What lies ahead?

- the experiment summary

PURPOSE	What is the hypothesis?
METHOD	In what order were operations performed?
RESULTS	What happened?
CONCLUSIONS	What does it all mean?

- the problem-statement summary

CONTEXT	What is the background of the problem?
DEFINITION	What are the complications?
OPTIONS	What are the alternatives?
RECOMMENDATIONS	What action should be taken?

- the proposal summary

CONTEXT	What is the background of the situation?
CONSIDERATIONS	What basic requirements/specifications are being addressed?
NEEDS	What time/money/effort is involved?
IMPLEMENTATION	What are the next steps?

Choose the formula that's most appropriate for your context. If your summary answers each of the questions in a sentence or two and adds nothing extra, it will be well-focused. More importantly, it will address the reader's needs exactly.

Here's a one-paragraph summary of a 17-page project report. Organized in chronological order, it satisfies the reader's needs by answering three questions: *What? So what? Now what?*

> In November 2019, the XYZ Film Lab in Toronto commissioned the design of a machine as an alternative to the equipment currently used for chipping thin hard plastic for recycling. The team developed and tested a functional prototype with a cylindrical blade and a flexible hopper. Tested in an office environment, the prototype handled up to 10 sheets of plastic simultaneously, with peak noise levels lower than 54 dBA. Existing commercial equipment achieved a similar processing rate but produced noise levels exceeding current health and safety regulations for office use. Proposed design research will lead to improvements in blade life, dust control, and further noise reduction. (106 words)

Summarizing the Work of Others

Sometimes you will be required to produce a summary of someone else's work, either as an academic exercise or on the job as a backgrounder for a busy colleague. This summary isn't like a review: it is not intended to evaluate, comment, or criticize.

Your summary of someone else's work simply records, as accurately as possible and in as few words as possible, your understanding of what the author has written. Whether you like what you have read is not the issue. Your job is to get to the heart of things—to separate what is important from what is not.

1. **Determine the author's purpose.** Every author writes for a reason: to cast some new light on a subject, to propose a theory, or to bring together the existing knowledge in a field. Whatever the purpose, you must discover it if you want to understand what guided the author's selection and arrangement of material. The best way to discover the author's intention is to check the preface, the introduction, and—if

there is one—the author's own summary or abstract. A glance at titles and subtitles, headings, and subheadings shows you what the author considers most important and what kind of evidence is presented. The details are much more understandable once you know the direction of the discussion.

2. **Read carefully and take notes.** A thorough reading will be the basis of your note taking. Because you have already determined the relative importance that the author gives to various ideas, you can be selective and avoid getting bogged down in less important details. Just be sure that you don't neglect any crucial passages or controversial claims.

    When taking notes, try to condense the ideas. Don't take them down word for word, and don't simply paraphrase them. You will have a much firmer grasp of the material if you resist the temptation to quote. Force yourself to summarize. This approach also helps you be concise. Remember: you want to be brief as well as clear. Condensing the material as you take notes ensures that your report is a true summary, not a string of quotations or paraphrases.

3. **Follow the same order of presentation as the original.** It's usually safer to follow the author's lead. That way your summary is a clear indication of what's in the original.

4. **Discriminate between primary and secondary ideas.** Give the same relative emphasis to each area that the author does. Don't just list headings or chapter titles or reiterate conclusions.

5. **Include the key evidence supporting the author's arguments.** Include supporting details. Without them, your reader will have no way of assessing the strength of the author's conclusions.

6. **Use bullet points when possible.** They help your reader see relationships.

Summarizing Work in an Annotated Bibliography

An annotated bibliography is a list of sources accompanied by a brief description of each item on the list. Such a list can be exceptionally helpful in reporting the results of literature research on a topic. If you read a collection of academic and industry documents on a topic, the best way to save what you have learned and share them with your colleagues or supervisor is through a good annotated bibliography.

The following example shows a simple annotated bibliography entry:

Bin Yang, Song Zhang, X. Fang, and Jilie Kong. 2019. "Double Signal Amplification Strategy for Ultrasensitive Electrochemical Biosensor Based on Nuclease and Quantum Dot-DNA Nanocomposites in the Detection of Breast Cancer 1 Gene Mutation." *Biosensors and Bioelectronics* 142 (October): 135–40.

> This paper describes the development and testing of a sensor using Quantum dots used to hybridize and activate single-stranded DNA in a HCl solution. The solution was used to condition a gold electrode, which was then transferred to a cyclic voltammetry setup for testing human serum extractions of miRNA. The paper describes methods to characterize the sensor, and validation using samples of miRNA. Optimal conditions were discussed, as were sensor stability.

Note that this example identifies the issues that were impressed upon the reader, and they reflect, to some extent, the purpose and interest that the reader had in reviewing the article. Many of the details of the article are not in this review because they were not relevant to the reader at the time. For example, the above article referred to a sensor for use in breast cancer detection, but the reviewer was purely concerned with DNA/RNA detection methods and the application the sensor was intended for was not of interest. It was not even mentioned in the comment. As such, an annotated bibliography is particular to the purpose that the compiler had in carrying out the research. The entries should help capture the relevance and importance of each paper reviewed in the research task at hand.

If you are asked to provide an annotated bibliography, begin by alphabetically arranging your entries for the bibliography and providing full details according to the referencing system you are following (see Appendix A for options). Then add your own summary (one to three sentences) of the contents of each source, including information of value to your reader. You want to ensure that each entry in the bibliography has an equivalent depth of review. Essentially, in your annotation you answer the same questions you ask when preparing an executive summary: *What is this?* and *What can we do with it?*

Use your own words and phrasing in answering these questions. It is tempting to reproduce the document's own summary or abstract or the "About Us" introduction that appears on a website, but the annotated bibliography needs to be more specifically tuned to the purpose for which you are conducting the literature research.

Editing for Economy and Precision

Whether you are writing a summary of your work or someone else's, it is essential to leave time for thorough editing. These two final guidelines are vital:

1. **Re-read and revise your summary to make sure it's coherent.** Summaries can often seem choppy or disconnected because so much of the original is missing. Use linking words and phrases to help create flow and give the writing a sense of logical development. Careful paragraph division will also help to frame the various sections of the summary.
2. **Revise to make every word count.** You may find that you must edit your work several times to eliminate unnecessary words and get your summary down to the required length. Be ruthless about eliminating wordy constructions (See chapter 5).

Chapter Checklist

- ☐ Read the original material carefully, noting what your audience needs to know about the subject and its context.
- ☐ Prepare a single sentence summary of the contents. Then, flesh out your summary by answering the following questions: What? So what? Now what?
- ☐ Keep to the assigned length.
- ☐ Take the time to edit thoroughly.

References

1. Bin Yang, Song Zhang, X. Fang, and Jilie Kong. 2019. "Double Signal Amplification Strategy for Ultrasensitive Electrochemical Biosensor Based on Nuclease and Quantum Dot-DNA Nanocomposites in the Detection of Breast Cancer 1 Gene Mutation." *Biosensors and Bioelectronics* 142 (October): 135–40.

9 Writing a Lab or Progress Report

Chapter Objectives

- Describe the five main sections of a technical report
- Identify which sections are needed in different types of reports
- List the three criteria needed to establish authorship
- Integrate strategies to create clear and measurable objectives
- Summarize the five details needed to ensure credibility of your results and observations
- Prepare effective questions to ensure your analysis is complete and accurate

Introduction

When you graduate, knowing how to write and interpret technical reports will be essential to the work you do. The lab and project progress reports that you create as a student are opportunities to practise this essential professional skill. Your reports communicate detailed scientific and technical results to your colleagues and supervisors. Developing the skill to quickly produce excellent reports for your colleagues will enable your observations, conclusions, and recommendations to be adopted by your team, and will play a role in developing your reputation as an effective professional.

This chapter will help you construct and draft a good report. While your individual instructors may have their own particular preferences, the advice we provide is a common set of guidelines. Whenever the guidelines conflict with specific preferences that your instructors express, always follow their preferences. If none are given, you will find these guidelines can help you produce a suitable document.

Format of a Technical Report

A technical report is usually broken into separate sections, each with its own heading. Your report will generally start with some initial archival information before outlining the context for your work and providing an explanation of what your original contribution will be. The next two sections will feature your raw results and observations, as well as your original interpretation of those results. The last pieces of your report will be end matter, such as references and additional raw data that should be available to the reader for archival purposes. The most common formats for reports will follow a standard order with the typical sections found within each of the five categories:

1. Initial archival information: *Title Page, Summary, Acknowledgements, Contents, List of Figures, Nomenclature.*
2. Explanation of context: *Introduction, Background, Purpose, Objectives, Materials, Equipment, Methods, Procedure, Safety Protocols.*
3. Original observations: *Results, Observations, Design Alternatives, Stakeholder Meetings, User Focus Groups, Financial Report, Project Management.*
4. Original interpretation: *Discussion, Analysis, Conclusions, Recommendations.*
5. End pieces: *References, Appendices, Detailed Drawings, Simulation Results, Program Code.*

You won't use all the headings in the list above in your report. The ones you pick will depend on the length, formality, and importance of the report that you are creating. Perhaps a 300-page thesis might contain most of the headings above, while your six-page lab report for a physics course might only have the following headings:

1. *Summary*
2. *Introduction*
3. *Materials*
4. *Results*
5. *Discussion*
6. *References*

Note that your brief lab report contains one heading from each of the five major categories listed above. The order of these sections is always the same, although some sections may be combined or given slightly different names, depending on how much information there is in each one. This basic structure of the five categories is found in all reports, although the categories are never explicitly named.

The order of presentation doesn't necessarily reflect the order in which you complete the lab work or, indeed, the order in which you do your write-up. Many authors write the Method and Materials sections first, then the Results and Discussion, leaving the Introduction, Abstract, and Conclusions for last. The remainder of this chapter will offer advice on each of these five main blocks of your technical report.

Initial Archival Material

Your report is one of many similar technical reports that readers will need to review. You need to make sure that they can distinguish your work from all the others, so it is your job to orient the reader and help them find the information again when they go looking.

Title Page

If your lab report is more than 10–15 pages, including a title page is often expected. For shorter reports, using a separate page might be excessive so it is common to put the same information on the top ¼ of the first page. Your title page information should include your name, the title of the experiment, the date it was performed, and the date you turn in the report. If the work is done for a specific class, it should also include the name of your course and instructor. If there is a standard title page format that your course instructor or department prefers, then follow that template. Your aim is to make it easy to categorize and store the report, so don't try to be unique with the format.

Titles should be brief (10 or 12 words) but informative, and you should make sure they clearly describe the topic and scope of the experiment. Avoid meaningless phrases, such as "A study of . . ." or "Observations on . . . ." Simply state what it is you are studying and be as specific as possible. For example, choose "Flow Rate Tests of Several Common Leaf- Blowers" as your title over something less descriptive like "Tests of Leaf-Blowers" or "Leaf Blowers."

Authors

Why think about whose name gets put in as an author? In some cases your work will produce a report that has contributions from several people on a team or lab group. Does every member deserve to be listed as an author? If so, in what order are the names placed? These can be prickly questions, so general guidelines have been widely accepted by the scientific and engineering communities for determining authorship.

In science and engineering, having your name listed as an author is warranted for only those people who satisfy *all three* of the criteria for:

- *Authorship:* you have actually written significant portions of the content and take responsibility for sections of the work.
- *Approval:* you acknowledge that you have reviewed and approved the document.
- *Integrity:* you are responsible for the content of some portions of the work, and you attest to the integrity of the work reported. (Tarkang et al., 2017; ICMJE, 1997)

The order of authorship often indicates the bulk of each person's contribution. In general, the lead author has taken primary responsibility for most of the work, controls the final copy, and has actually submitted the work for publication or grading. The remaining authors listed are not in any particular order of importance, so some agreement between authors regarding placement can be reached.

Abstract or Summary

The *Abstract* appears alone on the page following the title page (or on the lines following the title and authors in a brief report). An abstract is a brief, standalone summary of your report. The abstract is not like a movie trailer: it's expected that your abstract will clearly give away the ending of the story. Anyone should be able to read it and know exactly what the experiment was about, as well as the important results and how they were interpreted. The abstract or summary should be shorter than 75 words; for a complex report, this could be stretched to a maximum length of 150 words.

Writing a good abstract is challenging and will take many iterations. In each edit, you should be able to cut out more and more phrases and reword sentences to make them clearer, as well as briefer. Your final abstract or summary should contain only four or five sentences.

Table of Contents

If the report is lengthy, extending over several pages and including attachments as appendices, provide a *Table of Contents* that lists section numbers, titles, and page numbers. In extended reports, you might also include a *List of Figures* and a *List of Tables* on separate pages following the *Table of Contents* page. If your report is done by hand in a bound notebook, it is especially helpful to include a table of contents and number all your pages, so that the person marking your lab can easily find where to start. For a brief report (under 10 pages, typically), a *Table of Contents* is not needed.

Nomenclature

A report that uses extensive derivation of mathematical equations or that relies upon a variety of variables should include a table that defines each variable at the start. This is not needed for work that may use commonly understood terms and variables or that has fewer than 10 uniquely defined variables. If your work has more than that, it will help the reader to give a single table that shows the variable symbol followed by a brief one-line definition. For example:

Re	Reynolds' number
Gr	Grashof number
V	Average velocity of water in free-stream
t	Time from start of heating
T_f	Temperature of front of model
T_t	Temperature on top of model
T_r	Temperature right of model
T_a	Average overall temperature of surface
C_c	Coefficient of drag for corner of mold

Explanation of Context

For your readers to understand your work, it is up to you to provide them with the appropriate level of background explanation. The reader, and their familiarity with your work, will dictate how detailed this will need to be. If you are writing a report for a large team of colleagues who are part of your work group but who are not involved with you on a daily basis, you might need to take them back to the start of the project and explain the design criteria, or the background problem that underpins your design. You might need to provide a basic explanation of the physical principles of heat transfer, or fluid flow, or quantum mechanics if they are needed to understand your work. If you know that the readers are familiar with your work, then your explanation of the context can be briefer by providing a quick frame of reference for where in the project this work is situated. In the parts of your report that provide the context, you may choose to use some or all of the following headings.

Introduction

In a clear, well-written report, your introduction will provide the reader with a starting point to understand the rest of your work. Thus, you need to introduce the following elements:

- **The report itself.** Your introduction should explain the scope of your report. For example, explain if this is a final report, an interim progress report, a lab report, or a literature survey.
- **The background science to the subject.** Provide the reader with enough technical and scientific explanation (and references) to bring them to a point that they can reasonably understand your explanations of the particular work. For example, if your work was measuring the drag coefficient of a sphere, you would need to explain the background theory and past experiments that have been widely published and accepted in the field.
- **The unique issues that were important.** Explain to the reader what issues made your work unusual or unique. For example, if you were measuring the drag coefficient of a sphere, you might need to explain that most other results were for room temperature (with citations) while your work was done using sub-zero temperatures.

Although you will certainly refer to outside sources—especially if you want to add legitimacy to an experiment you've developed yourself—you should still put the emphasis on using this pre-existing work to explain your own work and its context.

Background

In some reports, the amount of material needed to properly introduce the work can become unwieldy. If this is the case, then it makes sense to separate the introduction into sections that give background on specific areas. For example, in your report on drag coefficients, you might require a section called "Background: traditional drag-body experiments" and another which might be "Background: low temperature gas flows" and perhaps a third being "Background: analytical basis for prediction of drag using wake vorticity." Creating these sections will make the topics clearer to the reader and enable your introduction section to better put your work in context.

The background section for engineering design reports can be very helpful in providing a catalogue and analysis of alternative solutions to the design goal. In this case, you might consider including a background section pointing out flaws in the designs of several competing solutions, or a section that breaks the competing designs into functional morphologies that enable you to compare specific design features and come up with a new design that recombines some of the different features in a novel, more effective way.

Purpose

Your report may require a detailed statement of purpose for the work you have undertaken. This will take on a slightly different appearance depending upon the type of report you are creating. A design or technical report will have a purpose section that might include the design goals and some form of "value statement" for the product design. For example, your team may be designing a product for separating plastic from compostable trash. Your purpose for the report might include the design intent and specific design criteria that you wish to optimize.

The purpose of a lab report is not just a section that your instructor wants you to write, it's a motivating reason for doing the lab. Make it real. Take the time in class or in lab to ask your instructor or TA why the lab is being conducted. Ask about the purpose, then decide for yourself before you actually do the experiments. When you think you've got the real reason why you are carrying out the lab, hone it down to one brief sentence: "the purpose of this experiment is to observe the behaviour of an ideal gas in near-adiabatic expansion" or "the purpose of this lab experiment is to evaluate the structural design of a small wooden structure under large loads."

Objectives

You may want to explicitly tell the reader what you hope to achieve with the work presented. As such, it is acceptable to write a brief bulleted list of achievable objectives. The best objectives will be testable. By the end of the report, the reader should be able to clearly tell that, for example, items one to four were successfully accomplished, while items five and six are still in question. In a lab experiment report, the objectives will be tied to the research purpose of the experiment. In the case of a design report or progress report, your objectives will cover those measurable results that your design activity encompasses. For example:

Lab Experiment Objectives:

- Measure the drag force on three different sizes of plastic sphere in crossflow of air at 3, 5, 10 m/s
- Photograph the turbulent wake of spheres tested

Design report objectives:

- Evaluate the selected design with leading competitive designs
- Generate 3D printable models for design prototype functional testing

In either of the above examples, the statements are clear and testable. The reader can look further in the report and determine that the objectives were met within the context of the work reported.

Materials

The *Materials* section presents a description of the materials and equipment you used and provides some explanation of how you set up the experiment. If you modified equipment or varied the setup at different points in the experiment, include a full list of the equipment and describe each separate arrangement. Your explanation of materials must be sufficient for a reader to find the same resources and reproduce the work you have reported.

A simple sketch or two—produced by computer or by hand—will help the reader visualize your arrangement of the equipment. If a diagram is too complicated to fit a regular page, include it as an appropriately labelled attachment at the back of the report and direct the reader to it with a reference.

Even if the apparatus or materials you are using are standard, commercially available items, note the name of the manufacturer, the model number (if applicable), and the name of the source or supplier: for example, "spectroscopic-grade carbon tetrachloride (99% pure) supplied by BDH Chemicals in St. John's."

Method or Procedure

The *Method* section is a step-by-step description of how you carried out the experiment, with procedures presented in the order you performed them. If your experiment consisted of several tests, begin this section with a summary identifying how many tests you ran. This way, your reader is prepared for the numbering of your series. When you describe the tests later in the report, use the same numbering system to prevent confusion.

Write this part of the report with enough specificity to permit anyone to duplicate the experiment in all its details. If you are following instructions in a lab manual, include page references. Summarize the instructions in your own words rather than copying directly. Verify conventions for acknowledging such sources with your lab instructor. Often a standard bibliographic reference is all that's required.

Although you should be concise in your description of the experimental method, make sure that you don't omit essential details. If you heated the contents of a test tube, for example, be sure to report at what temperature you heated them and for how long. If you performed a chromatography or other process at a faster or slower rate than usual, it's important to indicate the rate. Readers need to know exactly what controls to apply if they try to perform the experiment themselves.

When reporting the results of experiments, it is standard practice to use the past tense. However, scientists regularly debate whether to use the active or passive voice (e.g., "*I tested* the sample" versus "The sample *was tested*"). Traditionally, the passive voice was preferred because its detachment seemed appropriate for scientific reports. More recently, writers have tended to use the active voice because it is less likely to produce convoluted sentences. Ask an instructor about your department's preferences but use your own judgment about what reads best. Your goal, whichever voice you use, is to be clear, concise, and objective.

Safety Protocol

In all labs, safety must always be considered before doing any experiments. In most university labs, a safety certificate is required before carrying out a series of experiments. This might be as simple as having the lab technician who is responsible for the space look over your setup before you start, or as complex as requiring a submission to the research safety committee for formal authorization. Regardless of how involved the process is at your institution, your lab report or design report should document the protocols that were observed for the work. It is very helpful to write this section in draft form before even arriving at the lab, but certainly it is worthwhile revising it after the experiments are complete so that any readers will understand that you followed clear rules, and that there are risks inherent in this experiment. Your safety protocols section should be complete and detailed so that a reader could prepare to carry out the same experiment with full awareness of the risks and mitigation strategies.

Original Observations

The most important sections of any report that you write as an engineer or a scientist will be your original observations. These could be anything from your data: a unique experimental setup, a clever or novel analytical solution to a problem, results from a unique user survey, or an innovative design concept. These original observations are the fruits of your labour and will be your contribution to the community of scholars in which you work.

Results or Observations

The *Results* section is of most interest and value to your colleagues, and they depend on its accuracy. It usually presents a blend of data and description. For it to be useful to others, you need to ensure that your derivation of equations and definition of parameters is detailed and correct. Depending on the style and the purpose of your report, you might include extensive calculations or derivations within the section or in an appendix. Whether or not all the detail is included in this section of your report, or in an appendix, you need to ensure that it can be available for those readers who need to understand the detail of your work.

There are certain details to which you should pay particular attention because these will influence the credibility of your results:

- **Underlying assumptions.** Implicit in your work, whether it is design or experimental investigation, you have relied upon a theoretical world view. Recognizing that your work is underpinned by certain assumptions is a form of scientific humility that, if not recognized and acknowledged, could put your results in question. Your work might be based upon an assumption of frictionless flow, or incompressibility, or that your design assumes the materials used have isotropic mechanical properties. In some cases, the design or experimental results would be different if those assumptions prove to be untrue.

- **Model simplifications.** We are not able to put the "real world" in an experiment or a design calculation fully. In order to make any headway, your work makes a variety of simplifications. In your reporting of results, you must declare the important simplifications that have enabled you to carry out the design analysis or experiment.

- **Uncertainty.** Measurements always contain some level of uncertainty. For example, you might measure the diameter of a sphere to be 10 mm. Your results will be more credible if you acknowledge that your method of measurement allows you to claim that the true diameter was 10.0 ±0.1 mm. If the results that you observe are still true with the widest range of these values applied in your subsequent analysis, then the conclusions that you will draw from the work are more valid than if you ignore the uncertainty.

- **Sources of error.** In addition to recognizing the fact of measurement uncertainty, your results' credibility will be enhanced if you can demonstrate to the reader that you understand and have taken steps to minimize or eliminate the sources of error. Reporting these efforts in your results is essential.

- **Statistical significance.** In any experimental results, there are some sources of error that are systematic and there are some that are random. Those random errors can be appreciated and accounted for by replication of tests. Doing so enables you to report the statistical significance of your test results and adds to the credibility of those results for the reader.

Each of the above details are the subject of much longer books and courses on the individual subjects of measurement and statistics. We encourage you to become more familiar with those topics and ensure that you can demonstrate to your readers that you are in command of the experiment and that you fully understand the limitations of your results.

Design Alternatives

In a design report, it is common to report some of the options that you have considered before coming to a design recommendation. The more fully you report the options that you have evaluated, the more faith the reader will have in the wisdom of your ultimate design decisions. Treat this section just like experimental results. Report accurately and completely the options that you have considered, the analysis that you have carried out to help weed out the best options, and some comparative estimates of your decisions.

In many design reports, the authors will try to codify the decision by presenting a design feature morphology table or a decision matrix to help justify the choice of design options. Whatever method that you prefer to use, or that your course instructor and project supervisor encourage you to apply, it should be explained and reported in this section. The best design reports will present design criteria to be used for evaluating options, and then will use good and well-detailed engineering calculations to show the comparative benefits of the different options.

Financial Report, Project Management, and Others

Your report may have a range of other management aspects that should be presented, depending on the context of your report. In general, you will do well to consider each of these as presentation of "data" to the reader. Whether that data is the experimental result from lab tests, or the accounting of project costs and time resources, it should be presented accurately and accompanied by a full explanation.

Original Interpretations

Independent of your raw results and analysis, the most important section of your report is the interpretation section. This is the place where you apply your engineering or scientific judgment to put the data and experimental results into perspective and make sense of what you have seen.

Discussion or Analysis

The *Discussion* or *Analysis* section of the lab report allows you the greatest input; it is here that you interpret the test results and comment on their significance. You want to show how the test produced its outcome—whether expected or unexpected—and to discuss elements that influenced the results.

In determining what details to include in the *Discussion* section, you might address the following questions:

- Do the results reflect the goal of the experiment?
- Do these results agree with previous findings, as reported in the literature on the subject? If not, how do you account for the discrepancy between your data and those accepted or obtained by other students and researchers?
- What may have gone wrong during your experiment, and why? Can you propose a source of error?
- Could the results have another explanation?
- Did the procedures you used make sense considering what you hoped to accomplish? Does your experience suggest a better approach for next time?

For a good discussion, think critically about how your own work relates to previous work that you have read about or done yourself. Remember to acknowledge primary and secondary sources.

For design or project progress reports, your discussion might consider the following questions:

- Have we met the design requirements with any of the options?
- Are there any design criteria that are especially hard to meet with the options available?
- What are the cost implications of each option evaluated?
- Have we missed any design alternatives?
- Will the design alternatives compete successfully with other state-of-the-art solutions?

Conclusions

The *Conclusions* section briefly lists the conclusions that may be drawn from the experiment and the analysis. You don't necessarily need a separate section for these in a brief report—they may also appear in a short paragraph at the end of the *Discussion* section.

Conclusions need to be logically drawn from all the work presented in the report. It is not okay to introduce new information in this section. The conclusions section should be brief and it should allow the reader to follow your reasoning in order to come to the same conclusions.

Recommendations

Not every type of report needs to present recommendations. A lab report need not typically recommend anything for further work. If it does, usually the recommendations simply encourage direction for further research.

Design reports and project reports are quite different in this regard. It is necessary that a design report recommend the decision to be taken in design. You need to tell the reader whether the design should proceed, what type of design is preferred based on the work, or what additional work needs to be done before a design decision can be taken with confidence.

If you opt to present recommendations, they should be brief and concrete. Bullet-form lists are very effective for recommendations. For example, design report recommendations might include:

> Both design options A and B will result in a prototype that satisfies all of the design requirements and is superior to other options in all criteria aside from the criteria #7: environmental impact.
>
> At this time, the analysis shows that design option A or B will both satisfy the requirements, but we do not have sufficient wind drag data to recommend a preferred alternative.
>
> Wind tunnel testing of the design options A and B should be carried out before prototyping.

End Material

After the bulk of the report is complete, there are a few sections that you may need to include. These aren't sections that the readers will look at unless they are looking for something specific.

References

List references to any outside sources used in your work, including the course textbook, on a separate page before the *Appendices*. There are many citation formats, and you should follow the ones recommended by your course instructor, or by the journal or publisher of the report that you are writing (see Appendix A). If they have no preferred format, then pick one that you are most comfortable with and learn to follow the detailed citation rules carefully.

Appendices

If you have extensive detailed results, particularly computer-generated ones that fill more than a page or two, include these at the end of your report. If you have more than one section, number them *Appendix 1*, *Appendix 2*, and so on. Make sure each has a title that identifies its contents (for example, *Appendix 2: MATHCAD Worksheet*), and list them, including the titles, in your *Contents*. In a lab book, you will simply paste these data or calculations in where they fit naturally.

Format, Style, and Writing

We have saved the topic of your detailed style of writing and formats for the final discussion in this chapter. While you might feel this is the first thing to worry about in your writing, really it is the final detail. If you craft the report with the right overall structure and include the correct amount of content in a topic format that makes sense to the reader, you will be forgiven somewhat for your actual writing. However, if you want your report to really be the best it can be, then you need to pay attention to the details of grammar and wording, the format and style of figures and figure captions, and the overall look of the report.

Your report should always be written in the past tense—after all, your report informs the reader about work that you have done in the past, not work you are doing in the present. You may choose to write in the first person (I did . . . , or We did . . .) if you wish, or you may choose to be more formal in the third person (. . . was done . . .). Either style is acceptable in most contexts in North America. Before you finish your writing, it would be a good idea to scan that section and look for any common mistakes.

Chapter Checklist

- ☐ Structure your report to include the appropriate front material for identifying and archiving your work.
- ☐ Provide context in the introduction sections for the report itself, as well as the science and decisions made.
- ☐ Present your original observations, calculations, and analysis with enough detail that others could reproduce your work.
- ☐ Present logical and justified original interpretations based on the observations.
- ☐ Provide complete and correct references.

10 Writing Tests and Examinations

Chapter Objectives

- Summarize the value of preparing for exams from the first day of term
- Formulate an effective study schedule
- Integrate practice problems into your study schedule to maximize retention
- Use visualization strategies in exam prep
- Identify tactics for effective time management during exams

Introduction

An undergraduate degree in engineering or science requires that you complete around 40 courses over your four-year degree. More than half of those courses will have test- or exam-based evaluations. Most of those will be written in an age-old format: a pencil and an exam booklet with a sheet of questions to answer. Even in an age when we do most of our work electronically, this exam format still retains a primary place in your success.

Most students feel nervous before tests and exams. It's not surprising. Writing an exam imposes special pressures because of the time restrictions, breadth of questions, and lack of access to reference material. These elements combine into a stressful and out-of-the-ordinary experience. To do your best, you need to feel calm. The following general guidelines should help you approach any test or exam with confidence.

Preparing for the Exam

Exam preparation begins long before the exam period itself. A daily or weekly review of lecture notes and class resources helps you remember important material and relate new information to old. If you don't review regularly, at the end of the term you'll be faced with relearning rather than remembering.

Read the Course Syllabus

During the first week of classes, carefully review the course syllabus provided by your instructor for each course you are taking. These syllabi are essentially the contract between you and your instructors, and they provide helpful advice and guidelines for being successful in your class.

An essential component of your course syllabus is the grading system. In this section, you'll find the due dates for assignments as well as their grading weight. Perhaps the class has a midterm exam and a final exam. Perhaps there are three tests in class and a final exam. Are those worth 100 per cent of the grade, or are they diluted by projects and reports? Knowing how long you must work on an assignment and what it's worth in your overall grade will help you plan your strategy for the semester.

Attend Class

The first step in successfully writing exams is to make sure that you attend every lecture or tutorial. Attending lectures keeps you aware of what section of the course you should be working on and gives you an opportunity to ask your instructor questions in a timely fashion.

Ask Questions

Most students are shy and don't want to stand out in front of the class. Most people in general are afraid of sounding foolish by asking a dumb question. Many students actually imagine that a professor will resent or be upset at a simple question. In fact, most professors love to have a good question. A question from the class is a good indication that students are engaged and trying to learn the material. Questions also help professors get a sense of what material the class finds difficult.

Whether you ask a question during the lecture, at a time when the instructor may pause and invite questions, or after the lecture, you shouldn't hesitate to ask a question about the content of the class or the course. When you ask your professor or teaching assistant a question, you will find that they are helpful one-on-one, enthusiastic about the topic, and can explain things differently to help you grasp the concepts.

Practice

When you have finished looking at the syllabi for all your courses, and you have made up your weekly schedule of classes, continue with your time management activity by breaking the rest of your time into "appointments" for yourself with the course materials. When doing so, try to set out one-hour or half-hour blocks of time that will regularly have you refresh your knowledge in each course. A great way to plan this is to think about interacting with each subject every single day. Daily practice with the concepts will help you layer your learning and really understand the concepts. Interacting with a course is a lot more effort than merely reviewing the notes: you need to connect with the material. Try putting the concepts into practice, analyzing concepts, creating a conceptual model, and deconstructing a design with your mind, pencil, paper, and hands.

Perhaps you have a Tuesday schedule in which you have a fluid mechanics class, a dynamics class, and a differential equations class with a tutorial in the afternoon. Attend those classes, take notes, and work on assignments fully committed to the courses that are scheduled. This should take up five hours or so of your day. Suppose that you plan to spend another four hours (two in the morning before class and two in the evening) working through the material at home. In those times, schedule yourself to work on studying or doing practice problems for your programming and your electric circuits course, the two classes that you did not have in the formal schedule on Tuesday. By the end of your workday, you will have interacted with every class, and you will have notes to show your progress, which will help you to know what is going on in every one of your courses. If you struggle with a concept, you can ask your instructor about it before or after your next class, keeping you on top of the course material.

How to Use Practice Problems

A key element of engineering classes is practice questions. Whether these come from a course textbook or are provided by the instructor, these questions are designed to help you understand the course material. More than that, they are there to help you test how well you understand the material.

Textbook problems follow a conventional format in science and engineering. They usually contain a simple sketch and provide data and parameters that relate back to the chapter content. The problems typically ask you to solve for one or more variables defined in the chapter. Try the following approach to your practice problems:

1. Rewrite the problem statement in your own words. If there is a figure, re-sketch it with variables and dimensions shown.
2. Make up a table of known properties and variables.
3. If you think you know an approach to solve the problem, try jotting down a point-form list of steps, and make sure to clearly note what physical principles that you will use at each step.
4. If the problem is connected to a section of your textbook or class notes, have a quick scan through them for other examples or relevant explanations. Look for similar parameters as mentioned in your problem. Look for similar questions and phrases in the chapter as used in your problem. This should ensure that you are on the right path.
5. Go back to your problem and try to apply concepts from the chapter, the equations used in the examples, and similar calculations to produce an answer.
6. If, anywhere along the way, you begin to get stuck, pause. Look back at your steps, and see if you have forgotten something. Look at the chapter in the book and see if there is a similar problem to review.
7. If you are still stuck, write down a one-sentence summary of the problem you are having. Put it aside and move to another problem.
8. Bring the sheets you've worked on with you to class. Make a point of asking the professor or the TA the very next day about this problem. Show them the steps you have taken and ask them to help get you unstuck.
9. Evaluate your solution. Is the result reasonable? Does it agree with an answer that may be given? Does it make logical sense? Can you put it in context to check its validity?

Notice one very important thing missing from these steps: checking the answer at the back of the book. The best way to learn is to develop the right approach yourself, not looking at someone else's method. Instead of looking at the back of the textbook or online for the solutions, talk to your instructor or your TA about the solutions. It will immensely improve your chances in the exam.

Plan Ahead

The time that you spend preparing to write an exam is an investment. If you invest your time early in the semester, by the time the exam rolls around, you'll have a bank of knowledge to withdraw from. The concepts in engineering and science build upon the early foundations. If you plan ahead, you will spend less time studying close to the date of the exam than you might have if you had invested all your time at the end.

For example, you are studying fluid mechanics and you are struggling with the first section on hydrostatic forces on submerged surfaces. You go to your professor and she explains it slightly differently than she did in lecture, and it makes sense to you. By asking for help early, the next topics of pipe flow and head loss and of drag and lift are clear to you. When exam time comes around, you don't have to practise hydrostatics, because your revision of drag and lift covered the same concepts, saving you time and stress. If you had waited to ask for help later in the semester, it would have taken you longer to learn the concepts and you would need to catch up on a lot more material. Planning ahead by making sure that you learn the basics through and through is the best way to save time in the end.

Last-Minute Preparations

It is the day before the big exam: you've done the practice problems, reviewed the course content, and asked a lot of questions of your instructors. You don't have to spend time cramming and talking about what you think might be on the exam or how hard it will be with your classmates will only stress you out, so you have some time on your hands. The best thing to do is to work on your own emotions by visualizing how you will feel during the exam.

Visualizing is most effective in the actual space where the exam will take place. If the exam is in a regular classroom, or some space that you can access afterhours when the place is empty, then plan to visit. Get comfortable in the space by sitting in one or two different seats where you might sit during the exam and by examining the room. After you've had some time to really look around you and to notice some small features in the room, imagine yourself with the exam paper in front of you and a pen in your hand. Now, go through each question and topic that you expect to be on the exam, and associate a different piece of the room around you with the important details and things to remember for that sort of question. For each of your imagined questions, picture yourself solving them in an orderly, business-like fashion. For example, suppose you're in a strength of materials exam and the first question is about the shear strain on a metal bolt. Look at the metal bolt above you that holds the projector in place. Ask yourself what its state of stress is and imagine the steps you will go through to solve a problem for that bolt. Picture the process as if it's a tag tied to the bolt. Imagine yourself solving the problem. By associating abstract concepts and processes with physical objects, you will more easily re-member the concepts when you look back at those objects when you get stuck.

Writing an Exam

When the day finally arrives to actually write an exam or a test, give yourself lots of time to get to an exam. If you have to travel by car or public transit, don't forget that busses can be late and traffic can jam. Always allow for a margin of error. The same advice applies if you are writing a test electronically on your course's learning management system. Don't wait until the last minute to sub-mit your answers, or you may find the drop box closed.

If you are late for an exam, or you miss it entirely, don't panic. Document the situation as best you can (for example, with a police report if you've been in a fender-bender or emergency-room record if it's worse). Let your professor and the department know about the situation immediately so that alternative arrangements can be made. The longer you wait to get in touch, the more your predicament will be met with skepticism.

Once you finally make it to your seat, with your pens and calculator at the ready, the following tips might help.

Read the Exam

Much as time seems limited, you are better off to be right than first to finish. Instead of starting to write immediately, take a few minutes at the beginning to read through all the questions and create a plan. Time spent thinking and organizing at the outset brings better results than the same time spent scrib-bling furiously. It's essential to read each question carefully to make sure you understand exactly what's being asked.

Choose Your Questions

Once you've read all the questions, decide the order that you want to complete them. Some people prefer to do the "easy" ones first, get them out of the way, and then move to the more difficult ones. The logic in doing this sequence is often that you can build confidence by doing the easy work first and then you can save the time later for the difficult ones. Some students prefer to just simply work in the order of the exam paper. You should choose whichever method suits you best.

Apportion Your Time

Read the instructions carefully to find out how many questions you must answer and to see what choices you have. Subtract five minutes or so for planning, and then divide the time you have left by the number of questions you have. If possible, allow for time at the end to review your answers. If the instructions on the exam indicate that not all questions are of equal value, apportion your time accordingly.

Keep Calm

If your first reaction on reading an exam is to panic, help yourself to be calm by taking slow, deep breaths to relax, and then decide which question you can answer best. Even if the exam looks impossible at first, there's always one question that seems manageable. If you had a chance to visit the room before this (see the previous section), look for the object in the room that relates to the topic of your first question. Try to remember the feeling you had when you sat in this place a few days ago and call up the tag that you attached to that object from your memory. Try to think about the specific topic, not about the circumstances that this is an exam. By the time you have finished the first question, you will find that your mind has calmed down and has automatically begun to consider the next question.

Read Each Question Carefully

As you consider each question, read it carefully and identify key words. The wording specifies the direction your answer should take. Be sure that you don't overlook or misinterpret anything (something that's easy to do when you're nervous). If you are required to complete the exam on the test paper itself, note the amount of space allotted for each answer. It tells you better than anything else how much detail your answer should contain.

Make Notes

As a preliminary strategy, jot down key ideas, details, and formulas on rough paper or the unlined pages of your answer book. These notes will keep you from forgetting something as you write. Use them to organize yourself once you start to answer in earnest. If these pages are part of the booklet to be submitted, just draw a box around the section and write "rough calculations" at the top.

Write and Sketch Neatly

Poor handwriting makes markers cranky. Tiny or messy sketches with no annotations make it difficult to understand your method. When the person correcting your exam has to struggle to read your answers, they may simply not understand you, and you may get lower marks than you deserve. Sketches of the solution geometry, or sketched graphs, need to be at least ¼ page in size, and they should be explained with a sentence or two, and key points or dimensions must be clearly shown. If you are using a geometry sketch to derive equations, then the variables need to be clearly shown on the sketch.

Keep to Your Time Plan

Keep to your plan for time per question. It's usually possible to score part marks for a question you can't fully answer, so put something down for every question if you can. If you find yourself short of time, summarize what you have written and move on. If you have time, you can always go back to complete an answer once you've answered the more valuable questions to the best of your ability. If you ever change an answer, cross out the old one neatly, don't use an eraser. It is common for students, towards the end of an exam to start second-guessing the first answer. It would be a shame to erase a correct solution because you are tired and stressed.

Reread Your Answers

No matter how tired you are, try to leave time to review your answers at the end of the exam. Check especially for readability. Revisions that make answers easier to follow are always worth the effort.

Open-Book Exams

Permission to take a formula sheet or textbook into the exam room doesn't guarantee an easy exam. In fact, allowing you to bring in reference materials actually gives the professor freedom to ask you more difficult questions. After all, the easy questions are already solved in your book or notes.

Make sure that you are fully comfortable with your reference material. Tabs on the pages you often turn to are a good idea. You can save time in an exam, and build confidence, by taping a tab label to the page with the table of material properties, or whatever element you kept using in the practice problems.

Formula Sheets

If you can bring in a formula sheet, be careful to follow directions exactly. Normally, you will be given a definition of what you're allowed to bring—for example, a standard-sized sheet of paper with writing on one side only. Follow the instructions precisely.

The real value of a formula sheet is not its handiness during the exam. The formula sheet is a tool that you can use to help you organize and prioritize the course content while you study. If you've spent 12 weeks covering the syllabus of the course, when you do your practice problems, you will start to get a sense of what questions are asked more frequently, and what principles are priorities. The formula sheet forces you to draw a complete picture of the course in one page. Typically, if you've studied effectively, and if you have spent quality time preparing a neat formula sheet, you will look at it only once or twice during the exam, but the time spent preparing it will have been invaluable.

Writing a Multiple-Choice Test

Multiple-choice tests are not particularly common in engineering and science, but you may encounter them. The main difficulty with these tests is that the questions are often designed to confuse students who are not certain of the correct answers. If you tend to second-guess yourself or if you are the sort of person who sees alternatives to every question, you may find such tests particularly difficult at first. Fortunately, practice almost always improves performance.

Preparation for multiple-choice tests is the same as for other kinds of exams that emphasize your ability to recall or apply information. Although there is no sure recipe for doing well, other than a thorough knowledge of the course material, the following suggestions may help.

Look at the Marking System

If marks are based solely on the number of right answers, pick an answer for every question, even if you aren't sure it's the right one. For a question with four possible answers, you have a 25 per cent chance of being right—even if you pick the answers at random.

On the other hand, if there is a penalty for wrong answers (with marks deducted for errors), make sure you guess only when you are fairly sure you are right, or when you are able to rule out most of the possibilities. Making wild guesses in these circumstances does more harm than good.

Do the Easy Questions First

Go through the test at least twice. On the first round, deal only with those questions that you can answer without difficulty, and don't waste time on troublesome questions. If all the questions are of equal value, start by getting all the marks you can on the ones you find easy. Save the more difficult questions to tackle the second time around. This approach has two advantages: first, you won't be forced by time to leave out questions that you could easily have answered correctly; second, when you come back to a harder question on the second round, you may find that you have figured out the answer in the meantime. Sometimes, reading other questions and answers reminds you of material you had forgotten.

Make Your Guesses Educated Ones

If you have to guess, at least increase your chances of getting the answer right. Forget about intuition, hunches, and lucky numbers. More importantly, forget about so-called patterns of correct answers—the idea that if there have been two "A" answers in a row, the next one can't possibly be "A" as well. Many test-setters either don't worry about patterns or else deliberately elude pattern-hunters by giving the right answer the same letter or number several times in a row.

James F. Shepherd [1] has suggested a number of tips that will increase your chances of making the right guess:

- Start by weeding out all the answers you know are wrong, rather than looking for the right one.
- Avoid any terms you don't recognize. Some students are taken in by anything that looks like sophisticated terminology and may assume that such answers must be correct. In fact, these answers are usually wrong (the unfamiliar term may well be a red herring, especially if it is close in sound to the correct one).
- Ignore jokes or humorous statements.
- Choose the best available answer, even if it is not indisputably true. Choose the long answer over the short (it's more likely to contain the

detail needed to make it correct) and the particular statement over the general (generalizations are usually too sweeping to be true).

- Choose "all of the above" over individual answers unless you can immediately spot a wrong answer. Test-setters know that students with a patchy knowledge of the course material often fasten on the one fact they know. Only those with a thorough knowledge recognize that all the answers listed are correct.

What If You Feel Overwhelmed?

Your university wants you to succeed. The structure of your program is challenging, and many students take the pressure and turn it inwards in ways that can be hard to deal with on your own. If you feel that, even sitting in the exam room beforehand, is simply too much, ask for help. Go to your professor, your department, your dorm, anywhere, and tell someone how you feel. Your classmates might be well-intentioned, but you need to talk to someone who is not a student. There are staff members at your university to help you find the right help at your student services office.

Chapter Checklist

- ☐ To prepare for exams effectively, practise sufficiently throughout the term.
- ☐ Do the practice problems yourself throughout the semester, and ask your instructors for help when you encounter problems.
- ☐ Review material you expect to be on the exam while visualizing, ensuring you connect questions and concepts with a physical object for easy remembrance.
- ☐ When taking an exam, read the questions carefully, making sure you fully understand what the question is asking before answering.
- ☐ If you feel overwhelmed before exams, tell someone. Ask for help.

References

1.   J.F. Shepherd, *College Study Skills*, 6th ed., Boston: Houghton Mifflin, 2002.

Part III
Writing for Others

11 Writing for Non-specialists

Chapter Objectives

- Summarize the steps of preparing to write
- Apply the Who-Why-No-No-Do questions when determining audience
- Apply three types of models when drafting your writing: GEST, TEPS, and TRC
- Develop questions to ask yourself when editing

Introduction

In your career, you will write a lot and you will share your sketches and ideas with many people from a wide diversity of backgrounds. You want your work to have the greatest positive impact on the world around you. That means your communication must educate and encourage people to act based on your professional opinion, your evidence, and your arguments. You will need to learn some ways to communicate your technical and scientific knowledge to people who don't have your background and who may not even understand some of your language.

Communicating with a non-science audience does not mean you must "dumb down" your work. Quite the contrary, the cleverest, clearest thinkers in science seem to effortlessly communicate complex theory to people from all disciplines. Your challenge is to clearly articulate your ideas to people who lack your background but who can still follow well-told stories. If you are successful, you will empower your audience to take informed decisions and actions.

Preparing to Write

The writing and illustrations that you have created from your notes and your reports form the raw material that you will draw upon to create work that will be read by non-specialists. All the planning advice given in Chapters 1, 2, and 4 still applies. Let's apply these to an example of creating a piece for an audience of non-scientists.

Know Your Reader

Before you start to construct your document, make a clear and definitive story about the target reader. Is this a report for a single person, for example, the president of your company, the deputy minister of your government department, or perhaps an elementary school teacher? Maybe this is a newspaper op-ed piece that you want to submit to explain an issue of importance to the community. Perhaps this is an executive council memo to send to your deputy minister for consideration by the government leaders. Whichever it is, the first step is to define your reader and what they know and don't know about your topic. From there, decide what language and wording is best.

Recall that in Chapter 1 we presented the simple Who-Why-No-No-Do mnemonic. We'll apply it here with an example of informing a non-technical executive about the impacts of tourism on the city:

WHO: The provincial deputy minister of environment and the provincial government executive council.

- Background: DM of environment: a business degree from Laurier in 1993.
- Worked as a stockbroker from 1995 to 2000.
- Moved to provincial govt after MBA at U of T in 2002.
- Managed projects in dept of env and treasury.
- In writing examples, seems very well-read, uses high-level vocabulary. No reference to science, but broad general and strong business background. I can use these examples as guides to what they will accept in writing level.
- The writing was very formal, so not good to use slang or to be too personal. Need to keep it clean and professional for them. They use bullet points quite a lot.
- Climate change: was on interdisciplinary committee in dept of Env, so knows background issues and language.

WHY: To get a clear understanding of the impacts in the city of Toronto resulting from increased tourism along the boardwalk.

KNOW (before): They know the province and the city plan to promote the city boardwalk as a summer destination for events.

KNOW (after): They need to understand the impact tourism will have on air quality, transit times, parking, and emergency services in the downtown core and the waterfront.

DO: I want them to ensure that support services are funded in keeping with increased traffic.

Decide What This Piece Will Be

Before you write a word, sketch out for yourself the basic parameters of the finished product. Will this be a three-page article with four figures, or will this be a one-page piece with room for three paragraphs and no figures? Your finished product must fit within those constraints. There is no value in writing a memo for the board of directors of your company that is three pages long if you know they will only have time and attention to read a single page.

You could, at this stage, create a storyboard for your finished piece. Storyboarding is a visual tool that divides the content of your piece into blocks so that your ideas can be better organized. Figure 11.1 shows an example storyboard for a small writing piece. The example shows the whole item will need to fit on a single page, and it will have one figure that will be ¼ page, leaving space for four paragraphs of text. The first paragraph will be an introduction of fewer than 70 words. The second paragraph will describe traffic flows into downtown Toronto in fewer than 70 words. The third paragraph will explain the impacts of greater traffic on city services in 100 words, and the final paragraph will be a call to action on providing funding support for workers. The figure will be a plot that illustrates the increase in ambulance calls on the vertical axis versus number of tourists on the waterfront based upon traffic data.

Create an Idea Map

Chapter 1 described how to create an Idea map of the writing and then to convert it into an outline. While the piece that we are considering here is only brief, it helps to create a map for the document to ensure that you remember to include each of the important points. An example idea map is shown in Figure 11.2. In this figure, we have drawn out the topics and ideas that we want to connect in the written work. The map can then be translated to an outline, although in this case the article is so short that it could be set up such that each bubble is a single sentence or two.

Figure 11.1 Storyboard for a one-page memo.

This shows the storyboard for a one-page memo intended to explain a complex technical problem to a non-technical executive. Each of the paragraphs is shown and the relative space that it should be allowed in the document.

Assemble Your Supporting Material

As an engineer or a professional scientist, non-specialists expect that you will be knowledgeable and rigorous in your understanding of all aspects of a topic about which you write. The material that you have produced before writing a document for the non-specialist is your background data. This will never be seen by the readers of your one page, but you need to be above reproach when you make statements about your science. The good news is that, so long as you are within a topic where you genuinely are expert, the background material is easy for you.

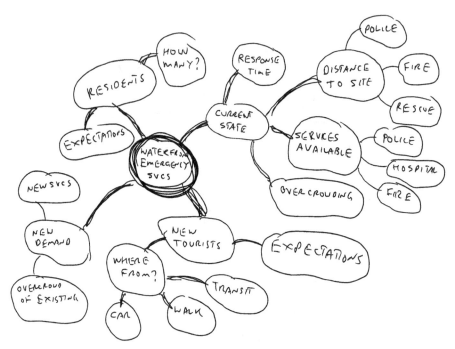

Figure 11.2 Idea map for a one-page memo.

The idea map for a one-page memo shows the major concepts and how they are connected. Each of the paragraphs in the final document will be formed from the second-level concepts, and sentences are created from the lowest level items.

Take the time to save background material to a folder related to the writing project at hand. Before you sit down to write your first draft, reread through all the material, just to remind yourself of the details, and refresh your memory of the important points.

One of the most difficult things for a writer is to start with a blank page. Luckily, you are not that writer! Your current piece of writing is the tip of the writing pyramid shown in Chapter 5. You have a huge mass of material that has come before. You can pull out your original notes from meetings, lab tests, class, design testing, and from all kinds of original content that you have already created for yourself. You also have the items that you have written for your colleagues and teammates.

Perhaps the most efficient way to start writing is to look through your previous work and clip out paragraphs, figures, notes, and sketches that you have already created. They don't need to be clean or clear, or anything other than raw examples of the ideas you've already written. You might be able to cut and paste five to 10 pages of examples that come from a variety of your own sources.

At this point, you aren't thinking about plagiarism, as long as you realize this cut-and-paste document will never be seen by anyone. This is just a way to get yourself started, and to have your background ideas populate the document at hand. Once you've pasted items in every section of the idea map or storyboard for your article, you are ready to start re-writing over what you have pasted.

Writing

It doesn't matter which paragraph or section of the document you start with. Some people like to start at the beginning, go on to the end, and then stop. Others like to write the introduction last. Decide on your own style and run with it. If you have brought in examples of your personal writing for all sections of the piece that you are writing, now you can go through that material and cut out the extra junk, rewrite the ideas, and rephrase explanations. You might take a full page of rough material that was captured from your personal notes and end up with only one paragraph. By the time you have finished, the original writing that you pasted won't exist. It will be distilled to share some of the same ideas in fewer words and better sentences.

Develop the Introduction

Introductions can often be the hardest part of a piece to write. You need to tell readers what you will be writing about, giving them a road map about what's to come, while being clear and succinct. As you develop the writing, remember that it has a purpose, and your wording needs to clearly articulate that purpose. If you have trouble getting an idea down in your work, then consider the basic **GEST** pattern below for the overall flow of the introduction to a brief piece of writing:

GENERAL STATEMENT (**G**):	the larger problem or topic of the article
EVIDENCE (**E**):	some applications/examples of the issue
SUMMARY STATEMENT (**S**):	applications/examples to show why you are writing this
THESIS (**T**):	primary focus of this article

Sheridan Baker [1] calls this the funnel approach because it works its way from broad to narrow in a few short sentences. The funnel introduction works for almost any kind of writing. The following example sets the stage for the introduction to a single-paragraph executive memo:

> (G) The City of Toronto and Province of Ontario are promoting Toronto's waterfront as a tourist destination. (E) Over the past year, our department has engaged in multiple inter-governmental initiatives relating to this effort. (S) Within the MoE, we have developed scenarios that show that increased tourism will demand multi-factored support across several services. (T) This memo proposes departmental action to scale appropriate support with increased visits.

In four brief sentences, the reader has a general background for the issue and has a clear idea of what the purpose and perspective is of the memo. It is important to note that knowledge of the reader governs the language used in the piece. While in general, an acronym should be defined the first time it is used, in this example we can rely upon the deputy minister of environment to be completely comfortable with the acronym of "MoE" as a reference to her department, the "Ministry of Environment." In this specific context, taking the space to define "Ministry of Environment (MoE)" might be simply annoying to the busy reader and give a sense that the author is not genuinely expert in this topic or context. In comparison, the reference to the province or the city might not have such a commonly seen acronym, so the full names are used.

Another consideration with acronyms is whether they will be used later in the piece. In the above example, the background context may indeed involve the City of Toronto and the provincial government, but once that has been stated as background, the reader may never need to be reminded of that. Hence, defining an acronym for those entities might be seen as a waste of space.

Consider an alternative version of the above example, one that is less effective:

> Tourism has been growing in the western world since Canada was founded. Tourist income is very important to Toronto. Even the fathers of confederation travelled to Charlottetown on a summer holiday that resulted in the forming of Canada. Tourism can have great results, like it did in this example. Toronto's waterfront is a great place for tourism. The City of Toronto (CoT) and Province of Ontario (PoO) want the waterfront to be a tourist destination. We want to increase tourism on the Toronto Waterfront (TW).

The second example starts with a much more broad background statement. It brings in unsubstantiated and somewhat vague claims ("since Canada was founded") and includes irrelevant details (what has Charlottetown to do with this?). It proposes some new acronyms that are not commonly used (CoT and PoO). In the end, the point of this article, which was to encourage appropriate scaling of support services, is never mentioned. The reader is left with a vague sense that this article will try to promote tourism. However you choose to start a paper, your reader must understand your purpose. Whether your article is one paragraph or several, make sure that by the end of it, your reader knows exactly what to expect from the paper that follows.

Develop the Body

It takes several paragraphs to develop a complex idea, and each new paragraph signals a change in the way you approach that idea. If you are struggling to write the body of your piece, then approach each paragraph independently. For each separate paragraph, try the **TEPS** format. This structure provides a basic pattern for each paragraph developing a topic in the body of an essay.

TOPIC SENTENCE (**T**):	The topic of this paragraph. (What's the point?)
ELABORATION (**E**):	This is how it will be focused. (Can you be more specific?)
PROOF/EXAMPLES (**P**)++:	These are some applications/examples. You should include as many as you think needed (P++) (Can you prove it?)
SUMMARY (**S**):	This is what it all means. (So what?)

The summary sentence often establishes the connection between the paragraph and the main point of the article. If this link is obvious, or if the next paragraph deals with a similar subject, the summary may not be needed. Still, the **TEPS** pattern is useful for confirming that you've kept your writing on topic.

(**T**) Traffic to the Toronto waterfront has increased over the past fifteen years. (**E**) The increase of traffic has led to an increase in demand for emergency support services. (**P**) The department of transportation has collected daily TTC ridership records showing 150 per cent increase in the daily visits to the lakeshore. (**P**) The Toronto Police Service records over the same time period show a trend of 300 per cent increased emergency calls to the waterfront. (S) These independent records show that there has been a disproportionate increase in demand for emergency services as traffic to the Toronto waterfront has grown.

Each of the subsequent paragraphs that you need to write can easily follow the same format. While this runs the risk of sounded formulaic and tedious, at least your article will cover the content if you ensure that each paragraph addresses one of the items in your outline or idea map.

Once you have written all the body paragraphs, if they follow the **TEPS** structure, then you can easily rearrange them to help the overall flow and logic. If you are happy with the order, then a read through the whole piece will give you a chance to adjust wording and sentences to avoid tedium, eliminate redundancy, and improve the flow.

Conclusion

Your work needs to come to a conclusion that will help the reader to make a decision and take some action. For a small article, this might be a single summary paragraph that follows the **TRC** model:

TOPIC REVIEW (T):   Restate the topic of this piece.

REITERATE (R):   Restate the most important evidence

CALL TO ACTION (C):   This is what you think should be done next.

Carrying on with our previous example, we might choose to finish up the memo to our deputy minister using the TRC structure. Keep in mind that there were some other paragraphs in the actual article, so our list of items that are being reiterated is longer than that mentioned in the earlier example.

(T) Tourism traffic to the Toronto waterfront has increased and will continue to rise over the next decade. (R) Data collected over the past fifteen years shows the demand for emergency services and support services has been increasing in step with tourism. (R) This trend is likely to continue based upon independent projections. (R) The MoE will need to increase its financial and staff support of services to the

Toronto waterfront in step with the tourism increases. (C) It is necessary for the MoE to anticipate these increases in its budget process.

With this, your brief memo to the deputy minister and executive council is complete. If you have established your evidence, and communicated it in a convincing way, then you have provided a clear direction that your expertise indicates should be taken. It is up to the reader to decide how well your evidence has convinced them to take the action you are suggesting.

Edit Carefully

Editing doesn't mean simply checking your work for errors in grammar or spelling. It means looking at the entire piece to see if the ideas are well organized, well documented, and well expressed. You might revise the structure of the essay by adding some paragraphs or sentences, deleting others, and moving others around. Experienced writers may be able to check several aspects of their work at the same time, but if you are inexperienced or in doubt about your writing, it's best to look at the organization of the ideas before you tackle sentence structure, diction, style, and documentation.

Below is a checklist of questions to ask yourself as you begin editing.

- Is my title concise and informative?
- Are the purpose and approach of this essay evident from the beginning?
- Are all sections of the paper relevant to the topic?
- Is the organization logical?
- Are all the ideas sufficiently developed? Is there enough evidence, explanation, and illustration?
- Would my reader understand everything I'm saying? Should I clarify some parts or add any explanatory material?
- In presenting my argument, do I take into account opposing arguments or evidence?
- Do my paragraph divisions make my ideas more coherent? Have I used them to keep similar ideas together and signal movement from one idea to another?
- Do any parts of the essay seem disjointed? Should I add more transitional words or logical indicators to make the sequence of ideas easier to follow?
- Do my conclusions accurately reflect my argument in the body of the work?

You might also devise your own checklist based on comments you have received on previous assignments. If you have a particular weak area (for example, wordiness or run-on sentences), be sure to give it special attention. Keeping a personal checklist will save you from repeating the same old mistakes.

Finally, once your article seems to flow, and the structure meets the needs that you intend for the piece, you should pay close attention to the details of wording and grammar. One of the most effective ways to improve the clarity of your draft writing is to read it aloud. If your own knowledge of grammar rules is weak, try reading the article to anyone you can cajole to listen. Ask them to stop you when they lose the story. That is usually an indication that your sentence structure and wording has become confusing. Revise and try again.

If you don't have anyone handy that is willing to listen, then simply read it aloud to an empty room. You will be surprised to find how many times you will come upon phrases that are hard to read and need to be revised. Also consider using your computer to read the text aloud for you. Most word programs have a read-aloud option, and even though the voice is typically flat, it helps to highlight the passages in your writing that are dull or confusing.

Once you have edited the document for structure and content by considering your list of questions, and you have tried editing for wording and grammar, don't stop improving. A piece of writing is always open for improvement, so the more times you read and revise the better it will become.

Chapter Checklist

- ☐ Create a storyboard for your writing piece.
- ☐ Create an idea map showing the ideas to be presented and develop the levels to help guide the writing of your work.
- ☐ Use the GEST model to produce a simple introduction.
- ☐ Draft body paragraphs following the TEPS model.
- ☐ Ensure that the writing finishes strongly using the TRC model.
- ☐ Apply the major questions when editing your work.
- ☐ Create your own custom list of editing questions based upon your past feedback.

12 Writing Proposals

Introduction

Your career in science and engineering is as much about imagining a vision of the future, and recruiting people to believe that vision, as it is about analysis and measurement of theoretical predictions. Throughout your professional life, you will need to find the financial, human, and equipment resources to make your vision come true, and to test your ideas in the marketplace or with a field experiment. If you want to make an impact in your career, you will need to write proposals.

What Is a Proposal?

A proposal is a formal communication that provides a persuasive summary of a project in order to convince its audience of the project's value. There are a variety of kinds—research, sales, improvement—but each is essentially asking for people to believe in you and to help you accomplish your ideas. Those people might be other scientists who sit on a grant review panel, senior management of a company, the principals in a venture capital firm, or potential customers for your business. They have the power to give you access to something you need to get a job done. The only thing in the way is their willingness to give you access.

Proposals are based on common human interaction. Think of a proposal using a simple example you may have encountered: Imagine that one of your classmates asks you to come along on a weekend camping trip. The first questions you might ask are:

- Where do you want to go?
- How long will it take us?
- Who is coming along?
- Have any of you ever camped before?
- Do you already have everything we need or do we need to get some stuff?
- What will it cost?
- What else do you need from me?

You could probably come up with a few more questions to ask, but we have captured most of the basic ones. If your friend responds with an unbelievable answer for any of those questions, or is evasive, then you will probably decide not to join them. You will likely only seriously consider joining the trip if all the questions are answered in a satisfactory way. Professional and scientific proposals are just the same, and the basic questions a funding agency or academic committee will look to be answered by your proposal will sound very similar to those ones you asked about the camping trip.

Preparing to Write

The steps required for the actual writing of your proposal are similar to what you've done for all your other writing projects. Start with the reader, and then use the Who-Why-No-No-Do model.

Who Is Your Reader?

In this case, your target reader is either the funding agency deciding on your pitch or some representative committee of that group. The reader is probably looking at several similar proposals, and will be comparing one to the next and with to internal agency expectations and wishes. You should find the level of technical language that is expected. If the reviewer is a scientist on a grant funding committee, it might be good to approach a research colleague in your institution who may have served on that committee in the past, or someone who has submitted a successful proposal to them. Acquiring a successful sample proposal from one of these sources will really help you find the right level of wording and explanation.

Break down your writing with the same Who-Why-No-No-Do mnemonic you used in the past. We'll use the example of applying for a research grant:

WHO: The NSERC panel for Physical Sciences Graduate research applications. The panel comprises senior research faculty members from across Canada.

WHY: To asses my merit to receive a graduate research grant to help fund my master's degree research at a Canadian University.

KNOW (before): They know the background science in my field, and some of them are familiar with the state-of-the art science in my field. A few are probably familiar with the larger research group in another university, but they do not know that my small team has been working on a parallel approach to this line of research.

KNOW (after): They need to understand how my research will complement the work done in the larger lab, how it is different, and how it may yield some interesting new insights.

DO: I want them to rank all the areas of my proposal as "excellent" and put my proposal at the top of the list to be funded.

Decide on the Finished Format

Just like any other writing project, imagine what the finished product will be. The tools you can use are storyboarding, mind maps, and a cut-and-paste initial version of the proposal (see Chapter 11). You will have some guidelines for how much space is allowed for each section if you are writing a proposal for a major funding agency (in Canada, this might be Natural Sciences and Engineering Research Canada [NSERC] or National Research Council [NRC]); they will have a template that you must follow. These templates have strict word count and letter count limits.

There is absolutely no flexibility in those limits, so your submissions must fit within them. In some cases, the format is a guide to show how much detail is expected. If you go over the limit of words or pages, the excess will simply be cut off. However, if you do not use all the space, your proposal could be penalized for not providing enough detail. It's a fine balance to perfect. Writing these sorts of proposals typically takes much longer than you would expect based upon the number of pages. You will spend more of your time revising and revising to hone the content within the word count limits.

Writing

Once you have a sense of the reader and what you want to achieve in your writing, the next step is to start writing. There are certain categories that need to be addressed in your proposal. We outline them below.

Defining the Project

Proposals are written and submitted to reviewers who either have asked for a proposal on a particular project they have in mind (solicited proposal), or a project that they have not asked for (unsolicited). Either way, it is your job to explain to the reviewer where you want to take them. Sometimes this is referred to as the "project scope" or "goals" or, in more detail, the "project plan." In most cases, the agency or person to whom you address the proposal will have a format that they want you to follow and it will include section headings they expect to find. One of these will demand that you clearly articulate the actual project plan.

If the proposal goes to a business or a government department that has issued a Request For Proposals (RFP), then they will have given you a list of their goals and objectives, as well as some clear standards that will be applied to the applicants' submissions. Your project plan will need to meet all the criteria, and it will need to explain to the reviewer what you and your team can do for them and how you will meet their needs in all ways. The reviewers will compare your proposals to other applicants' in order to choose which to support. Typically you won't know which criteria they will value the most. Whether or not they communicate it to you at some point, they want you to explain your plan to them so they can decide you are going in the same direction they want to go.

In the case of unsolicited proposals, your task is even more challenging. Before you can convince the reviewers to choose your proposal, you need to convince them that they should support the direction that you want to go with the project. Despite this extra challenge, your job is the same: to convince the readers of your proposal that you have a great project concept that, when successful, will have been an important venture.

Your project description could contain a wide range of description specific to the reviewers' need and your concept. As a minimum, you need to answer the following questions in your project description:

- Is there a current problem this project, if successful, will solve?
- What is the specific goal of the project?
- How far will this project take us towards a solution?
- What background science or technology do we need to understand in order to evaluate this project?
- What other solutions to this problem exist or are starting up?
- What will a successful completion of the project look like?

Outlining the Project Timeline

Your proposal will always need to explain a "project timeline" that shows the stages of the project. Readers of your proposal are unlikely to invest in your project or idea if they don't know there is a realistic plan to complete it. Depending on the requirements of the proposal recipient and the size of the project, your project plan will be more or less detailed.

One of the most common ways to communicate that you have a plan that is achievable in a reasonable amount of time is to describe the project in terms of phases. Each phase would be concluded by reaching a set of pre-determined milestones. The Gantt charts described in Chapter 7 are a great way to communicate the timeline of a project. The Gantt chart outlines both major phases and the milestones needed to accomplish the phase. The phases are collections of tasks that make some logical sense, while the milestones are measurable accomplishments. Eventually, the success of your project will be measured by how many of the milestones you have actually achieved, so it is essential that these milestones be concrete and measurable.

The phases and milestones are related to the tasks required to complete the project, but they are not the same. For example, on your camping trip, the milestone "completion of shopping for food" can only be reached by undertaking several tasks, including "go to superstore" and "go to bakery," and even "make up shopping list." Clear communication of the milestones and dates for those to occur will give the reviewer of your proposal some confidence that you understand the scale of the work, and that you are equipped to handle it.

The level of detail that you will require in the proposal will depend upon the expectation of the reviewer. If you are unsure how much detail to include, it is a good idea to ask the reviewer before you submit the proposal, or try to find examples of successful proposals in your field. Some proposals that ask for hundreds of thousands of dollars per year over several years may only expect a brief project plan comprised of five or six milestones and a dozen or so tasks. In other cases, a proposal for a few thousand dollars may require you to break the project into several weekly or monthly milestones and dozens of tasks. The only general rule is that the reviewer gets to make the rules.

Describing the Team

All proposals need to clearly define who will be the proponents responsible for the work and who will be called upon to help. Often, your proposal reviewer will expect to see a description of "the team" and will rely heavily on this in deciding who to award a grant or contract. The track record of the team helps to establish the credibility of the proposal. The track record and experience also helps the reviewer decide if they are confident that the team can actually succeed to accomplish what is promised.

The level of detail required will, just as with the project plan, be up to the reviewer. In some cases, you will be able to write a few sentences about each member of the team, while in others the reviewer asks for a complete resume or Curriculum Vitae (CV) of every member of the team. Regardless of how much detail you provide, you should always make sure that the biographical information is written to address the specific needs of the proposed project. For example, if the proposal is for a start-up company, the funders may need to know that some members of your team have started companies before this. Make sure that your biographical information is correct and relevant. Credibility in the field is essential for you to establish if you hope to submit a winning proposal. No matter the field in which you work, the reviewer of your proposal needs to know that they can trust your skill and can trust that you will complete the project should it be awarded. They need to believe that you know what you are doing.

This section will require that you also explain why your team is the right one by showing the experience is relevant and that all the skill within the team will be needed. This could be in the form of a detailed list of past projects that you have completed that were similar or led to this new proposal. In research, your CV should list all the published and non-published research you have completed. Alternatively, in business this list might be a catalogue of your team's past clients. The more substantial, complete, and relevant your team's past experience, the greater will be the chance that the reader will see your entire proposal as genuine and credible. If the reviewer doesn't believe your team is sufficient, the proposal won't succeed regardless of how well the rest of the sections are presented.

Defining the Resources You Have and Those You Need

It might seem odd that in a proposal where you might be asking for someone to supply you with money, ship-time, or the use of a piece of equipment that you should answer the question of what equipment and material you already have, but thinking of things from the point of view of the proposal reviewer, it makes sense. For example, you propose to create a fast car-charger station. In your proposal, you ask for $1,000,000 to make the charger station. That probably seems like a lot of money, but if you are proposing to build a charger that will require you to have the use of a $500,000 milling machine, as well as a $300,000 3D printer, then you really will only have $200,000 left of the original $1,000,000 with which to work. Imagine the reaction of the reviewer if someone else comes along and proposes to make a similar charger. They happen to already have a milling machine and a big 3D printer. They might also be asking for $1,000,000. Who should the funder support?

From the point of view of the funder, they want their money to go to the place that will have the greatest chance of success. Regardless of the merits of the project you propose, the safest bet is to pick the proposal from the team that already has the equipment. If they encounter problems along the way, they will still have most of the money to fix them. If the money went to you, you would only have the $200,000 to make the final result. Your chances of success will be much lower.

In your proposal, you must explain to the reviewer what you will need to complete the work and what items on that list you already own or that you have arranged to borrow or rent. It might even work to your favour if you can explain why your project does not require some resources that alternative approaches will use. Ideally, you can convince the reviewer that you have almost everything you need and all that is left is the piece they bring.

Outlining Your Budget

Every proposal can be translated into money. In your proposal, you need to clearly calculate and explain what finances you will need. This is important but not always as important as the other factors listed above. Regardless how much weight the reviewer puts on the price tag, your proposal will fail if you don't correctly estimate the costs or if you fail to list the costs at all. Correct and detailed cost estimation helps to support your credibility.

The budget for your proposal is never just a list of dollars and cents. It needs to communicate the relative importance that you place on different aspects of the proposed project. Suppose that you are proposing to build a new community centre in a small town. If your proposal shows that there is no money allotted for consultation with the hockey association, but you intend to host a meeting with the model train club to discuss the project, it is clear where your priorities lie. If your proposal shows that there is no budget for meeting members of the town, then that too shows your priorities in the project.

When you create a budget for a proposal, ensure that you have read and understand the conditions that the reviewer has put on their funding. In some cases, a particular funding agency will not cover equipment costs, or will not cover staff costs of researchers, but will cover contract employees. There are many other conditions that are unique to different funding sources. Before you prepare your budget, make sure you know what they will and will not cover.

The budget should be clearly connected to the proposal goals. As above, your budget indicates the values and priorities that you hold, but it also shows the order and plan that you have for completing the project. If possible, you should use the same headings for major project phases and tasks in the budget as you have in any other section of the proposal. Consistency is important, since any questions that come up when the reviewer looks at your budget will weaken your credibility and might erode the confidence that you have earned from the reviewer.

Finally, just putting a stand-alone spreadsheet in your proposal is typically not enough. You will need to write a "Budget Justification" section of your proposal where you will explain in a few paragraphs the purpose of the major and minor expenditures, and you will relate them to the overall project goals. After reading your budget justification, you want your reviewer to know that you have been smart and frugal with the plan for the financing of this project.

Editing Carefully

Once you've developed the sections of your proposal and have written all your ideas down, the next step is to clarify your writing through careful editing.

Developing Your Argument: Three Common Strategies

If you are unsure how to lay out your ideas to convince the reviewer of your viewpoint, consider using one of the following patterns for *defining*, *listing*, or *comparing*.

Defining

Your concepts depend upon ideas that may not be commonly known. Consider explaining the meaning of a key term that is complicated, controversial, or simply important to your field of study: for example, *bias* in measurements, *ergonomics* in design, *dendrites* in geology, *fidelity* in electronics. Often, all it takes is a single sentence or even just a quick definition in parentheses. The clear understanding of one of those examples might be essential to understand the importance of your proposal. A reviewer may not understand the value of your idea for the design of a desk chair if they aren't clearly aware of the issues in ergonomic design. By defining the term in the context of your proposal, you can ensure the idea is clear, and the linkage is clearly made with your proposal.

If you decide a definition is necessary for your context, perhaps because you are preparing a problem statement, begin with a general statement to introduce the term. Then make your definition more precise: it should be broad enough to include all the things that belong in the category but narrow enough to fit the context in which you want to use it for your proposal. For example, the ergonomics definition could include features that refer to improved health, productivity, and comfort for the user. These aspects of a definition allow you to connect your own proposal's features as they improve the health of the worker and their productivity. A good definition sets the stage for your proposal's main arguments.

In your definition, it's fair to point out the differences between your use of a term in the proposal and how it might differ from any other usages that may be generally applied or confused with it. For instance, if you are defining *precision*, you will want to ensure that you are only defining the term as it relates to the overshoot of heating in your temperature controller. You may not want to extend your definition beyond the bounds of the need in your context.

Listing

One way to organize material persuasively is to *prioritize* information, arranging things in their order of importance. At the heart of this structure is the bullet list, which can introduce any lineup of details: causes, effects, criteria, constraints, objectives, advantages, disadvantages, costs, findings, or recommendations. This approach helps readers recognize priorities right away, with minimal additional explanation to justify the order in which you have placed the items.

A list, like a heading, is an aid to a quick understanding of any sequence of three items or more. If you will be referring to the items in the list later, number each one; otherwise use a simple bullet (•). Whenever you list items, make sure all your points are consistent and parallel. For example, if you phrase one point as a complete sentence, make all your points complete sentences. Or if some of your points begin with verbs, make all of them begin with verbs. If your list is introduced with an incomplete sentence, make sure each point in the list properly completes the sentence

Comparing

When you want to explain why your proposal concept is the best choice, you will necessarily compare your ideas to other options. It is difficult to strike the right balance between sounding like an over-exuberant used-car salesperson versus being unconvinced yourself of which option is best. Presenting information that is as credible as possible is absolutely essential, and selectively leaving out issues of comparison will backfire on your argument. You will, if you compare ideas or solutions, need to make sure that your writing explains all of the important issues fairly, and justifies why your option is optimum and under what circumstance it might be best.

If you have several options to compare, then consider listing all logically and concisely in a table. Your table will be supplemented with a paragraph or two justifying your conclusion of the comparison. In this sort of a presentation of options, you will define the criteria and justify why you have weighted some of these as more important than others. Once the reviewer understands your ranking of criteria, it should be logical to argue the preferred solution or method that is the subject of your proposal.

Organizing the Parts

The guidelines and expectation of the proposal reviewer will usually determine the organization and sections required in your proposal. Regardless of what the funding agency or reviewer calls each section, the general topics outlined in this chapter will need to be present. You might be required to submit a section called "Project Description." You could decide, based upon the amount of space allowed, to use this section to address the project's goals as well as the project timeline. In other cases, the project budget section might be a better place to give detailed information about timing and amount of each of the project milestones. Regardless of how the funding agency has created their template, your job is to make sure that your message communicates what they want to know in each of the categories outlined in this chapter.

Getting Feedback

Proposals are the common vehicle used to recruit funding and resources to do the things you think are important, whether in academia, research, government, or business. It is important to prepare your drafts with enough time before the submission deadlines to allow for review comments from friendly, knowledgeable reviewers. Seek out as many reviewers as you can. The best reviewers are ones who will give you detailed and honest questions. The least helpful are those who don't want to hurt your feelings, or are too busy to commit serious time to the review, and send you back a note which says "This is great!" You need the reviewer who says, "I didn't understand why you . . ." or "why don't you consider this . . . ."

Once you've gotten some review comments, take them seriously, and don't be afraid to make big changes. Go through every single comment and think about why the reader thought that based upon what you wrote. Did you lose the reader with one aspect of your argument? Did you assume they knew too much? Did you aim the level too low for the reader? It's easier to try a different approach in your proposal or ask another reader to look at it for you and then go back to the original based upon their review than it would be to submit a sub-standard proposal which won't be successful. In the end, the only test of a great proposal is whether or not it is awarded the grant or contract.

Chapter Checklist

- ☐ Prepare an outline of a proposal showing the main sections required.
- ☐ Develop a list of project phases, tasks, and milestones.
- ☐ Develop a simple project budget showing the application of funds you are requesting.
- ☐ Prepare a relevant and complete bio or Curriculum Vitae of everyone on your team.
- ☐ Make a list of potential reviewers for your proposal.

13 Giving Presentations

Chapter Objectives

- Summarize what needs to be included in the three overarching sections of a talk in the scientific and technical fields
- Manipulate strategies for producing effective slideshows
- Incorporate strategies for delivering effective presentations
- Describe measures for answering questions from a scientific audience

Introduction

A successful professional scientist or engineer shares their knowledge. This book has touched on a variety of written and graphical forms that are common in our field. One remaining mode that we use is live and in person: the oral presentation. You will certainly be called upon in your professional life to stand up in front of an audience and tell your story.

The most common presentation formats are those given during conferences and workshops. Thirty or so colleagues, perhaps from a wide range of backgrounds, or perhaps all very specialized, sit down in rows, fill a room, and listen to you speak. You have prepared comments and have slides to show. They will listen and then ask questions. While most people do not relish this sort of event, we all get through it, and some of us even learn to enjoy standing up and telling an interesting tale of science, discovery, or design. This chapter is intended to give the novice scientific speaker some practical ways to start.

Plan Your Presentation

Consider the characteristics of classes or seminars you have enjoyed. What made them so good was likely the confidence, know-how, and enthusiasm of the speaker. Most audiences prefer presenters who seem well prepared, who speak without reading from notes, who use a range of relevant visual aids, and who look animated and interested in what they are talking about. Those talks were the result of good planning first and confident presentation second. Good planning starts with understanding your audience.

Know Your Audience

A presentation is just like any other form of communication that we have covered in this book. It must start with your audience. As with the other examples in this book, let's start with a quick summary of Who-Why-No-No-Do using the example of presenting at a conference as a graduate student:

> **WHO:** Engineers, professors and grad students attending an international conference on impacts from human activity on the deep ocean.
> **WHY:** To listen to my graduate school research on plastic wastes and their impacts in deep water.
> **KNOW (before):** They know a lot about oceanography, deep sea sediment transport, ocean physics, global chemical cycles, and environmental impacts of pollution.
> **KNOW (after):** The cycle time of microplastics in the ocean as compared with macro-plastics, and the relative harmful impacts of the different sources. Mechanics of conversion from macro- to microplastics and implications for ocean transport.
> **DO:** I want them to reconsider the current models and look at ways to include this mechanism in predictions. Further, I want to open opportunities for fieldwork and collaboration.

Your audience at a conference or workshop will be experts in the field. They may be your supervisor, or they may even be the author of one of the research articles you relied on in your own work. Even though they are experts, when planning your presentation, remember that you know more about your specific focus than anyone else in the room. Another person may be an expert in much of what you have done, but they are not you! They did not use the same data or carry out the same experiments that you did. You know more about your own work than anyone—even the person who is a leader in your field. Being prepared means that you will have a good understanding of the work some of these expert have done before you, and you will show them how your own work provides some added insights that will extend or refine their ideas. And while it may seem intimidating, having those experts in the room is a great opportunity to even further develop and refine your ideas.

You will find that the most successful talks are those that generate the most questions. Scientists and engineers, when they are engaged in a subject, will ask you questions that challenge your ideas. Think of your audience as collaborators in your project: they have now become colleagues, people to bounce ideas off of and to point out gaps to fill in your ideas. A lot of what we do in presentations is think about "what if?" What if the model used was larger? What if the plastic had a different density? What if the size distribution were smaller? If your audience asks hard questions, take that as a mark of pride. You got through to them. If the leading expert in your field asks you questions, then you have gotten their attention. They might be thinking about further research that can build on what you have done, leapfrogging your science ahead. They might be skeptical of some of your results. That is, in fact, the way science advances. You, as the expert, can challenge, support, or extend the accepted results. If you do so effectively, your work will have a lasting impact. This presentation you are giving is your chance to make an impact!

Organize Your Presentation

Except for very formal presentations of conference papers, never simply read a prepared text out loud. (Unless you are a skilled public speaker it's hard to keep such a presentation sounding lively.) That isn't to say that you shouldn't write it all out first—doing so will help you be better organized and perhaps less nervous. But if you have the full text in front of you at the presentation, the temptation to read from it can be overpowering. It's better to be prepared, but not memorized.

In most science and engineering presentations, we use graphical aids. These can really help to both reduce your nervousness and keep you organized. As you develop your series of slides, you are essentially planning the presentation. It's a great idea to put together a storyboard of all the slides in your presentation. When you do so, you will certainly recognize the need to have an introduction slide or slides, a content or discussion set where you offer most of your original ideas and content, and finally a conclusion slide. Your storyboard will help you decide how many graphics you are allowed for each section. The mistake most speakers make is including too many slides.

Starting with a storyboard will help you avoid that mistake. Take note of the special demands for each section.

1. **Introduction.** Establish the context for your presentation by relating it to topics your audience understands. Start by posing a question to be answered, or by making a provocative statement to catch the audience's attention and to identify your subject. It is important to hit the right tone. If your opening remarks are hyperbole, in science and engineering, the remainder of your presentation will meet with a skeptical audience. If your opening remarks are too timid, then your presentation might just meet with disinterest.

   a. **Begin with a title slide.** A title slide orients your audience. It should contain the title of the presentation, your name, the date, and perhaps the name of the course or conference. Have your title slide on the screen as people enter. Wait for everyone to be seated before you begin to speak.

   b. **Have an overview slide.** Put an overview of your presentation on the screen as you introduce your topic. This has the advantage of helping your audience estimate your timing. Do not, therefore, include so many points that your audience fears you will never get finished.

2. **Discussion.** Follow a clear order, just as you would in writing. Include a title or caption on each slide and take advantage of bullets to list specifics. Every slide must have a reason for being shown. If the graphics you show are not on point, then cut the slide out.

   a. **Use headings and subheadings.** Most of your slides should be in point form, using numbers or bullets, with headings and subheadings. If you do this, the audience will be able to distinguish between the main points and the elaborations. Remember to be consistent: if you're using numbers, don't switch needlessly between Arabic and Roman numerals; if you're using bullets, use the same style throughout. As a general rule, five or six bullet points is the maximum per slide.

   b. **Give the audience a "progress bar" for the talk.** Either graphically, or by returning to the overview list of topics, keep reminding them when you move from one item to the next.

3. **Conclusion.** Use the final minutes of the presentation to summarize and reinforce your main points. Make sure that you keep to the

purpose of your talk and what you hope the audience will do with this new perspective you have presented. Bring the presentation to a satisfying conclusion for your audience by referring to the question or issue raised in your introduction.

a. **Finish the journey.** Show the audience that the topic overviews declared at the start have all been covered.

b. **End with a summary and/or conclusions slide.** If you have been discussing an ongoing project, list the questions you want to pose to the audience at the end. If you are making a proposal, your final slide should identify *next steps* (your suggestions for follow-up or future planning).

c. **Avoid having a last slide that features the words "Questions?" or "Thank you!"** A summary of your main points is much more useful. Include your name and contact information, and those of your co-authors.

Keep your presentation strictly within the time you have been allotted. It's a good habit, when you run through a practice of the presentation, to make your talk a little shorter than the amount of time. Most speakers, due to nervousness and perhaps audience interaction, seem to speak for a bit longer when doing a presentation for real. As a rough guide, it takes a minute or two to read a page of double-spaced text; time yourself accordingly by rehearsing with a written-out copy of your presentation. Use your text to prepare your slideshow and take advantage of the notes feature if you need prompts while presenting. Generally, each slide takes about two minutes of talking to cover, so for a 20-minute presentation at a conference you should plan for around 10 slides.

Creating Your Slides

The demand for clarity and simplicity governs every aspect of visual aids. It is better to put too little information on a slide than too much. Your slides should help you make your point, so it is effective to put simple language/phrases on the slide and allow yourself to extend the concept while talking about the slide. The following suggestions will help you keep things simple:

- **Use a plain font.** Any word processing or graphics software includes dozens of font options. Stay with the clean, simple ones like Courier or Arial, reserving Comic Sans for informal occasions only. Avoid all fancy font formats, including italics. Use a bold format instead if you want to emphasize something.

- **Choose an appropriate font size.** Verify that your slides can be read from the back of the room in which you will be giving the presentation. Remember that the size of any type you use will depend on how far your projector is from the screen, not on the font size you used to prepare the slide. If you keep to a font size from 20 to 36 point, you should be fine.

- **Use a simple format.** No matter how tempting it is to try out the variety of colourful themes, bullets, backgrounds, and borders, choose a plain, light-coloured theme. If your school or department has a standard template, use it. Avoid complex graphical images as backgrounds, they will merely make your points and graphics harder to see by the audience.

- **Don't overuse colour or other effects.** Using fonts of different colours can provide effective contrast but using too many is distracting. It's worth noting that a simple illustration in black and white is often easier to interpret than a photograph. Avoid flashy effects, which get tiresome for the audience. Slideshow software offers the option of introducing text in a variety of ways, even letter by letter. Don't be tempted by exotic possibilities. Use the screen to display everything related to a single point at the same time. It is annoying for an audience to have information displayed in tiny portions. No one likes to be kept in suspense.

- **Don't pack too much information on one slide.** If you treat your slides as your script, you will be tempted to read directly from them. Instead, use bullets as prompts to allow yourself the time to elaborate as you talk. Whenever you have a table, diagram, or graph, use the simplest, cleanest version possible and explain it thoroughly to your audience. If you are standing right next to the screen, use broad gestures to point to relevant parts of your slides (it gives you something to do with your hands). Laser pointers or an electronic mouse, while popular, tend to bounce around annoyingly, so it's better to avoid them unless you are very practiced.

- **Avoid distracting or irrelevant visuals.** Clipart is easy to paste on a slide but contributes very little to your talk. If you find that your slide has too much blank space, find some relevant graphics or consider combining it with another slide. Pasting a humanoid figure holding a cartoon pen or a giant question mark doesn't help the audience's focus. Keep it simple and stay on topic.

- **Use only the most basic tools to get the point across.** In some cases, you can communicate a point most easily with an animation or a short video clip. Use it if you feel you must but keep it short (less than 20 seconds) and make sure that it is clearly showing what you need to communicate. All other graphics that you use should follow the quotation attributed to Einstein "Everything should be made as simple as possible, but no simpler."

Rehearse Your Presentation

As you progress through your career, you will find that your level of comfort and skill for public speaking will evolve. For the beginner, just keeping your legs from buckling and your voice from trembling seems to be a challenge. Practising your presentation will help.

Once you have prepared your slides, take the time to run through your presentation at least once. See if it's possible to book the actual room to rehearse in. If so, take the opportunity to check the equipment and the readability of your visual aids while you get used to standing at the front. It's best if you can rehearse with someone whose opinion you trust. Take advantage of any feedback to improve your delivery. A couple of dry runs will help you identify areas you need to strengthen and let you know if you are keeping to your time limit. Keep the following points in mind as you rehearse:

- **Speak slowly and deliberately.** Make sure your voice can be heard at the back of the room. Remember that a room full of people will muffle sound, so you must talk even louder at the official presentation.
- **Practise looking around the room as you talk.** Choose three focal points where you will direct your gaze during your presentation—left, right, and centre. By looking from one place to the next, you appear to include everyone. That way you seem less wooden and more comfortable addressing your audience.
- **Time your delivery accurately.** Be prepared to cut out sections rather than go over time. In fact, as you rehearse, mark places where you could shorten your discussion if necessary. Then, during the presentation, you can just move to the next section smoothly as you keep to your time limit. After your rehearsal, be ruthless about editing slides you don't need. Your audience won't even notice what you've left out.

Delivering the Presentation

When the day arrives to give your talk, there are a few tips that will help it go smoothly. These are discussed below.

Dress Comfortably

Dressing comfortably means dressing for the occasion, not overdressing. Don't wear anything that you feel awkward in, including new shoes. There's no need for a business suit unless you know the rest of the audience will be wearing one too. A good rule of thumb is to dress the way your instructors and TAs do. Something that's clean, neat, and casual sets the right tone.

Leave Yourself Plenty of Time to Get There

Don't arrive at the last minute. Leave yourself time to set things up and make sure all the equipment works. There's nothing more disconcerting for you or your audience than to have a projector fail or a slideshow go missing. If everything is ready before you're scheduled to begin, you can take time to relax. Best of all, you won't get flustered rushing to set things up with your audience looking on.

If, in a worst-case scenario, there is a complete equipment failure, take advantage of whatever visual aids are available—blackboard, white board, flip chart, or overhead projector. The well-prepared presenter has a hard copy and can chalk-talk their way through the ideas with a whiteboard and a pen if all else fails.

Don't Apologize

Never start with excuses: "You'll have to forgive me. I'm really nervous about this" or "I sure hope this equipment is going to work properly." Audiences are more receptive if you focus on your topic rather than on your nervousness. After all, you don't want to suggest that you are unsure of your material. Most of your audience won't even notice your discomfort—as long as you don't draw attention to yourself by apologizing.

If you are someone who finds it difficult to stand up in front of a crowd, consider options for confronting your discomfort. Many colleges and universities offer courses in public speaking, and some local organizations even host regular meetings of Toastmasters International. If your future involves regular presentations and you are naturally reticent, consider getting some practice to make yourself more comfortable. Start by checking with the career services department on your campus.

Speak in a Calm, Clear Voice

When you speak, be sure you're loud enough that everyone in the room can hear you. Also, try to put some energy into what you are saying. (It is difficult to remain attentive to even the most interesting presentation delivered in a monotone.) One of the tricks of professional speakers is careful breathing. Taking a silent, deep, slow breath before you begin is a way to master nervousness. (It's like counting to 10 to avoid losing your temper.) Breathing slowly and deliberately while you deliver your presentation not only gives the impression that you are in control, but it also relaxes your audience.

Maintain Eye Contact with Your Audience

Look around the room as you speak, shifting your gaze from one to the other of your focal points. When you look at people, you involve them in what you are saying. As you scan the faces in front of you, you can watch for signs that your audience is following. If you sense confusion, adjust your talk accordingly by explaining a difficult point or slowing your pace.

Work with Your Visual Aids

Take full advantage of your slides (while remembering that the visual material should enhance your presentation, not deliver it for you). Some guidelines for using visual aids effectively include the following:

- If you are using your own laptop, remember to turn off pop-up features and audio to prevent incoming messages from interfering with your presentation.
- When referring to a point on a slide, use different words to elaborate on what appears there. Use your slide as a set of notes to expand on. Don't simply read the words on the screen.

- Be sure to leave your audience enough time to make sense of each visual. It is frustrating to watch slides flash by without having a chance to take them in. It is better to delete a visual than to rush it by your audience. This is another reason why it's better to have only a few uncluttered, uncrowded slides. Audiences need time to understand something new. You don't want people to become frustrated and negative because they feel rushed.
- Explain your figures. If it's a graph, make it clear what the x- and y-axes represent, then explain what the graph shows. If it's a diagram, take the audience through it step by step. Remember that you are much more familiar with the material than your audience is. Never take for granted that anything is so obvious that it doesn't need to be explained.
- During your presentation, move around periodically so that you are not permanently blocking anyone from seeing the screen. Avoid putting yourself in front of the projector: it's distracting to an audience to see a presenter lit up by text from a slide. Staying at the side of the screen or board allows you to point effectively to important material while guiding your audience's eye.

Pace Yourself

As you speak, adjust your speed to your content. If you're discussing background information that is familiar to the audience, you can go a little faster. If you're describing something complex or new, slow down. It often helps to explain a complicated point a couple of times in slightly different ways. Don't be afraid to ask your audience if they understand. Almost certainly, someone will speak up if there is a problem. But don't let this rattle you. A one-sentence answer will allow you to continue on schedule.

Monitor Your Time

Stand so that you can see a clock throughout your presentation, but don't make a big deal of positioning your smartphone or watch at the beginning. (Many of those who make elaborate gestures like this go over time anyway.) If you've carefully rehearsed your presentation, you should know roughly how long it will take. Always leave extra time for questions that people might ask.

End Confidently

Bring your presentation to a strong finish by summarizing the main points you have made and drawing conclusions. Remember to have these available on a concluding slide so that they can be left there for the ensuing discussion. If you raise questions in your conclusions, you can use them to help structure the question period to follow.

Be Prepared for Questions

The question period is the time when you can make the best impression. It is an opportunity for you to demonstrate your thorough understanding of the topic and even to reinforce one or two points that you think you may have missed. If you know your material well, you should have no problem dealing with the content of the questions, but the way you answer these questions is important, too.

- Don't introduce the question period with a hurried "Any questions?" Such an abrupt approach makes you seem anxious to rush through or altogether dodge the finale. You appear sincere about welcoming questions if you phrase your request slowly this way: "Thank you for attending. I welcome your questions at this time."
- Listen carefully to the question, and don't try to answer until they finish speaking. When you do answer, it's always nice to begin with something like "Thank you, that is an excellent question" or "I'm delighted you asked that . . . ." This shows that you are having a dialogue with them, not defending your position.
- It's a good idea to repeat a question for the audience, especially if you are in a large room where everyone may not have heard it. Repeating the question can clarify it for you and buy you time to think before you answer.
- If you didn't quite hear or didn't understand a question, don't be afraid to ask the person who asked it to repeat or clarify it.
- Keep answers short and to the point. Rambling is neither helpful nor convincing. Long answers often confuse the audience, so it's best to start briefly and then elaborate if necessary.

- Sometimes the questions are asking for clarification of a point you made in the talk. If so, take the time to rewind the slides to one that might help you clarify. Don't refer to a slide in the middle of the presentation unless the audience can see it too; they don't know your slides as fully as you may.
- If you don't have an answer, say so. It's also okay to ask your audience for suggestions or refer the question to the course instructor if the presentation is for class. Certainly, it's better to admit that you don't know an answer than to guess or to make up a response that everyone knows is not correct.

Whether you are speaking alone or as part of a team, you have the best chance of success if you take your time to prepare, rehearse, and refine your presentation. The most important thing to remember is that your audience has a reason for being in attendance. Rather than concentrating on how you feel about speaking publicly, focus your attention on delivering the interesting, new information your audience expects.

Chapter Checklist

- ☐ Plan your presentation with your purpose, topic, audience, and time limit in mind.
- ☐ Keep the information on your slides clean and simple.
- ☐ Time your delivery carefully and rehearse until you are comfortable with your material.
- ☐ Treat your audience as collaborators to share ideas with: answer questions thoughtfully, clearly, and respectfully.

Writing a Resumé and Letter of Application

Introduction

Whether you are looking for a co-op placement, an apprenticeship, a summer job, admission to graduate school, or permanent employment, you will have to produce a resumé and a cover letter in order to apply for most positions. Even with the advent of Artificial Intelligence bots to pre-screen applications for some companies, your resumé will usually be viewed by someone who sees hundreds of them at a sitting. If we assume that the reader can concentrate on scanning resumés for one hour, and they have a hundred resumés, then you might think they could spend 3,600 seconds/100 resumés = 36 seconds on each resumé! In reality, an experienced reader will do a rough cut first for 20 minutes and choose 10–15 resumés to look at more closely. From that pile, they might choose five or six to call for an interview. Those numbers mean that most resumés get only 12 seconds of eyeball time. The lucky ones might get as much as three minutes of the reviewer's attention. It is critical for you to make that first 12 seconds you have with the reader as effective as possible.

If you can't get the reader to stop and notice your resumé in 12 seconds, it won't be selected from the pile and you won't be invited to an interview for the job. Your goal is to design a resumé that grabs the reviewer's attention, gets them to select it for a second look, and then has them look closer at what you have to offer. Once your resumé passes this review pipeline, then you get the chance to meet them and show them how awesome you can be. This chapter will offer some advice for creating a successful resumé and give you tips on making a good first impression.

Preparing to Write a Resumé

Before you start writing your resumé, collect the job ads or application guides for the jobs that you want. You don't typically make a custom resumé for every different job application, but it is good to tailor a few resumés for specific clusters of job types. If you want to apply to a few jobs that emphasize skills with Computer Aided Design, your resumé should certainly highlight the skills and projects that you have completed in that area of work. In another cluster of applications, the job ads might emphasize teamwork, so your alternate resumé might highlight some of your proven team skills. Both resumés must correctly and accurately represent your skills and background, but you simply would rearrange your experience so that relevant items are most evident, and are explained in more detail, while the less-relevant ones are given lower priority.

Analyzing the Job Advertisement

To get started on your application, find each job ad, then print it out and highlight the skills that are mentioned in the description. The advertisement for a summer student job below is an example:

> *Summer Student Position in Physics*
> *Our research team is seeking one research assistant to work on a project to analyze design details, fabricate, and evaluate a prototype biomedical research device. Your responsibilities will include optimizing electrical interface connections and overall circuit board architecture, as well as testing the thermal transient effects within prototypes. The ideal candidate will possess demonstrated excellence in CAD modelling, experience in testing and evaluating of electrical and mechanical systems and have excellent communication skills. The successful candidate must be currently enrolled in an undergraduate physics or*

engineering program in Canada. The successful applicant must hold a valid Government of Canada security clearance or be able to pass the clearance check prior to the start of the work term.

Looking at this ad, the first thing you should do is decide if you seriously want this position. In this example, do you know the professors involved, and if so, do you really want to work for them? Based upon the description, can you imagine this position will be something you'd like? If your answer to both those questions is a fervent "Yes!", then start looking at the details. For summer positions, entry-level positions, or other professional jobs, some additional questions you should ask yourself are: Will this job help advance my career? Also, on a practical level, can I commute to this job and will I be able to manage my bills on the salary or honorarium it might offer? If you can't answer yes to those questions, then consider moving on and focusing your efforts on finding those jobs that work for you and your career. But be sure to prioritize which questions matter most: maybe the job is an unpaid internship, which will make paying the bills for that short period of time a challenge, but the experience and networking opportunities outweigh the temporary instability, and, at the end, it could lead to a job offer. Whichever way you prioritize and answer your questions, most importantly, don't waste your time, or a company's time, applying for jobs that you would not accept, if offered.

Once you have decided to apply, have a close look at the ad and pull out the important terms. From our example, the key terms would be those below:

Must-have:
- Current undergrad physics or engineering student
- GoC security clearance

Ideal qualifications:
- Excellent communication skills
- Experience testing and evaluating electrical systems
- Experience testing and evaluating mechanical systems
- Excellence in CAD

Responsibilities:
- Optimizing electrical interface connections
- Optimizing overall circuit board architecture
- Testing thermal transient effects within prototypes

With the above list, you can proceed to revise or adapt your resumé to apply for the job. When doing so, you will be able to ensure that the package you send gives the most relevant and clear expression that your skills and experience are suited to the job. The rest of this chapter will provide some concrete ways to build your resumé.

Know Your Reader

Before you start to construct your document, find out whatever you can about the person or people who have posted the ad. In the example above, this might be a professor that you have known in a course. What were they like? Was this a formal sort of instructor or were they much more informal? You can use that background to know how your resumé and cover letter need to appear.

Do some research into the company or research group. Through online and peer-reviewed sources, look up all you can for research on the work of the professor, or, if this is a business, find out about their products and their market. Every piece of information you can find will help you create the best application to highlight your skills. The more you know about the position, the more your resumé and subsequent interview will stand out. You may find that the more you learn about the work, the more enthusiastic you will become about the job, and this too will help your chances.

If it is an on-campus position, it might be worth your time to visit the professor's office during their office hours to ask more about the job and to find out more about the research. This will give you a better idea of which skills are really a priority and a sense of how your own skills might be applied on the job, should you be hired. In addition to helping you decide how to pitch your skills, a good visit will give you a bit of name recognition when the professor goes through all the applications.

Once you have learned everything you can about the employer and the position, apply the simple Who-Why-No-No-Do mnemonic to your resumé writing. Considering the example job ad from above:

> **WHO**: The lead engineer in a small tech start-up company started by my professor.
> **WHY**: To see if I have the necessary skills for the job and if I would be someone to call in for an interview.

KNOW (before): They know I am an engineering student at a Canadian University that they hire co-op students from each year. I am one of a hundred applicants for the co-op placement. The company founder was one of my profs and I did okay but not great in the course.

KNOW (after): I am one of the people they should interview because I have proven skills and enthusiasm that will make me a good fit for their company.

DO: *I want them to invite me for an interview.*

Decide How Your Resumé Will Look

The resumé should begin with your contact information at the top, or in a prominent position if you choose a non-traditional format. No matter the orientation or format, your resumé will likely be read on a screen and you need to have your name and the most important items visible together as soon as the file is opened or the screen is viewed. Because of the size format of most devices, only the top half or one-third of a letter-size page will typically be seen on one screen. This top half of the page is your prime real estate. Use it wisely!

Beyond that first top of page with your name, modern resumés can follow any of a wide range of formats. Don't obsess on the graphical style or invest time or money in resumé templates with fancy colours or fonts. Your resumé will not be chosen for its graphical style if you are working in engineering and the sciences. The employer will appreciate a clear, simple, black and white layout that gets across the content. More than anything, the format you choose should be appropriate to the industry and job that you want to work in. A very artistic, cool layout might be great for a sophisticated design firm or a Silicon Valley tech firm, whereas a nuts-and-bolts manufacturer may expect resumés to be more traditional.

Whatever format you choose, your goal is to keep the resumé concise (one page for an undergraduate student). Common sections that appear in resumés are listed below. You don't need to include every item in the list, but these are generally common.

Keep in mind that you are not required to state anything about your age, place of birth, race, religion, or gender. Do not include a photograph of yourself on the resumé. To be sure that your application will be considered, of course, you must provide all the information requested when you are completing an application form that has set questions. Professional human resources departments are trained to follow hiring rules in their jurisdiction, so the questions should be appropriate. If you have concerns, that may signal something about the company values and should not be ignored.

Name

Begin with your name in a font that is one size larger than the one you use in the rest of your resumé. To ensure that your resumé is given an unbiased chance, it is a good idea to simply use your first initials and last name on the resumé. This step is often effective in minimizing any gender or racial stereotypes that are inappropriate in a job search.

Contact Information

This includes your home address, phone numbers, e-mail address, and website (if you have a professional one that presents samples of your work). If you have a temporary student address, remember to indicate where you can be reached after the term is over. If you're applying for a co-op or student position, for your own credibility, use your school e-mail address rather than a social one. Make sure you check it regularly. It is also wise to make sure that your voice-mail message is short and professional, to ensure that a prospective employer will even leave you a message.

Career Objective

It may be helpful to remind a hiring committee of your current aim for employment. Without naming the employer, use the job name provided in the ad. Some hiring managers find this is wasted space, and some like it. Use your discretion.

Summary of Qualifications

This section lists the most significant experience and skills that qualify you for the position. The most effective approach is to highlight five or six items in your work experience that reflect what the employer has requested. People will hire you for excellence in the skills they really value. If they've already decided you are a front-runner, they won't discount you for "proficient" skills, but neither will they prize them. Some examples:

Good examples

- Advanced CAD modelling experience with solidworks and NX
- Experience completing the complete CAD assembly and renderings of a complex set of machine parts

- Manager of busy team of software and technical professionals in three-month project delivered on time
- Lead in design project workshops that were awarded first place in hack-a-thon learning sessions

Examples to avoid
- Proficient in Microsoft excel
- Entry-level database, CAD, machining
- Hard worker
- Team player

The first set of skills shows enough detail that the reader has a sense that you really did excel, and that you are very familiar with the field. The jargon used is acceptable since the reader will be your future supervisor, and if those skills are valuable to the job, they will be familiar terms. In the case of the teamwork and leadership points, there is a brief statement pointing to more than a vague claim to be a "team player."

The best approach is to accurately reflect what you have done. In some cases being a "hard worker" can better be shown by what you specifically did, for example, "Manager of busy team of software and technical professionals in three-month project delivered on time," which certainly implies that you are a hard worker in a much more credible way. However, don't exaggerate your role, and never claim more for yourself than is true. Including false information in a resumé is grounds for dismissal if it is discovered.

Education

Recent practice has gotten away from including all of your degrees and diplomas or certificates, but you certainly will want to include your highest degree. You can choose how far back to go with the list, but it should be in reverse-chronological order (newest to oldest). In most cases, your high school and middle schools aren't listed, so you should stop with post-secondary degrees and diplomas. If you are currently a student, then you should list that degree and preface it with "candidate for . . . ." For each degree, include the name and location of institutions that granted them and the year obtained. If it will help your case, you can also list courses you have completed that are relevant to the job.

Academic Awards or Honours

If you have three or more, list them in a separate section along with the years they were awarded. Include them with your education details if you have only one or two, especially if they are no longer recent.

Work Experience

Give the name and location of your most recent employers, along with your job title and the dates of employment. List one or two relevant accomplishments, using point form and action verbs. Here are two examples:

- Designed, administered, and reported result of a resource management survey
- Supervised a three-member field survey crew in northern Alberta

If you have worked as a research or teaching assistant, be sure to state the type of work you did and the name of your supervisor. Include such details, either in the chronological listing of previous employment or in a separate category, this way:

- May–August 2014. Research assistant for Professor A. Trivett, independently designing and conducting optical filter experiments for biotechnology start-up company, University of PEI, Charlottetown, PEI, Canada.

If relevant, include volunteer experience, clearly indicated as such, either as a separate section (if you have a lot in addition to paid positions) or as part of your list of work experience.

Extracurricular Activities

If you believe they are relevant to your story, list extracurricular expertise not mentioned in your Summary of Qualifications. Naming a few achievements, such as athletic prizes, music, or travel, confirms that you are well rounded or especially disciplined. Avoid listing general activities that show passive or minimal involvement. For example, while reading is a commendable activity, including it says nothing about your versatility as an employee. Include only activities that set you apart from the average applicant.

References

Do not write "References available upon request" at the end of a resumé. Either you will have been asked to include them (which you do on a separate sheet), or you will be expected to bring the list with you to an interview. Only include people whom you have personally asked for a reference and who will give you a strong recommendation. List the full name, complete title, address, phone number, and e-mail address of each one.

Writing a Cover Letter

Most employers judge the writing of the letter that accompanies a resumé. Not every applicant even supplies a cover letter, so taking the time to craft a good one is a way to increase your chances of success. If you intend to submit a cover letter, make sure your letter is specially drafted with the company in mind. Don't use the same letter for all applications. Instead, each cover letter will follow a standard pattern.

As with any of your writing, keep the reader foremost in your mind. The reader might be the kindest person imaginable, but their concern is not that you need/want a job. Every applicant they will review wants the job, not just you. Your letter should not read as a plea for help, or a request that they do you a favour by hiring you. The employer is looking for someone that will get the work done, so your tone should focus on the work and the role you could fill. Craft your letter to highlight the items in your resumé and explain how they link to your fit for the position. Don't simply repeat what's in your resumé. Make each paragraph fulfill a specific function:

1. Identify the specific position advertised and state your interest in applying for it.
2. State your best qualification and refer the reader to your resumé.
3. State your next best qualifications.
4. Politely state your availability for an interview.

The challenge in writing a letter of application is to tell your reader about yourself and your qualifications without seeming too self-focused. Two tips can help:

1. Limit the number of sentences beginning with *I*. Instead, try burying *I* in the middle of some sentences, where it will be less noticeable, for example, "For two months last summer, I worked as a . . . ."

2. Avoid, as much as possible, making unsupported, subjective claims. Instead of saying "I am a highly skilled manager," offer specifics like, "Last summer I managed a $90,000 field study with a crew of seven assistants." Rather than claim "I have excellent research skills," you might say, "Based on my volunteer work with first-year students, Professor Anson Park hired me as a lab assistant for CIVE 221 (Advanced Calculus) in Fall 2019."

Formatting the Application E-mail

Most employers post job opportunities on their organization's website and on standard sites like Workopolis, Indeed, or the Government of Canada's Job Bank. Your university or college co-op office will help you find links to job advertisements. For most employers, e-mail applications are the standard. To make sure your application gets the best chance of being read:

- Make sure your e-mail is not designated as spam, use the subject line to identify the job exactly as it is posted, for example, "Process Engineer - JO189."
- Whenever possible address your message to a specific person. Use a formal greeting in your e-mail ("Dear Ms. Shimodo" not "Hi Karen!"). If a name has not been linked to the e-mail address listed with the job description, check the company's electronic directory. Use "Attention: Human Resources" as a last resort.
- Keep the text of your e-mail brief. It has three aims:
  - Name the position and indicate your interest in it.
  - Indicate that your cover letter and resumé are attached.
  - Thank the reader for considering your application.
- Add your letter and resumé as separate attachments rather than put them in the body of the e-mail message. PDF format (with embedded fonts) is best because it will appear to the reader exactly as you intended. To confirm that you recognize the conventions of applying for a job, always attach a signed cover letter. Make sure that the PDF files are small, with no large graphics backgrounds. Mail that is sent unsolicited with a large attachment will be tagged as spam. Try to make your PDF files smaller than 80 kb.
- Before pressing the "send" button, proofread your e-mail message carefully. A job application is too important for you to run the risk of looking sloppy. Pay special attention to the spelling of people's names.

- If your application is the result of an online search on Indeed, Monster .ca, or Workopolis, or through another online submission portal, make sure that your submission meets all the format rules, both for the site and those specific to the employer.

Making a Good First Impression

When you apply for a job, your application will be one of many. Of course, it must pass a screening process before you will be invited to an interview. For this reason, it is essential that you submit a package that looks as professional as you will when you present yourself in person. With job interviews, as with applications, first impressions count. When you are asked to an interview, you want to confirm that you are as professional as your resumé promised. Dress professionally and be prepared with answers to both questions you think they will ask and questions you'd like to ask them. While you're a student, take advantage of your school's career centre advisors to help you prepare. Then, if everything comes together just right, you can look forward to a job offer that's well deserved.

Chapter Checklist

- ☐ Take advantage of career services advisors and writing centres to help get you started.
- ☐ Research both the position you want and the company it's with.
- ☐ Match your skills and experience to the job description and prepare your Summary of Qualifications accordingly.
- ☐ Summarize your education, awards, and experience in reverse chronological order, followed by skills and extracurricular activities.
- ☐ Write a cover letter that introduces you and your best qualifications.
- ☐ Write an e-mail message to the hiring committee and attach your resumé and letter.
- ☐ Proofread slowly and carefully all documents at least twice before sending.

Appendix A
Documentation

Introduction

Much of the writing you do requires you to consult secondary sources for project ideas as well as to keep up with current research. Although scientific writing calls for few direct quotations, it is still essential to acknowledge your sources, not just if you quote directly from them but also when you refer to observations, conclusions, theories, or ideas presented in them. If you don't acknowledge these sources, you let your reader assume that the words, ideas, or concepts are yours. Such an omission is considered plagiarism, and penalties are severe (see pp. 68–74).

Of course, the purpose of documentation is less to avoid charges of plagiarism than to situate your work within the body of knowledge in your discipline. Academic writing is based on the premise that researchers are indebted both to scholars who came before them and to colleagues. By documenting your sources, you show that you recognize your indebtedness and are ready to make your own contribution to your field.

Documenting Your Sources

Your purpose for including a list of references at the end of your document is to make it as easy as possible for any reader to track your sources. That's why each reference includes as much of the following information as possible:

- name of author or authors, in the order listed in the original work
- publication date
- title of article, posting, paper, or chapter
- title of book, journal, periodical, or collection, including edition if applicable
- name of editor or translator, identified by the abbreviations "ed." or "trans."
- place of publication and publisher, for books only

- volume number, issue number, and page numbers for journals and periodicals
- site sponsor/organization for websites
- DOI (digital object identifier) or URL for electronic sources

List only those works that you have actually referred to in the text of your writing. As well, it's important to cite the exact source you consulted. Don't list a print version if your source was electronic.

There are many systems of documentation, and the one you use depends both on your subject and on the preference of your instructor, your department, or your employer. It makes sense from the beginning to find out whether there is a preferred documentation style and set of guidelines for its use. For easy reference, the most common systems are presented later in this chapter. Remember, though, that style guides are constantly undergoing revision, especially with the wealth of electronic information available. Always check the website or the latest edition of the relevant manual to be sure that you have the most up-to-date information.

Be aware as well that technical societies may produce their own specifications, spelled out on their websites. If you are preparing a paper for publication, you are expected to follow the guidelines of the organization exactly, and there may be major or minor variations from the standards you follow in other contexts. It is a mark of professionalism to keep to requirements exactly.

There is one absolute principle in documenting anything—the demand for consistency. Once you have committed to following a particular referencing style, you must continue to use it throughout whatever it is that you are writing.

Even if you have not been told to follow a specific style manual or set of guidelines, you are still expected to acknowledge your sources. In scientific writing, the most common system of documentation is also the simplest and most economical. The following guidelines outline the system for IEEE publications [1], which we use in this handbook. Keep to these conventions if no others have been specified for you.

Using Direct Quotations

Direct quotations are rarely seen in scientific and technical papers. However, if you are not writing a technical paper, judicious use of direct quotations can add authority to your writing. Never quote a passage just because it sounds impressive; be sure that it really adds to the discussion. Maybe it expresses an idea with special force or gives substance to a debatable point. Quote directly only when you need to present the source's exact words. The following are situations that justify word-for-word quotations from primary or secondary sources:

- **Literary content.** An analysis or evaluation of someone's writings (prose or poetry) calls for exact quotations of the literary text.
- **Expert opinion.** A representative statement or a memorable comment from a recognized authority is worth citing, especially if it is the subject for discussion.
- **First-hand reports.** In media accounts and news releases, an accurate record from witnesses adds necessary specificity.

When you are convinced that only a direct quotation will serve your purposes, follow the guidelines below:

1. Integrate the quotation so that it makes sense in the context of your discussion and fits grammatically into your sentence:

    ✗ Bill Gates could not foresee the future. "640K ought to be enough for anybody" is highly ironic.

    ✔ Bill Gates's 1981 prediction that "640K ought to be enough for anybody" is ironic in light of exponential leaps in computer engineering.

2. If the quotation is fewer than four lines long, include it as part of your text, enclosed in quotation marks. If the quotation is four lines or longer, set it as a block of free-standing text, double-spaced and indented from the left-hand margin (without quotation marks). If the quotation consists of more than one paragraph, indent the first line of the second and all subsequent paragraphs an additional three spaces.

3. Be accurate whenever you are using quotation marks. Reproduce the exact wording, punctuation, and spelling of the original. (You can always acknowledge a typo or mistake in the original by inserting the word *sic* in square brackets after it—see p. 220). If you want to insert an explanatory comment of your own into a quotation, enclose it in square brackets:

    As Jones points out, "Biology has a statistical machine [cladistics] to order the world."

4. If you want to omit something from the original, use ellipsis points. (See p. 228 for details.)

Standard Style Sheets

If you have professors, colleagues, or situations calling for a specific reference style, it is likely to be one of IEEE, APA, or Chicago. Below you will find examples of these formats. There are minor differences distinguishing each of these, so be sure to follow the conventions exactly. Many other style formats exist that are less commonly seen in the sciences (MLA, for example). For specific formats that are not mentioned in this chapter, you will find numerous references available through your library. If you have access to RefWorks or other bibliographic software, simply click on your chosen style sheet to have your references formatted automatically.

IEEE Style

The Institute of Electrical and Electronics Engineering (IEEE) is a well-established engineering professional society that publishes numerous periodicals on engineering and science topics. It is a great example of a style to emulate both in the articles published, and certainly in the style of citations.

In-Text Citation Sequencing

Number your citations consecutively, putting the reference numbers in square brackets and punctuating afterwards if necessary. The first reference in your text will be [1], the next new reference will be [2], and so on. Once a source has been assigned a number, it is referred to by that number whenever it appears in the text:

> Labossière's groundbreaking study [1] was first challenged by Gormon [2] and later disputed by Huang [3]. Gormon's later work [4] confirmed the validity of Labossière's original hypothesis [1].

Putting reference numbers in square brackets both in the text and in the list of references is a preferred alternative to raised numerals that might be confused with superscript in scientific abbreviations or exponents. If you are referencing several sources at once, include all reference numbers in the same citation, giving each its own set of square brackets. Refer to multiple references this way:

> Ultrasound images contain speckle noise [1]–[3] that makes tumours difficult to detect by eye alone.

If you make a later reference to a work you have already cited, use the number you assigned the work originally. List the work only once by number in your reference list.

Reference Lists

The IEEE regularly refers writers to the *Chicago Manual of Style* (see p. 180) for questions of style, but the reference guidelines outlined in the *IEEE Editorial Style Manual* [1] provide formatting advice. This method for preparing a comprehensive list of sources at the end of your work merges traditional formats for endnotes and bibliographies. If you are using the in-text citation method, you list references in numerical order, according to their order of appearance in your work. Put the bracketed number flush with the left margin and use a hanging indent if your entry extends beyond the initial line. To conserve space, use initials rather than first names for authors, and use standard abbreviations for the names of journals, conferences, conference proceedings, and organizations. If you are referring to a page or two, rather than the entire work, list only the page numbers. Follow the punctuation conventions illustrated below:

> [1] I. Author and U. Writer, "Title of chapter," in *Book*, T. Smith, Ed. City, State, Country: Publisher, Year, pp. xx–xx.
>
> [2] I. Author and U. Writer, "Title of article," *Abbrev. Title of Periodical, vol. x,* no. x, pp. xx–xx, Abbrev. Month, Year.
>
> [3] I.M. Author. (year, month, day). Title. *Source* [Medium]. *volume* (issue), pp. xx–xx. Available: URL or DOI.

The models above italicize titles and volume numbers but use regular type for the titles of chapters or articles. Always check with your instructor or a librarian if you are in doubt.

The following examples provide IEEE models for scientific references including titles in italics. Remember to give as much information as necessary for your reader to locate each source.

Book with One Author

The author's name follows the citation number and is not inverted. Capitalize important words in the title:

[1] R. Van Meter, *Quantum Networking*. Hoboken, NJ, USA: John Wiley & Sons, 2014.

Book with More Than One Author

If the book you are citing has two or more authors, list all the names, separated by "and" (and commas, in the case of three or more authors).

[2] J.P. Goedbloed, R. Keppens, and S. Poedts, *Advanced Magnetohydrodynamics*. New York, NY, USA: Cambridge University Press, 2010.

Book with a Group or Corporate Author

[3] University of Chicago Press, *The Chicago Manual of Style*, 17th ed. Chicago, IL, USA: University of Chicago Press, 2017.

In the case of a revised or subsequent edition, include this information following the title, as shown above. (A revised edition would be shown as "rev. ed.")

Book with an Editor, a Compiler, or a Translator

If the book has an editor or compiler and no author, give the editor's or compiler's name followed by "Ed." or "Comp.":

[4] V. I. Kodolov, Ed., *Nanostructures, Nanomaterials, and Nanotechnologies to Nanoindustry*. Toronto, Canada: Apple Academic Press, 2015.

If the book has a translator, editor, or compiler as well as an author, put the author's name before the title and the other name after the title, introduced by the appropriate abbreviation.

[5] N. Copernicus, *On the Revolutions of the Heavenly Spheres*. Trans. A. M. Duncan. New York, NY, USA: Barnes & Noble, 1976.

Selection in an Edited Work

The title of the selection is placed in quotation marks and in lower case but for the first letter of the first word of the title and subtitle. It follows the author's name and precedes the name of the edited work. Notice that the word *in* precedes the name of an edited book but is *not* used before the names of journals, periodicals, magazines, or newspapers containing a referenced article:

> [6] R.F. Miller, "Geotourism, mining and tourism development in the Bay of Fundy," in *Mining Heritage and Tourism: A Global Synthesis*, M.V. Conlin and L. Jolliffe, Eds. New York, NY, USA: Routledge, 2011. pp. 211–225.

Article in a Journal or Periodical

> [7] J. Shapiro, "Electromagnetic compatibility for system engineers," *IETE Technical Review*, vol. 28, no. 3, pp.70–77, May–June 2011. doi:10.4103/0256-4602.74505

Most electronic articles have a DOI (digital object identifier), which offers a permanent link to the publication. To find a missing DOI, use http://www .crossref.org.

If the work has not yet appeared in print, put "to be published" if the work has been accepted for publication. Use "submitted for publication" if it has not yet been accepted:

> [8] M. Foumani, A. Khajepour, and M. Durali, "Optimization of engine mount characteristics using experimental numerical analysis," *J. Vibration and Control*, to be published.

Article in a Newspaper

If the section of the newspaper containing the article you are referencing is identified, give its name, number, or letter:

> [9] J. Ball, "Wind power hits a trough," *Wall Street Journal*, p. A20, April 6, 2011.

If the article is unsigned, begin your reference with the title of the article.

Technical Report

Even if a technical report has been printed in house (i.e., by the organization itself), you list it as a publication. Include all necessary information for locating it, including the report number abbreviated as "Rep."

> [10] "A summary of NRC construction housing activities for 2012: A report prepared for the Canadian Home Builders' Association," NRC Institute for Research in Construction, NRC, Rep. 68187, Feb. 2013.

Paper Presented at a Conference

Cite this as you would a journal article, but include the words "presented at" to indicate that you are referencing a paper you attended:

[11] B. Richter, "Chasing water: The imperative to move from scarcity to sustainability," presented at the 10th Intl. Symp. on Ecohydraulics, Trondheim, Norway, June 26, 2014.

Otherwise, use the conventional reference format for a publication.

Dissertation

Refer to an unpublished dissertation this way:

[12] V. Bevan, "Sediment budget of an urban creek in Toronto." PhD dissertation. Dept. Civ. Eng, Univ. Waterloo, Waterloo, Canada 2014.

Lecture Notes

Give as much detail as necessary for the reader to locate the material. For material included in courseware packs, give original publication information as well:

[13] M.P. Anderson and W.W. Woessner, "Profile models," in *Applied Groundwater Modeling*, 2nd ed. Elsevier: Academic Press, 2011. pp. 172–194. Included in C. MacGregor, course notes. SD 347, Conestoga College, Waterloo, Canada, Fall 2014.

For references to material (a slide, for example, or notes on the board) coming from a class you attended, acknowledge the source by providing the details, the course name, institutional information, and date.

[14] C.R. Ellis, "Pavement stress graphs: Highway 404, 2011," CIVL 460, Queen's Univ., ON, Nov. 23, 2014.

Patent

Include the inventor's name, the title of the invention, the patent number, and date of issue:

[15] M. Bureau, "Fluid Recovery," Can. Patent CA 2610221, Sept. 2, 2014.

Multimedia Sources

Specify the type in square brackets:

[16] D. Suzuki, Chris Hatfield: The Man who Tweeted Earth [DVD], 44 min. CBC, 2013.

Website

The most up-to-date information is available instantly, but it can change. Especially if you are citing a wiki, you should identify the date you accessed the site (to show when your information was current). List this information at the end of your citation. References must include enough information about the material, the site, and the sponsoring organization that the reader can access the source. For all online sources, then, provide the full DOI if available; otherwise, provide the URL, not just the home-page address. Be sure to report the DOI or the URL accurately.

[17] S. Arbesman. (2014, Oct. 2). From 53 kilobytes of RAM in 1953. [Online]. Available: http://www.wired.com/2014/10/53-kilobytes-ram-1953/

Note that if you have to break a URL so that it fits properly on a line, do so after a slash. Don't add extra spaces or use hyphens.

Alphabetical Referencing

Some professors will ask you to list your references in alphabetical order at the end of your document rather than in their order of appearance in the text. Follow their recommendations by assigning a number to each reference only once everything has been alphabetized. (For entries, use the same format as that described above, but reversing first names and surnames.) Thus your reference list will be in numerical and alphabetical order at the same time. To complete the process, go back to your document and make sure your references are keyed to the numbers listed at the end. When the reference list is alphabetized, numbers in the text will therefore not appear in sequence:

Ultrasound images contain speckle noise [2],[5],[6] that makes tumours difficult to detect by eye alone.

APA Style

The American Psychological Association system of documentation is the one most commonly used in the social sciences, business, and nursing. The APA system uses in-text citations, which name authors and dates in parentheses after the information cited, rather than providing reference or note numbers. Complete bibliographical information is included in a list of references at the end. Some examples are listed below. For more detailed information, consult the *Publication*

Manual of the American Psychological Association (7th ed.). The APA website at http://apastyle.apa.org/ also provides current information on APA Style.

In-Text Citations

Source with One Author
If the author's name is given in the text, cite only the year of publication in parentheses.

> Helmsteadt (2014) made a significant contribution to the climate change debate.

Otherwise, give both the name and the year:

> The latest analysis (Christensen, 2015) has disproved government statements.

Source with More than One Author
If the work you are citing has two authors, include both names every time you cite the reference in the text. APA uses an ampersand (&) when the names are in parentheses, but uses "and" in the text:

> Earlier research showed that it was possible to redesign agro ecosystems for environmental sustainability (Hill & Henning, 2013). Todd and Voisin (2014) later showed that rural communities could afford to implement such systems only with heavy government subsidies.

If there are three, four, or five authors, cite only the first two names, followed by "et al.":

> Reid, Jensen, et al. (2015) offered new insights on sustainability projects. [. . .] Research showed that public school students were capable innovators (Reid et al., 2015).

If the work you are citing has six or more authors, cite only the surname of the first author followed by "et al."

Source with a Group or Corporate Author
Corporations, associations, and government agencies serving as authors are usually given in full each time they appear. Some group authors may be named in full the first time and abbreviated in subsequent citations if this provides the reader with enough information to easily locate the entry in the reference list:

A recent study examines the effectiveness of treating low-back pain in the first two weeks following injury (Institute for Work & Health [IWH], 2014) . . . . The same study also looks at the effectiveness of bed rest in speeding up recovery (IWH, 2014).

Work with No Known or Declared Author

If the work you are referencing has no known or declared author, cite the first few words of the title, as well as the year:

In the pyroelectric sensor, the infrared light generates surface electric charge off a substrate ("Motion Sensing Lights," 2015).

[The full title of the source is "Motion Sensing Lights and Burglar Systems Work, Study Shows."]

Specific Parts of a Source

If you are referring to a particular part of a source, indicate the page, chapter, figure, table, or equation. Always give page numbers for quotations:

(Felderhaus, 2012, p. 299)

(Christenssen & Schor, 2014, pp. 2601–2602)

(Stenson, 2013, Chapter 2)

Note that the APA abbreviates page numbers with "p." for a single page and "pp." for several pages.

Online Sources

In-text citations for electronic sources use the same formatting principles outlined above for print sources, with the following exceptions:

- If your source has no page numbers, use the paragraph number, if one is available, preceded by the abbreviation "para.":

    (Edson, 2015, para. 10)

- If sections, pages, and paragraphs are not numbered, cite the heading and the number of the paragraph following it to direct the reader to the specific location you are referring to:

    (Black, 2014, Introduction, para. 6)

References

The following conventions are used for recording entries in an APA *References* section:

- Entries begin with the author's surname, followed by his or her initials with a space between initials (full given names are not used).
- In entries for works with more than one author, all authors' names are reversed, with the name of the last author preceded by an ampersand (&) rather than "and."
- The date of publication appears immediately in parentheses after the names of the author(s).
- Entries for different works by the same author are listed chronologically. Two or more works by the same author with the same publication year are arranged alphabetically by title.
- For titles of books and articles, only proper nouns and the first word of the title and of the subtitle (if there is one) are capitalized. However, titles of journals are capitalized as usual.
- Include the DOI (digital object identifier) for articles from databases and e-journals.
- Titles of articles or selections in books are *not* enclosed in quotation marks. Book and journal titles are italicized.

For references to electronic sources, no retrieval date is needed. Provide the URL if you are providing a web address that is freely accessible or with "Available from" if it comes from a source that must be purchased (a database or subscription service, for example).

Book with One Author

Lane, C. A. (2013). *On fracking*. Rocky Mountain Books.

Book with More than One Author

Bell, M., & Buckley, C. (2010). *Solid states: Concrete in transition*. Princeton Architectural Press.

For books with 21 or more authors, list the first 20 followed by three ellipses and the last author's name.

Book with a Group or Corporate Author

European Commission Directorate-General for Energy. (2011). *Renewables make the difference*. Publications Office of the European Union.

Book with an Editor or Editors

Weiss, N., & Koschak, A. (Eds.). (2014). *Pathologies of calcium channels*. Springer.

Selection in an Edited Book

Galison, P. L. (2011). Tools and innovation. In R. Y. Chiao, (Ed.), *Visions of discovery: New light on physics, cosmology, and consciousness* (pp. 23–30). Cambridge University Press.

Note that the page numbers of the selection are given, preceded by "pp."

Article in a Journal or Magazine

Arjoranta, J. (2014). Game definitions: A Wittgensteinian approach. *Game Studies, 14*(1). http://gamestudies.org/1401/articles/arjoranta

If there is a volume number, the page range is given without "pp."

When a journal has continuous pagination, the issue number should not be included. If each issue begins on page 1, give the issue number in parentheses before the page numbers and immediately following the volume number, with no punctuation separating them and a comma following the parentheses. The volume number is italicized or underlined; the issue number and its parentheses are not. Include the digital object identifier (DOI), if one is provided; otherwise, provide the URL:

Osoba, L. O., Sidhu, R. K., & Ojo, O. A. (2011). On preventing HAZ cracking in laser welded DS Rene 80 superalloy. *Materials Science and Technology, 27*(5), 897–902. https://doi.org/10.1179/026708309X12560332736593

For monthly or bimonthly magazines, give the month(s) in full; for weekly magazines, give the month (in full) and day.

Multimedia Sources

Be sure to include either the DOI or URL for electronic sources.

> Walters, R. (2013, April 27). *Reusing spray foam cans* [Video]. YouTube. http://www.youtube.com/watch?v=PVOfoUD5Mvl

Website

> Environment Canada. (2014, October 19). *Air quality health index*. http://weather.gc.ca/airquality/pages/onaq-004_e.html

Remember to break a URL that goes to another line after a slash or before a period. Do not insert (or allow your word processing program to insert) a hyphen at the break.

Message Posted to a Newsgroup or Mailing List

Give as much information as possible to allow a reader to track the source.

> Bryant, M. D. (2015, February 4). *DNAPL contamination* [Electronic mailing list message]. news://sci.aptenv.poll

Because e-mail messages and tweets are not recoverable, do not list such communications in the *References* section, but do reference them in the text of your document as personal communication.

Chicago Manual of Style

The Chicago Manual of Style (CMS) outlines two methods of documentation. The *author–date* system, preferred in the natural and social sciences, follows the same principles as APA style with only minor stylistic differences. The *notes-and-bibliography* method uses superscript numerals to direct the reader to footnotes at the bottom of the page or endnotes listed separately at the end of the document. In scientific writing, footnotes or endnotes are used not to cite references but to expand upon the content of the paper—on the very rare occasions where such elaboration is impossible in the text. Some journals, for example, will use a footnote to provide biographical details of the author(s). In most of your work, you can include the reference in the text itself by name, year, and page in parentheses like so: (Northey and Jewinski 2016, 34).

Despite the convenience of footnoting software, use notes *only* if you are specifically directed to do so. The following are some examples of notes using the Chicago notes-and-bibliography method. For additional examples, consult *The Chicago Manual of Style: The Essential Guide for Writers, Editors, and Publishers* (17th ed.) or the University of Chicago Press/Questions & Answers website, available at http://www.chicagomanualofstyle.org/qanda/latest.html

Notes

Footnotes appear at the bottom of the page or column that contains the reference. Endnotes are placed on a *Notes* page after any appendices and before a bibliography. All notes are single-spaced and typed with an indented first line (as in the examples below). Although the note numbers are superscript where they appear in the text, the note numbers that precede the notes themselves are not. If you have been asked to cite your references with CMS notes, prepare them to meet the following conventions.

Book with One Author

The name of the author follows the note number and is not inverted. It is followed by a comma and the italicized title of the book, with all important words capitalized. The publication details follow the title in parentheses, and the page numbers are added without an abbreviated "p.":

1. Dan Marinescu, *Classical and Quantum Information* (Maryland Heights, MO: Academic Press, 2012), 87.

Book with More than One Author

If the book you are referencing has two or three authors, all of the authors' names are given, separated by "and" and (in the case of three or more authors) commas:

2. James Ambrose and Patrick Tripeny, *Simplified Engineering for Architects and Builders*, 11th ed. (Hoboken, NJ: Wiley, 2011), 155.

If the book you are referencing has more than three authors, you can use the name of only the first author, followed by either "et al." or "and others" and a period, without intervening punctuation.

Book with a Group or Corporate Author

3. University of Chicago Press, *The Chicago Manual of Style*, 17th ed. (Chicago: University of Chicago Press, 2017), 244.

In the case of a revised or subsequent edition, include this information following the title, as shown above. A revised edition would be "rev. ed."

Book with an Editor, a Compiler, or a Translator
If the book you are referencing has an editor or compiler and no author, give the editor's or compiler's name first, followed by "ed." or "comp.":

4. Kent Pinkerton and William N. Rom, eds., *Global Climate Change and Public Health*. (New York: Humana Press, 2014), 48.

If the book you are referencing has a translator, editor, or compiler as well as an author, the author's name should come before the title with the translator's, editor's, or compiler's name following the title, introduced by the appropriate abbreviation:

5. Madeleine Ferrier, *Sacred Cow, Mad Cow: A History of Food Fears*, trans. Jody Gladding (New York: Columbia University Press, 2006), 24–31.

Selection in an Edited Book
The title of the selection, set in quotation marks, follows the author's name and precedes the name of the edited work. Note that a title within a title is enclosed in quotation marks:

6. Elizabeth A. Gibson and Anders Hagfeldt, "Solar Energy Materials," in *Energy Materials*, ed. Duncan W. Bruce, Dermot O'Hare, and Richard I. Walton (Chichester, West Sussex: Wiley, 2011), 246–278.

Article in a Journal
If an issue number is given, it follows the volume number, separated by a comma and "no." In a reference to the article as a whole, the entire page range should be included. A reference to a particular section should give relevant page numbers only. Include the DOI (digital object indicator) if the article comes from an online journal:

7. Ron Zevenhoven, Martin Falt, and Luis Pedro Gomes, "Thermal Radiation Heat Transfer: Including Wavelength Dependence into Modelling, *International Journal of Thermal Sciences* 86, (Dec. 2014): 189–197. doi:10.1016/j.ijthermalsci.2014.07.003

Article in a Magazine

Even if a magazine is numbered by volume and issue, it is usually cited by date only:

> 8. Charlie Gillis and Chris Sorensen, "Finding Franklin," *Maclean's*, Sept. 22, 2–14, 40–44.

Website

To cite a website or other electronic source, include as much of the following as can be determined: author of the content, title of the page, title or owner of the site, and URL or DOI.

> 9. "Aggressive Driving and Road Rage," Government of Ontario. http://www.mto.gov.on.ca/english/safety/topics/aggressive.shtml.

Bibliography

The bibliography is a list of all the sources you have used in your paper, including works you may have consulted but not referred to directly. It is placed on a separate page at the end, arranged alphabetically by the authors' last names, single-spaced, with hanging indents. If you are asked to keep primary and secondary source materials separate, or list online sources separately from paper sources, use subheadings. Do not number your entries.

Book with One Author

> Funk, McKenzie. Windfall: The Booming Business of Global Warming. New York: Penguin, 2014.

Book with More than One Author

If the book you are referencing has two authors, invert the name of the first author only and separate the names with a comma and "and":

> Tomecek, Stephen M., and Steve Tomecek, *Global Warming and Climate Change.* New York: Chelsea House Publications, 2011.

If the book you are citing has four to 10 authors, list only the first author, followed by "et al." in your note, but your bibliography should list all authors. For works of more than ten authors, you may also follow the first author's name (inverted) with a comma and "et al." or "and others":

Hausladen, Gerhard, Michael de Saldanha, Petra Liedl, Hermann Kaufmann, Gerd Hauser, Klaus Fitzner, Christian Bartenbach, et al. *ClimateSkin: Building-skin Concepts that Can Do More with Less Energy*. Basel: Birkhauser, 2008.

Book with a Group or Corporate Author

United Nations Development Programme. *Global Environmental Outlook 3*. London: Earthscan, 2002.

Book with an Editor or a Translator

If the book has an editor and no author, give the editor's name first, followed by the abbreviation "ed." or "eds." if there are multiple editors:

Nicholson, Simon, and Paul Kevin Wapner, eds. *Global Environmental Politics: From Person to Planet*. Boulder, CO: Paradigm Press, 2015.

If the book has an editor or translator as well as an author, give the author's name first and give the translator's or editor's name after the title, introduced by "Edited by" or "Translated by":

Ferrier, Madeleine. *Sacred Cow, Mad Cow: A History of Food Fears*. Translated by Jody Gladding. New York: Columbia University Press, 2006.

Selection in an Edited Book

Spielgelman, Jonah. "Management to Industrial Ecology." In *Linking Industry and Ecology: A Question of Design*, edited by Raymond Côté, James Tansey, and Ann Dale, 225–241. Vancouver: UBC Press, 2006.

Article in a Journal

Because a bibliographic entry is a reference to the article as a whole, the entire page range should be given:

Mwafy, Aman. "Assessment of Seismic Design Response Factors of Concrete Wall Buildings." *Earthquake Engineering and Engineering Vibration* 10, no. 1 (March 2011): 115–127. doi:10.1007/s11803-011-0051-7

If you are referencing an unsigned article, the entry should begin with the title of the article.

The preceding example lists an electronic journal, but the same guidelines apply to electronic magazines and newspapers: follow the format of the print counterparts, with the addition of the DOI or URL and, if the information is time-sensitive, the date of access. To list a website, include as much of the following as can be determined: the author of the content, the title of the page, the title or owner of the site, and the URL or DOI.

Kukulka, David et al. "Thermal Conductivity of Natural Rubber Using Molecular Dynamics Simulation." *Journal of Nanoscience and Nanotechnology* 15, no. 4 (April 2015): 3244–3248. doi:10.1166/jnn.2015.9640

Multimedia Source

Laszewski, Nick. "DIY Battery Backup Sump Pump." *Lifestyle*. YouTube. Mar. 4, 2014. 10:15. http://www.youtube.com/watch?v=7twLj5MDCO4

Because electronic communications can be difficult or impossible to access, Chicago style recommends making only in-text references to such sources as e-mails or tweets. They are not normally mentioned in a bibliography although you still must cite them in a footnote or endnote.

References

1. IEEE. (2014) IEEE Editorial Style Manual. [Online]. Available: http://www.ieee.org/documents/style_manual.pdf

Appendix B
Grammar and Usage

Part 1 Common Errors in Grammar and Usage
Introduction

This appendix surveys those areas where students most often make mistakes. It will help you watch for weaknesses as you edit your work. Once you get into the habit of checking, it won't be long before you avoid potential problems as you write.

As you work to increase your writing proficiency, keep track of mistakes you typically make and focus on eliminating them as you edit. It is also a good idea to have your writing reviewed by a colleague whom you know to be a clear reader. This person can point out errors and issues of clarity that you may have missed.

The suggestions and guidelines below will help you finesse your writing so that your reader focuses on what you're saying and not how you said it.

Problems with Sentence Unity

Sentence Fragments

To be complete, a sentence must have both a subject and a predicate in an independent clause. If not, it's a fragment. There are times in informal writing when it is acceptable to use a sentence fragment in order to give emphasis to a point, as in

✔ Will the municipality reduce property taxes? Not likely.

The sentence fragment *Not likely* is deliberate. Because the writer was speaking directly to an audience, it is an appropriate shortening of *It is not likely that the municipality will reduce property taxes.* Unintentional sentence fragments, on the other hand, usually seem incomplete rather than shortened:

✘ One application is the algorithm for a chess program. Based on an actual game situation.

The last "sentence" is incomplete because it has neither a subject nor a verb. (Remember that a participle such as *based* is a verbal, or "part-verb," not a verb.) The fragment can be made into a complete sentence by adding a subject and a verb:

✔ It is based on an actual game situation.

More economically, you could join the fragment to the preceding sentence:

✔ One application is the algorithm for a chess program based on an actual game situation.

Be particularly careful not to separate dependent clauses from the previous sentence. Watch for such subordinators as *whereas, while,* and *because.*

✗ Some companies are exemplary corporate citizens. <u>Whereas others are interested only in making profits.</u>

One good test for a complete sentence is to make sure that it fits naturally into the following space: "It is true that _____." If the result sounds wrong—as it would with the sentence fragment beginning *whereas* above—it makes sense to revise it:

✔ Some companies are exemplary corporate citizens, whereas others are interested only in making profits.

Run-on Sentences

Many people consider a run-on sentence one that continues beyond the point where it should have stopped:

✗ Mosquitoes and blackflies are annoying, but they don't stop tourists from coming to spend their holidays in Canada, and such is the case in Ontario's northland.

This example reveals a problem of over-coordination. The sentence could be improved by removing the word *and* and replacing the comma after Canada with a semicolon or period.

The grammatical problem called a run-on sentence occurs when two independent clauses are jammed together without any punctuation at all. (An independent clause is always a complete sentence.) Two independent clauses should not run together, as they seem to do in the following example:

✘   Glaciers are retreating so fast scientists are concerned about global water levels.

✔   Glaciers are retreating so fast that scientists are concerned about global water levels.

Here the problem is corrected by adding the word *that*, which makes it clear that the second clause (*scientists are concerned about global water levels*) is a dependent, or subordinate, clause. The problem cannot be corrected by simply adding a comma, as the writer of the next example has done:

✘   In physics there is matter and antimatter, everything must be balanced.

This error is known as a comma splice. There are three ways of correcting it:

1. by putting a period after *antimatter* and starting a new sentence:

    ✔   . . . and antimatter. Everything . . .

2. by replacing the comma with a semicolon:

    ✔   . . . and antimatter; everything . . .

3. by making one of the independent clauses subordinate to the other so that it can't stand by itself:

    ✔   In physics, because there is matter and antimatter, everything must be balanced.

The comma splice is occasionally forgivable when clauses are very short and arranged in tight sequence:

orig.   We noted the contrast: the flow geometry was simple, the flow pattern was complex.

However, it's still better to revise such a sentence:

> ✔ We noted the contrast: the flow geometry was simple, and the flow pattern was complex.

Contrary to what many people think, words such as *however, therefore,* and *thus* should not be used with a comma to join independent clauses:

> ✘ The coefficient used for the calculation is still correct, therefore no new modelling has been done.

Correct this mistake by beginning a new sentence after *correct* or by replacing the comma with a semicolon:

> ✔ The coefficient used for the calculation is still correct; therefore, no new modelling has been done.

The only words that can be used without a semicolon to join independent clauses are the coordinating conjunctions—*and, or, nor, but, for, yet,* and *so.* (Subordinating conjunctions such as *if, because, since, while, when, where, after, before,* and *until* reduce the construction to a dependent clause.)

> ✔ The coefficient used for the calculation is still correct, so no new modelling has been done.

Faulty Predication

When the subject of a sentence is not grammatically connected to what follows (the predicate), the result is called *faulty predication*:

> ✘ The reason they chose this design is because it is well suited to indoor environments.

The problem with this sentence is that *because* means essentially the same thing as *the reason (that)*. The subject needs a noun clause to complete it:

> ✔ The reason they chose this design is that it is well suited to indoor environments.

Another solution is to rephrase the sentence:

✔ They <u>chose</u> the design <u>because</u> it is well suited to indoor environments.

Faulty predication also occurs with *is when* and *is where* constructions:

✘ The best time for the tests <u>is when</u> the subjects are well rested.

Again, you can correct this error in one of two ways:

1. Follow the *is* with a noun phrase to complete the sentence:

   ✔ The best time for the tests <u>is the morning, when</u> the subjects are well rested.

2. Change the sentence:

   ✔ Run the tests in the morning, when the subjects are well rested.

Problems with Subject–Verb Agreement

Identifying the Subject

Formal writing always requires the verb to agree in number with its subject. In other words, singular subjects call for singular verbs; plural subjects call for plural verbs. Sometimes, however, when the subject does not come at the beginning of the sentence, or when it is separated from the verb by other information, you may inadvertently use a verb form that does not agree, as in the example that follows:

✘ Our design <u>work</u>, including earthwork calculations and cost estimates, <u>are based</u> on these figures.

The subject here is *work*, not *calculations and estimates*; therefore, the verb should be singular:

✔ Our design <u>work</u>, including earthwork calculations and cost estimates, <u>is based</u> on these figures.

Either, Neither, Each

The indefinite pronouns *either*, *neither*, and *each* always take singular verbs:

- ✘   Neither of the models <u>are</u> flawless.

- ✔   Neither of the models <u>is</u> flawless.

- ✔   Each of them <u>has</u> flaws.

Compound Subjects

When you use *or*, *either . . . or*, or *neither . . . nor* to create a compound subject, the verb is expected to agree with the last item in the subject:

- ✔   Neither the TA nor <u>her students</u> <u>were</u> able to solve the equation.

- ✔   Either the students or <u>the TA</u> <u>was</u> misinformed.

You may find that it sounds awkward to use a singular verb when a singular item follows a plural item:

orig.   Neither the transistors <u>nor the circuit was</u> modified.

In such instances, it's worth rephrasing the sentence:

rev.   Neither the circuit nor <u>the transistors were</u> modified.

Unlike the word *and*, which creates a compound subject and therefore takes a plural verb, the phrases *as well as* and *in addition to* do not themselves make a subject plural. The verb agrees with the original subject:

- ✔   Noise, interference, and channel distortion corrupt information transmissions.

- ✔   Noise, as well as interference and channel distortion, corrupts information transmissions.

When the main verb is a form of *be* (*is*, *are*, *was*, or *were*), you often have a choice of sentence order. Note the subject–verb agreements below:

✔ My <u>area of research</u> <u>is</u> biomechanics and motor control.

✔ Biomechanics and motor control are what I study.

Remember that you can always revise your sentences to make them stronger.

Subject–verb agreement is often ignored in spoken English (which is much less formal than writing, remember). Orally, sentences beginning with *there*, for example, tend to be followed by the singular verb, even when the subject is a plural. Avoid such casual structures in writing:

✘ There's a number of <u>problems</u> to be resolved.

✔ There <u>are</u> a number of <u>problems</u> to be resolved.

✔ A number of <u>problems</u> <u>need</u> to be resolved.

Subject–verb agreement errors sometimes result from a misunderstanding of the true subject in phrases containing *of*. In the example above, *a number of* is grammatically equivalent to *many*, so it is appropriate to use a plural verb. But many similar constructions are singular, not plural, because the true subject comes after the definite or indefinite article (*the* or *a*), not *of*. When you use the following, be sure to use a singular verb:

a series of _____
the set of _____
a range of _____ } <u>is</u> available.
the group of _____
a multitude of _____

Collective Nouns

A collective noun is a singular noun that represents a number of members (examples include words such as *family*, *class*, *group*, and *team*). If the noun refers to the members as one unit, it takes a singular verb:

✔ The <u>class</u> <u>is</u> studying communication systems.

If, in the context of the sentence, the noun refers to the members as individuals, the verb becomes plural:

✔   The <u>class</u> <u>are</u> submitting their projects on Friday.

It's advisable to rewrite such a sentence to avoid the awkward sound of the singular and plural together:

✗   The <u>class</u> <u>is</u> submitting <u>their</u> projects on Friday.

✔   The <u>class</u> <u>is</u> submitting <u>the</u> projects on Friday.

✔   The <u>students</u> <u>are</u> submitting <u>their</u> projects on Friday.

Quantities

A number of nouns and pronouns are used to measure quantities that can be either enumerated or portioned out (see pp. 206–10 for a discussion of countable and uncountable nouns). You must be especially careful to distinguish between singulars and plurals so that your choice of verb will be appropriate:

✔   <u>Most</u> of the <u>noise</u> <u>was</u> eliminated.

✔   <u>Most</u> of the <u>noises</u> <u>were</u> accounted for.

    With the words that follow, the rule is to use a plural verb if you are measuring a number of individual items (*microchips, electrodes, test tubes*) and a singular verb if you are measuring a portion of something that cannot be counted (*equipment, software, water*):

all	
some	
none	
most	of the _____ [singular] <u>is</u>
half	of the _____ [plural] <u>are</u>
two-thirds	
a majority/minority	
a percentage	

The following sentences show the difference:

- ✔ None of the experiment was videotaped.

- ✔ None of the experiments were videotaped.

Unusual Plurals

A number of nouns cause real trouble for writers because they do not follow the traditional pattern of forming plurals by adding an *s*.

Singular	Plural
datum	data
criterion	criteria
phenomenon	phenomena
stratum	strata

Watch for these words in your writing, and be sure to use them correctly:

- ✖ The criteria was met.

- ✔ One criterion was met.

- ✔ One of the criteria was met.

- ✔ All the criteria were met.

In addition to these, there are a number of words that form plurals by adding *s* only in certain instances and have alternative plural forms in other contexts. Consult a dictionary before using words like *medium* and *antenna* in the plural.

Finally, be aware that in scientific writing, *data* is considered plural. In non-scientific contexts, however, *data* is accepted as a singular synonym for *information*.

Titles

The name of a business or an organization is always treated as a singular noun, even if it contains plural words. The same is true of book titles. Use a singular verb with these:

- ✔ Essentials of Optics is an excellent textbook.

- ✔ Goodman & Goodman is handling the legal dispute.

Tense Problems

When you are speaking, your tenses usually come automatically, but it's easy to run into difficulty when writing. A few general rules can help you avoid problems.

The Past Perfect

If you have a reference point in the past and you want to mention something that happened *prior to* that time, use the *past perfect* (*had* followed by the past participle). The time sequence will *not* be clear if you use the simple past for both:

> ✘ The second study <u>revealed</u> that the earlier results <u>were misinterpreted</u>.

> ✔ The second study <u>revealed</u> that the earlier results <u>had been misinterpreted</u>.

Similarly, when you are reporting what someone said in the past—that is, when you are using *past indirect discourse*—use the past perfect form to distinguish what's happening at the time from what happened prior to that time:

> ✘ The CEO said that the project <u>was approved</u>.

> ✔ The CEO said that the project <u>had been approved</u>.

If–Then Conditions

When you are describing regularly occurring consequences, use the present tense in both the condition (*if*) clause and the consequence (*then*) clause:

> ✔ If the temperature ever <u>drops</u> below −6°, the liquid <u>freezes</u>.

> ✔ Whenever the temperature <u>drops</u> below −6°, the liquid <u>freezes</u>.

When you are predicting a specific future consequence, use the present tense in the *if* clause and the future in the *then* clause:

> ✔ If the temperature <u>drops</u> below −6° tonight, the liquid <u>will freeze</u>.

When the situation is hypothetical, it is conventional—especially in formal writing—to use the *subjunctive* form in the condition clause and *would* + the base verb in the consequence clause:

✔ The experiment <u>would fail</u> if the solution <u>precipitated</u>.

Note that the subjunctive form is exactly the same as the past tense. The subjunctive form of the verb *be* is always *were*. Another way of expressing this subjunctive is to use *were to* + the base verb:

✔ If the solution <u>were to precipitate</u>, the experiment <u>would fail</u>.

When you are describing a hypothetical instance in the past, use the *past subjunctive* (it has the same form as the past perfect) in the *if* clause and *would have* + the past participle for the consequence. It is an error to use *would have* in both clauses:

✘ If the solution would have precipitated, the experiment would have failed.

✔ If the solution had precipitated, the experiment would have failed.

Writing about Technology

When you are describing a situation with a historical context, use the past tense:

✔ In 1993, Claude Berron <u>introduced</u> a new class of channel encoders, which he <u>named</u> turbo codes.

To discuss applications that are timeless (sometimes called "scientific truths") use the present tense:

✔ Turbo codes <u>achieve</u> high rates with low interference.

To establish a relationship between past and present in writing, use the present perfect form (*have* + the past participle):

✔ Recently, LPDC codes <u>have outperformed</u> turbo codes.

Do not hesitate to combine past and present tenses in the same paragraph as long as the contexts are appropriate. Never shift without good reason:

✔ Tests <u>were performed</u> on 14 November, and results <u>have been ana-lyzed</u>. The company now <u>recommends</u> further study.

Maintain the present tense for all reports of current or timeless actions, processes, or states.

Pronoun Problems

Pronoun Reference

The noun a pronoun refers to is called a *referent* or an *antecedent*. There needs to be a clear antecedent for every pronoun. If the referent doesn't appear in the same sentence, it must appear in the preceding one:

✖ <u>Groundwater</u> specialists have developed a variety of strategies to de-contaminate <u>it</u>.

Even though *groundwater* appears in the sentence, it is used here as a modifier, not a noun. Therefore, it cannot serve as referent or antecedent for the pronoun *it*. Either replace it or rephrase your sentence:

✔ <u>Specialists</u> have developed a variety of strategies to decontaminate <u>groundwater</u>.

When a sentence contains more than one noun, make sure there is no ambiguity about the antecedent:

✖ The public wants increased <u>environmental responsibility</u> along with <u>lower taxation</u>, but the government does not favour <u>it</u>.

What does the pronoun *it* refer to: *responsibility, taxes,* or even *the public*?

✔ The public wants increased <u>environmental responsibility</u> along with <u>lower taxes</u>, but the government does not advocate <u>spending increases</u>.

Another problem with pronouns relates to the same singular–plural agreement issues that occur with subjects and verbs (see pp. 190–3). Singular pronouns have singular nouns as antecedents; plural pronouns refer to plural nouns:

✖ A spokesperson for GVA <u>Transit</u> said that <u>their</u> ridership had doubled in the past year.

✔ A spokesperson for GVA <u>Transit</u> said that ridership had doubled in the past year.

In speaking, it is common to use *they* and *their* to refer to a singular noun—particularly when the noun is a person of unknown gender—but this practice does not yet always extend to formal writing. Rewrite the sentence to avoid the problem, either by pluralizing everything or dropping the pronouns:

✖ <u>Every</u> co-op <u>student</u> must submit <u>their</u> work report by the beginning of <u>their</u> next school term.

✔ <u>All</u> co-op <u>students</u> must submit <u>their</u> work <u>reports</u> by the beginning of <u>their</u> next school term.

✔ <u>Every</u> co-op <u>student</u> must submit <u>a</u> work report by the beginning of <u>the</u> next school term.

Using "It," "Which," and "This"

Using *it*, *which*, and *this* without a clear referent can lead to confusion:

✖ Although the directors wanted to meet in January, <u>it</u> [<u>this</u>] didn't take place until March.

✔ Although the directors wanted to meet in January, <u>the conference</u> didn't take place until March.

When you use *which*, make sure that it refers to its noun antecedent and not to a general idea:

✖ The directors wanted to meet in January, <u>which</u> didn't take place until March.

✔ The directors wanted <u>a winter meeting</u>, <u>which</u> didn't take place until March.

If you don't want your sentences to confuse readers, make sure that your pronoun clearly refers to a specific, identifiable referent.

Using "One"

People sometimes use the pronoun *one* to avoid *I* in formal writing. Although common in Britain, such a reference is often too formal for a North American audience:

orig.   If one were to apply for the grant, one would find oneself engulfed in endless red tape.

While there is nothing grammatically incorrect in this example, it sounds pretentious. The best alternative is to recast the sentence with a plural subject:

rev.   Researchers applying for the grant could find themselves engulfed in endless red tape.

If you avoid using *one*, you automatically avoid making the error of shifting point of view (mixing the third-person *one* with the second-person *you)*:

✘   When one uses a bank machine, you are using a CNC system.

✔   A person using a bank machine is using a CNC system.

Using "Me" and Other Object Pronouns

Remembering that it is wrong to say "My supervisor and me were invited," many people use the subject form (*I*) of the pronoun when the object form (*me*) is correct:

✘   The committee invited Damian and I to present our findings.

✔   The committee invited Damian and me to present our findings.

The verb *invited* requires an object; *me* is the objective case. A good way to tell which form is correct is to ask yourself how the sentence would sound with only the pronoun. You will know by ear that the subject form—"The committee invited *I*"—is inappropriate.

Knowing that *I* should be avoided in the previous example, some people prefer to substitute *myself*, but this usage is equally ungrammatical. *Myself, yourself, ourselves*, and so on, are reflexive pronouns used when their referent has already appeared, usually as the subject, in the sentence:

✔ <u>She</u> wrote <u>herself</u> a note to remind <u>herself</u> to return the book.

Avoid using reflexive pronouns as substitutes for object forms:

✘ The final exam schedule causes problems for <u>myself</u>.

✔ The final exam schedule causes problems for <u>me</u>.

Problems also arise with prepositions, which should be followed by a noun or pronoun in the objective case:

✘ <u>Between</u> you and <u>I</u>, this result doesn't make sense.

✔ <u>Between</u> you and <u>me</u>, this result doesn't make sense.

There are times, however, when the correct case can sound stiff or awkward:

orig.   The reporter wanted to know to <u>whom</u> the award had been given.

Rather than keep to a correct but awkward form, feel free to reword the sentence:

rev.   The reporter wanted to know <u>who</u> had received the award.

Exceptions for Pronouns Following Prepositions

The rule that a pronoun following a preposition takes the objective case has exceptions. When the preposition is followed by a clause, the pronoun should take the case required by its position in the clause:

✘ The students were curious <u>about whom would be elected</u>.

Although the pronoun follows the preposition *about*, it is also the subject of the verb *would be elected* and therefore requires the subjective case:

✔ The students were curious <u>about who would be elected</u>.

Similarly, when a gerund (an *-ing* word that acts partly as a noun and partly as a verb) is the subject of a clause or phrase, the word that modifies it takes the possessive form:

- ✘ Our drafting instructor objected to <u>us</u> asking for an extension.
- ✔ Our drafting instructor objected to <u>our</u> asking for an extension.
- ✔ The drafting instructor objected to the <u>students'</u> asking for an extension.

Problems with Modifiers

Adjectives modify nouns; adverbs modify verbs, adjectives, and other adverbs. Never use an adjective to modify a verb:

- ✘ He played <u>good</u>. (adjective with verb)
- ✔ He played <u>well</u>. (adverb modifying verb)
- ✔ He played <u>very well</u>. (adverb modifying adverb)
- ✔ He had a <u>fine style</u>. (adjective modifying noun)
- ✔ He had a <u>very fine style</u>. (adverb modifying adjective)

The examples above feature one-word adjectives and adverbs. Many combinations can act in similar ways—as adjectival and adverbial modifiers. The following represent some of the most common ones:

She is a student <u>in residence</u>. (*adjectival*)

The students live <u>in residence</u>. (*adverbial*)

Here is a place <u>to begin</u>. (*adjectival*)

<u>To begin</u>, open the book. (*adverbial*)

The TA <u>preparing the slides</u> is new. (*adjectival*)

The TA discovered an error <u>while preparing the slides</u>. (*adverbial*)

Everyone understood the material <u>prepared by the TA</u>. (*adjectival*)

Being familiar with these types of modifiers will help you to avoid the problems described below.

Misplaced Modifiers

Modifiers need to be put as close as possible to the words they refer to. If there is some distance between a modifier and the word it modifies, a reader may misinterpret the sentence.

- ✘ Students can access information about eating nutritiously <u>with this app</u>. [*Are they eating with the app?*]

- ✔ <u>With this app</u>, students can access information about eating nutritiously.

Be particularly attentive to words like *hardly, nearly, even, only,* and *almost,* which can modify many of the words in a sentence. Put them directly before the words they are meant to modify—just so that there is no room for misinterpretation:

- ✔ <u>Only</u> this study surveys the transformations.
- ✔ This study <u>only</u> surveys the transformations.
- ✔ This study surveys <u>only</u> the transformations.
- ✔ This study surveys the <u>only</u> transformations.
- ✔ This study surveys the transformations <u>only</u>.

Squinting Modifiers

Remember that clarity largely depends on word order: to avoid confusion, make connections between the different parts of a sentence clear. Keep modifiers as close as possible to the words they modify. A *squinting modifier* is one that, because of its position, seems to be working in two directions at the same time:

- ✘ Resistors that malfunction <u>often</u> need to be replaced.

Does *often* refer to the rate of malfunction or the rate of replacement? Changing the order of the sentence or rephrasing it will make the meaning clearer:

- ✔ Resistors need replacing if they malfunction <u>often</u>.
- ✔ <u>Often</u>, resistors that malfunction need to be replaced.

Other ambiguous modifiers can be corrected in the same way:

✘   Dr. Hutt gave a lecture on nanorobotics, <u>which</u> has several extended applications.

✔   Dr. Hutt's <u>lecture</u> on nanorobotics <u>has</u> several extended applications.

✔   Dr. Hutt lectured on <u>nanorobotics</u>, <u>which</u> has several extended applications.

Split Infinitives

Many readers object to the positioning of modifiers between the two parts of an infinitive (*to* and the base verb). Indeed, it's often more elegant to move the modifier to another position, either earlier or later, in the phrase. This revision is recommended whenever it is easy to make:

orig.   To <u>graphically</u> represent time requires four coordinates.

rev.   To represent time <u>graphically</u> requires four coordinates.

Dangling Modifiers

Modifiers that have no grammatical connection with anything else in the sentence are said to be *dangling*. Sentences that begin with modifiers need special care. If it isn't clear who or what is doing the action expressed by the modifier, the dangling construction needs to be repaired:

✘   <u>Developing</u> a third model, <u>success</u> was eventually achieved.

It is unclear who is doing the developing. Here are two more examples:

✘   Before <u>setting out</u> to model the system, <u>it</u> is important to define the intended benefits.

✘   To <u>understand</u> the concept, <u>knowledge</u> of market risk is essential.

It is unclear who is doing the setting out or the understanding. Clarify meaning by putting the subject for the modifier close to it:

✔   <u>Developing</u> a third model, <u>the designers</u> finally achieved success.

✔ Before <u>setting out</u> to model the system, <u>the project team</u> must define the intended benefits.

✔ To <u>understand</u> the concept, <u>students</u> need a knowledge of market risk.

One type of dangling modifier occurs when the subject is hidden by a passive verb:

✘ To <u>maximize</u> the validity, a target user <u>group</u> has to <u>be designated</u>.

✔ To <u>maximize</u> the validity, <u>testers</u> <u>must designate</u> a target user group.

In another situation, changing an active verb in the modifier to a passive verb will solve the problem:

✘ After <u>modifying</u> the filter, it performed extremely well.

✔ After the filter <u>was modified</u>, it performed extremely well.

In conclusion, it makes sense to watch for problem modifiers when you are editing, for they occur far too frequently in scientific and other kinds of writing.

Problems with Pairs and Parallels

Comparisons

Make sure that your comparisons are complete. The second element in a comparison should be equivalent to the first, whether the equivalence is stated or merely implied:

✘ Today's students understand <u>calculus</u> better than <u>their parents</u>.

This sentence suggests that the two things being compared are *calculus* and *parents*. Adding a second verb (*do*) that matches the first one (*understand*) shows that the two things being compared are parents' understanding and students' understanding:

✔ Today's students <u>understand</u> calculus better than their parents <u>do</u>.

A similar problem arises in the following comparisons:

✘ A design engineer's <u>responsibilities</u> are similar to an <u>architect</u>.

✘ <u>The area</u> of the landfill site is twice as large as the proposed <u>development</u>.

In both cases, the writer is neglecting one of the primary principles of comparison—that the left side and right side must be equal and comparable:

✔ A design <u>engineer's</u> responsibilities are similar to an <u>architect's</u>.

✔ <u>The area</u> of the landfill site is twice as large as <u>that of</u> the proposed development.

Parallel Phrasing

A series of items in a sentence should be phrased in parallel wording. Make sure that all the parts of a parallel construction (A, B, and C) are in fact equal:

✘ He liked <u>the pay</u>, <u>being able</u> to vary his hours, and also <u>appreciated</u> the many benefits.

✔ He liked the pay, the flexible hours, and the many benefits.

Once you have decided to use the same pattern in the first two elements, the third must have it as well. For clarity as well as elegance, keep similar ideas in similar form:

✘ The products are extremely strong, dimensionally stable, and they do not contain formaldehyde.

✔ The products are extremely strong, dimensionally stable, and free of formaldehyde.

The rule applies to lists as well, where bullets, with their implied *and*, call for parallel phrasing:

✘ Communications system use coding for three major reasons:
- <u>reducing</u> the volume of information
- <u>protection</u> against intruders
- <u>to personalize</u> it

✔ Communication systems use coding for three major reasons:
- to reduce the volume of information
- to protect it against intruders
- to personalize it

Correlatives (Coordinate Constructions)

Constructions such as *both . . . and, not only . . . but also,* and *neither . . . nor* demand special care. The coordinating term must not come too early or else one of the parts that come after will not connect with the common element. For the implied comparison to work, the two parts that come after the coordinating terms must be grammatically equivalent:

✖ Mechanical systems should be not only simple and reliable but require little maintenance.

✔ Mechanical systems should not only be simple and reliable but require little maintenance.

Problems for English Language Learners

If English is not your first language, you have likely spent more time in English grammar and writing classes than the average student. The following explanations point out some of the most persistent trouble spots to watch for as you edit your work. When in doubt about vocabulary or idioms, consult the latest editions of the *Oxford Advanced Learner's Dictionary* and the *Oxford Collocations Dictionary*.

Noun Rules

Use the Determiner That's Right for the Context

Most nouns can be introduced by a word called a *determiner*. (The articles *a, an,* and *the* are the most common determiners, but others, called *quantifiers*, have similar functions.) Because nouns can be singular or plural, countable or uncountable, general or specific, it is usually the determiner that tells what kind of noun will follow. Choosing the appropriate determiner for the context will prevent you from sending mixed messages to your reader about the kind of noun you are using.

English nouns can be categorized in terms of quantity either by number or by amount. Singular countable nouns (such as *lake* or *contaminant*) are easily confused with uncountable nouns (such as *water* or *pollution*) because they both take singular verbs and because neither of them has an added *-s*. Plural countable nouns (*lakes*, *contaminants*) are easier to spot, but many nouns play dual roles, acting as countable or uncountable according to the context. It's the choice of determiners that makes the difference.

1. Use the determiners *a, an, one, another, each, every, either*, and *neither* only with singular countable nouns. If you remember the rule that every singular countable noun *must* have a determiner of some sort or other, you will avoid making errors like the one below:

   ✘ ITS encourages commuters to take bus rather than drive car.

   ✔ ITS encourages commuters to take a̲ bus rather than drive a̲ car.

2. Animals and people are always countable. It is a mistake not to use a determiner when they are used in the singular.

   ✘ The computer is often compared to the brain of human being.

   ✔ The computer is often compared to the brain of a̲ human being.

3. Do not use singular countable determiners with uncountable nouns:

   ✘ E̲v̲e̲r̲y̲ slang or jargon must be avoided in formal writing.

   ✔ A̲l̲l̲ slang or jargon must be avoided in formal writing.

4. Uncountable nouns don't need a determiner when they are used in a general sense. If you use a singular word without a determiner, you automatically tell the reader that it's uncountable. Be sure that's what you intend.

   ✔ Many people are afraid of c̲h̲a̲n̲g̲e̲.

   ✘ There's been c̲h̲a̲n̲g̲e̲ in plans.

   ✔ There's been a̲ c̲h̲a̲n̲g̲e̲ in plans.

5. The following determiners can all be used before plural (countable) nouns: *other, all, some, more, most, a lot of*:

other courses	all students
some books	more requirements
most colleges and universities	a lot of exams

   But these determiners are also used to introduce uncountable nouns:

other coursework	all software
some research	more evidence
most equipment	a lot of studying

Be careful not to confuse your singulars and plurals:

✖ <u>Some lab</u> need <u>more spaces</u> for machinery.

✔ <u>Some labs</u> need <u>more space</u> for machinery.

6. Watch out especially for nouns that can be either countable (one ____) or uncountable (a lot of ____) according to the context. For example, the word *experience* as a countable noun refers to a single eventful occurrence: "Meeting the astronaut was quite *an experience*." When referring to someone's background, however, use uncountable determiners: "He doesn't have *much experience*." Always use determiners that clarify your meaning:

✖ Dr. Frank had <u>a</u> trouble solving the equation.

✔ Dr. Frank had <u>some</u> trouble solving the equation.

Words like attention, *difficulty, damage, effort, exercise, interest, life, power, promise, proof, respect,* and *time* are only a few of those that create similar difficulties for English language learners.

7. All numbers higher than *one* are used only with countable plurals (*two eyes, three wheels, four legs,* and so on), as are the following quantifiers: *these, those, many, several, few, fewer, both,* and *a couple of.* Be sure that the noun following them is indeed a plural. Sometimes, you will have to use a countable word or phrase like *a piece of* together with an uncountable noun:

✖ Imperial measures are still used in <u>many equipment</u>.

✔ Imperial measures are still used in <u>many pieces of equipment</u>.

8. The following quantifiers introduce uncountable nouns only: *much, little, less,* and *an amount of.* You will make a mistake if you use one of them in front of a plural:

✖ Channel coding produces <u>less errors</u> than expected.

✔ Channel coding produces <u>fewer errors</u> than expected.

9. The definite article *the*, the possessive pronouns (*my, your, his, her, its, our, their, whose*), the interrogatives *what* and *which*, and the determiners *no* and *any* can be used before any noun at all. But when you

use *the*, you must already have a specific context for your noun. It is a mistake to use *the* when you mean *any*:

✖ The groundwater is an important source of water for agriculture.

✔ Groundwater is an important source of water for agriculture.

10. Before using a proper name, be sure you know whether it takes the determiner *the*. Nouns that are capitalized won't normally be introduced by *the* unless they also contain a phrase with *of*: it's *Vancouver*, but the *City* of *Vancouver*; *Waterloo College*, but the *University* of *Waterloo*; *Scotiabank*, but the *Bank* of *Montreal*. When the proper noun is included as a modifier, however (as in *the* English *language* or *the* Calgary *Flames*), you must use *the* for the sake of specificity:

✖ They went to a conference in United States.

✔ They went to a conference in the United States.

Verb Rules

Watch Agreement with Singulars and Plurals

Countable nouns can be singular or plural, where uncountable nouns have only a singular form. In addition to regular rules for subject–verb agreement, you must pay careful attention to the following situations.

1. With present-tense verbs and a *singular* subject, be sure to add *-s* to the verb:

   ✖ An RGP lens offer high oxygen transmissibility.

   ✔ An RGP lens offers high oxygen transmissibility.

   The verb must be singular as well when one of the following singular pronouns is the subject of the sentence: *one, each, either, neither, another, much, little, less*.

   ✖ Of the two sets of figures, neither are easy to manipulate.

   ✔ Of the two sets of figures, neither is easy to manipulate.

2. When referring to countable items in a set, you may use the prepositional phrase *of the* before the item to measure quantities. Remember that the word following *of the* will always be plural: "one of the *books*,"

"both of the *tests*," "some of the *results*." Remember also that the verb agrees with the word before *of*: "*one* of the books *is*," "*both* of the tests *are*," "*some* of the results *were*." Such constructions are worth checking twice to avoid errors:

✖ One of the most complicated <u>application</u> of AI <u>are</u> computer games.

✔ One of the most complicated <u>applications</u> of AI <u>is</u> computer games.

With sets of uncountables, the word following *of the* is always singular and the verb is singular as well: "*much* of the *test is* invalid"; "*some* of the *equipment was* missing."

With pronouns that can be either uncountable or plural (*all, any, more, most, some, none*), subject–verb agreement depends on whether the pronoun's referent is singular or plural: "*all* of the *material is* ready"; "*all* of the *materials are* ready."

3. In classifications, expressions like *type of*, *sort of*, and *kind of* are quite restrictive in terms of what follows: agreement will depend on whether the main noun is countable or uncountable. With countable nouns, agreement rules require everything to be all singular or all plural: "What *sort* of *label is* required?" "What *kinds* of *labels are* needed?"

With uncountable nouns, the expression can be singular or plural, but the noun itself must always remain singular:

✖ The program could handle various types of <u>informations</u>.

✔ The program could handle various types of <u>information</u>.

4. Rules for subject–verb agreement do not apply to modal auxiliaries (*can, could, shall, should, will, would, may, might, must*), which do not have separate singular and plural forms. If you aren't sure whether a subject is singular or plural, you will be safe if you can use a modal:

✔ The criteria will need validating.

Be sure, however, that you use the root form of the verb following a modal auxiliary:

✖ Later, the principal investigators <u>could discussed</u> the project.

✔ Later, the principal investigators <u>could discuss</u> the project.

Verb Forms

Use Be and Have with Care

Be is the verb most often used in English—both as a main verb and as an auxiliary. *Have* is the next most common one. It makes sense, then, to watch how you use these two verbs in particular.

Use Continuous Verbs for Action in Progress

Be followed by the present participle forms the continuous verb form to emphasize action in progress at a point in time in the past ("she *was reading*"), present ("she *is reading*"), or future ("she *will be reading*"). Use the continuous to add the meaning of "being in the process of" to your context: "I am [in the process of] studying for my finals." Verbs that express states of being and sense perceptions instead of action do not take the continuous form, however. Among these are the verbs *appreciate, believe, contain, hear, intend, know, mean, need, own, possess, see, understand*, and *want*.

When the verbs *be* and *have* are used in the continuous form, they have specific meanings: *be* means "behave" ("Joshua *is being* unusually cooperative today"), and *have* refers to temporary duration ("He *is having* dinner"; "she *is having* a party"). Always be careful to choose the appropriate form.

✖ We assume that everyone is understanding the academic integrity policy.

✔ We assume that everyone understands the academic integrity policy.

Use Perfect Forms to Express Completion

Have followed by the past participle produces the perfect form, which suggests completion of an activity prior to a point in time in the past, present, or future. Use the present perfect rather than the past tense to bring things up to date:

✖ We will be interviewing all next week because seventeen candidates submitted impressive CVs.

✔ We will be interviewing all next week because seventeen candidates have submitted impressive CVs.

Be Careful with Passive Forms

Be followed by the past participle produces the *passive voice* (see pp. 57–8), which shows the subject of the sentence *receiving* the action of the verb rather than *doing* it. Be sure to keep such relationships distinct:

✘ An atom <u>composes</u> of a nucleus surrounded by orbiting electrons.

✔ An atom <u>is composed</u> of a nucleus surrounded by orbiting electrons.

Differentiate your Participles

Because *be* can be used as an auxiliary with both the past and present participles, it is especially important to choose the appropriate participle form for the context. In other words, always be sure to distinguish between *doing* an action (verb + *ing*) and *receiving* an action (verb + *ed*):

✘ I am <u>interesting</u> in applying for a position with your company.

✔ I am <u>interested</u> in applying for a position with your company. (The position interests me.)

Use Only Gerunds in Prepositional Phrases

Prepositions like *in, of, on, for,* and so on may be followed by only one possible form of a verb: the verb ending in -*ing*, which is called a *gerund*. Be sure to use only this form in prepositional phrases:

✘ Designers enhance the SNR either <u>by reduce</u> the noise effects or <u>by increase</u> the signal level.

✔ Designers enhance the SNR either <u>by reducing</u> the noise effects or <u>by increasing</u> the signal level.

An apparent exception to this rule is the word *to*, which may be followed by a gerund or the base form of a verb, depending on the context. When *to* is being used as a preposition, it must be followed by a gerund; when it is being used as part of an infinitive, however, it is followed by the base form of the verb. This double role explains the difference between "She used to do calculus" (but she no longer does) and "She is used to doing calculus" (so ask her to help you). Be sure that you know which *to* is called for by the context:

✘ I am looking forward <u>to meet</u> you.

✔ I am looking forward <u>to meeting</u> you.

✔ I hope <u>to meet</u> you soon.

Include Required Verbs

Don't leave out the auxiliaries or the main verbs that convey the meaning in the sentence:

- ✘ He <u>working</u> for that oil company since February.

- ✔ He <u>has been</u> working for that oil company since February.

Idiom Rules

Idiom is the term used for a construction we can't explain except to say that it "sounds right." Idioms aren't predictable, and they aren't logical. The following are typical situations where you want to be careful that things sound the way they should.

Pay Attention to Word Endings

As you add to your vocabulary, it's worth noting the suffixes that mark the various parts of speech (*-ment*, *-ness*, *-er*, *-ence* for nouns; *-ify*, *-ate*, *-en*, *-ize* for verbs; *-al*, *-ful*, *-ent*, *-like*, *-less* for adjectives; *-ly* for adverbs). Be sure to use the appropriate word for the context:

- ✘ Please send the following files at your <u>convenient</u>.

- ✔ Please send the following files at your <u>convenience</u>.

Be sure the suffix you have used is legitimate:

- ✘ This insulation is valued for its <u>strongness</u> and <u>durableness</u>.

- ✔ This insulation is valued for its <u>strength</u> and <u>durability</u>.

Include Expected Prepositions

1. Some prepositions (words such as *of, for, in, on,* and so on) express conventional relationships. The following sentences represent typical examples:

   - ✔ I am a student <u>in</u> the Faculty of Engineering and Applied Science <u>at</u> Queen's University <u>in</u> Kingston, Ontario.

   - ✔ I'll meet you <u>at</u> noon <u>on</u> Monday <u>at</u> the lab <u>on</u> King Street.

   Although *at* specifies time or place here and *on* generalizes, the relationships cannot be applied to other situations haphazardly:

   - ✘ This work will be presented <u>in</u> the graduate research conference <u>at</u> August 2–4, 2016.

    ✔ This work will be presented <u>at</u> the graduate research conference <u>on</u> August 2–4, 2016.

2. Verb or adjective constructions completed with prepositions don't usually allow for any choice. From *consist of* to *insist on* and *convenient to*, it is worth maintaining a list to refer to whenever you are writing.

Avoid Unneeded Prepositions

1. Do not include prepositions after verbs that do not require them:

    ✖ He lacked <u>of</u> motivation to find a job.

    ✔ He lacked motivation to find a job.

Lack is used as a noun followed by *of* in the expression *have a lack of.* But because it uses four words instead of one, you should prefer the single verb *lack* for the sake of sentence economy.

2. With time expressions introduced by *last, next, this,* or *every* (*last night, next Monday, this month,* or *every week*), it is redundant to use a preposition:

    ✖ The midterm is <u>on</u> next Monday.

    ✔ The midterm is <u>next Monday</u>.

3. A few key idioms are completed by either gerund phrases or prepositional phrases:

    to have trouble/difficulty/a problem <u>doing</u> something

or

    to have trouble/difficulty/a problem <u>with</u> a topic (*or* in a subject)

    to spend or waste time/money <u>doing</u> something

or

    to spend or waste time/money <u>on</u> it

    to keep busy <u>doing</u> something

or

    to keep busy <u>at</u> it.

It's redundant to use the gerund and the preposition together:

    ✖ The professor spent three hours <u>on explaining</u> the project.

    ✔ The professor spent three hours <u>explaining</u> the project.

Use the Idiomatic Verb Form Called for by the Main Verb

1. Some verbs must be followed by an infinitive; others, by a gerund. Some (*begin, cease, continue, dread, forget, hate, like, love, prefer, remember, start, stop, try*) are followed by either form, sometimes with a change in meaning. Be sure you use the right idiom:

   ✘ Chemical reactions result when atoms <u>try sharing</u> electrons with other atoms.

   ✔ Chemical reactions result when atoms <u>try</u> to share electrons with other atoms.

2. There are eight verbs (*have, make, let, help, see, watch, hear,* and *feel*) that are followed by an object and the root form: "They *made* you *learn* this." Memorize these idioms, and avoid mistakes with them in your writing:

   ✘ Because of her high average, her faculty <u>let</u> her <u>to take</u> six courses in the winter term.

   ✔ Because of her high average, her faculty <u>let</u> her <u>take</u> six courses in the winter term.

3. Nine verbs (*ask, demand, insist, prefer, recommend, request, require, suggest, urge*) may be followed by a *that*-clause containing a verb in the subjunctive (the uninflected root form of the verb): "She *suggested that* he *be* consulted." Only four of these verbs (*ask, prefer, require, urge*) allow the clause to be rephrased with an infinitive phrase: "They urged her *to accept* the job." Do not use infinitive phrases with the other five verbs:

   ✘ She suggested <u>him to take</u> some time off before finding a job.

   ✔ She suggested <u>that he take</u> some time off before finding a job.

Watch Word Order

1. Word order in declarative sentences follows a basic pattern of subject followed by verb. The order is inverted in questions, whether they are information questions beginning with an interrogative (*What* is the density? *How long* does the reaction take?) or questions where the expected answer is "yes" or "no" (Is the frequency modulated? Did the program work?). When these questions are reported in sentences,

however, the original word order is preserved. Be careful, then, to respect the difference between *direct* and *indirect* questions:

✘ <u>Why</u> the e number <u>is</u> so important to scientists? (*direct*)

✔ <u>Why is</u> the e number so important to scientists? (*direct*)

✔ The student asked <u>why the</u> e <u>number is</u> so important to scientists. (*indirect*)

2. The subject–verb word order is also reversed when a sentence begins with a restrictive modifier introduced by *only* or a negative like *not*, *never*, or *seldom*. Regular word order applies if such modifiers appear later in the sentence:

✔ <u>Only once has</u> the computer lost a match.

✔ <u>Rarely does</u> the computer <u>lose</u> a match.

✔ The computer <u>rarely loses</u> a match.

The same principles apply to sentences introduced by *not only* and *neither* and/or *nor*. It is a mistake not to invert the subject and verb after these correlative conjunctions if you use them to join complete sentences:

✘ Not only <u>CNC performs</u> operations that people used to do, but it does work that was previously impossible to do.

✔ Not only <u>does</u> CNC <u>perform</u> operations that people used to do, but it does work that was previously impossible to do.

Avoid Ungrammatical Repetition

1. When you combine two sentences, use either coordination or subordination. It is redundant to use both:

✘ <u>Although</u> there are some limitations, <u>but</u> this method does identify clear trends.

✔ There are some limitations, <u>but</u> this method does identify clear trends. (*coordination*)

✔ <u>Although</u> there are some limitations, this method does identify clear trends. (*subordination*)

2. Avoid repetition in relative clauses. Once you've used a relative pro-
    noun or adverb, be sure to delete the original referent:

    ✖ Seismologists are needed in countries <u>where</u> there have been
    major earthquakes <u>there</u>.

    ✔ Seismologists are needed in countries <u>where</u> there have been
    major earthquakes.

Distinguish between "It Is" and "There Is"

Despite sharing the main verb *be*, *it is* and *there is* (or *there are*) constructions
are idiomatically quite different. They cannot substitute for each other: *It is time
to work* is different from *There is time to work*. One test of whether it is appropriate to use *there is* is to try substituting *exists* for *is* (or *exist* for *are* if you are
trying to use *there are*). If you can't make the substitution, try another idiom:

✖ <u>It is</u> a number of applications for packet filtering.

✔ <u>There are</u> a number of applications for packet filtering.

✔ <u>There exist</u> a number of applications for packet filtering. (*test*)

Be careful to include *it* or *there* in front of *is*. Even though neither word
conveys much meaning, each one is essential idiomatically:

✖ <u>Is</u> theoretically possible to control traffic flow even in a large city.

✔ <u>It is</u> theoretically possible to control traffic flow even in a large city.

Avoid Errors with Comparisons

1. One- and two-syllable adjectives and some adverbs express the com-
    parative by adding *-er* and a phrase beginning with *than*: *harder than
    x, easier than y, sooner than z*. Longer words and nouns show the
    comparison with *more* instead: *more difficult than x, more research
    than y*. It is redundant to use both methods of comparison together:

    ✖ Coding makes communication <u>more</u> faster and cheaper.

    ✔ Coding makes communication <u>much</u> faster and cheaper.

    If you can use *more* in a comparison, then you can express the
    opposite with *less*, as long as you are comparing modifiers. (If you

are using nouns, use *fewer* if the noun is plural and countable [see p. 206].) If your comparison uses *-er* rather than *more*, you can express the opposite with the phrase *not as . . . as* instead.

✖ Plastics are <u>less hard</u> than ceramics but have higher impact resistance.

✔ Plastics are <u>not as hard as</u> ceramics but have higher impact resistance.

2. Don't forget to complete phrases including *so, such, too,* and *enough* for expressions of degree. Follow *so* or *such* with a *that*-clause: *The paper had so many errors that it was rejected.* With *too*, use an infinitive phrase: *It was too complicated to correct.* With *enough*, use either construction. In writing, it is an error not to complete such expressions. Revise to avoid the problem:

✖ Nature presents <u>so many</u> examples of symmetry.

✔ Nature presents <u>many</u> examples of symmetry.

3. Use standard phrases to establish comparisons: *different from* (not *than*), *similar to*, and *the same as*. Be sure that you always include *the* when you use the word *same*:

✖ At equilibrium, forward and reverse reactions occur at <u>same</u> rates.

✔ At equilibrium, forward and reverse reactions occur at <u>the same</u> rates.

Readers expect writing to be free of distracting or disruptive mistakes. Errors in grammar and usage, whether unconscious or careless, give the reader a negative impression. Being aware of the most likely mistakes and learning to avoid them are worthwhile practices.

Part 2 Punctuation

Introduction

Punctuation can be tricky for anybody. If your punctuation is flawed, your readers may be confused and forced to backtrack; worse, they may not be convinced that you are in control as a writer. Punctuation marks are the traffic signals of writing. Use them with precision to keep readers moving smoothly through your work.

Note: Items in this section are arranged alphabetically.

Apostrophe [']

1. **Use an apostrophe to indicate the possessive form for nouns and some indefinite pronouns**.

    • Add an apostrophe followed by "s" to all singular and plural nouns not already ending in "s":

    Schrödinger's cat; women's studies.

    • Add an apostrophe followed by "s" to indefinite pronouns:

    no one's fault; anybody's guess

    • Add an apostrophe followed by "s" to singular nouns and short names ending in "s" when you pronounce the new ending "iz":

    his boss's proposal; Ross's idea; Willis's autobiography

    Note, however, that you omit the second "s" when the word has more than two syllables:

    Socrates' disciples; Copernicus' discovery

    • Add only an apostrophe to plural nouns ending in "s", remembering to avoid confusing singulars and plurals:

    the Board of Directors' decision; several students' projects (but one student's project)

2. **Use an apostrophe before or after "s" (according to the rules above) to show time or distance measurements:**

   a month's notice; two weeks' time; a stone's throw

3. **Use an apostrophe to show contractions of words in informal writing:**

   we'll see; you're welcome; the '90s

   Caution! Don't confuse *it's* (the contraction of *it is* or *it has*) with *its* (the possessive of *it*), which has no apostrophe.

4. **Do not use an apostrophe to signal plurals of acronyms and numbers.**

   ✖ URL's were standardized in the 1990's.

   ✔ URLs were standardized in the 1990s.

Brackets [ ]

Brackets are square enclosures, not to be confused with parentheses (which are round).

1. **Use brackets to set off an editorial remark within a quotation.** They show that the words enclosed are not those of the person quoted:

   Before her marriage soured, Mileva Einstein Maric liked to joke that she and Albert were "one stone [ein Stein]."

   When a direct quotation is unavoidable, use brackets to enclose *sic* after an error, such as a misspelling, to show that the mistake appeared in the original. (Most of the time you paraphrase to avoid reporting errors):

   Banting's discovery of insulin can be traced to brief jottings in his lab book: "Diabetus [*sic*]. Ligate pancreatic ducts of dog."

2. **Use brackets to indicate references in scientific writing.** Include the number of the citation in brackets when you make the reference in the text of your work:

   Dr. Knuth named the approach "literate programming" [3].

   Then use the same number in brackets in the *References* section at the end to provide full documentation of the source. See p. 171.

3. **Use brackets within parentheses to indicate an additional parenthetical insertion** (This is the inverse of mathematical "fences"):

> The National Research Council (which delivers Canada's Business Innovation Access Program [BIAP]) encourages applications for short-term and long-term projects.

Colon [:]

A colon indicates that something will follow: an elaboration, a list, a quotation.

1. **Use a colon before a formal statement or series:**

> ✔ In physics, matter exists in four states: solid, liquid, gas, or plasma.

It is considered informal to use a colon if the words preceding it do not form a complete sentence:

> ✘ In physics, matter exists as: solid, liquid, gas, or plasma.

> ✔ In physics, matter exists as solid, liquid, gas, or plasma.

On the other hand, it is conventional to use a colon to introduce a vertical list, even when the introductory part is not a complete sentence:

> ✔ In physics, matter exists as:
>   – solid
>   – liquid
>   – gas
>   – plasma

Even so, professional writers usually recast the introductory phrase as a complete sentence.

2. **Use a colon for formality before a direct quotation, especially when introduced by a complete sentence:**

> If you seek success, remember the words of Thomas Edison: "Genius is 1% inspiration and 99% perspiration."

3. **Use a colon between numbers expressing time and ratios:**

> 4:30 p.m.

> The ratio of calcium to potassium should be 7:1.

Comma [,]

Commas are the trickiest of all punctuation marks; even experts differ on when to use them. Most agree, however, that too many commas are as bad as too few because they can make writing choppy and awkward to read. Certainly, writers now use fewer commas. When in doubt, let clarity be your guide. The following are the most widely accepted conventions.

1. **Use a comma to separate two independent clauses joined by a co-ordinating conjunction (*and, but, for, or, nor, yet, so*).** By signalling that there are two clauses, the comma will prevent the reader from confusing the beginning of the second clause with the end of the first:

   ✘ Pine is softer than oak and cedar is harder than oak.

   ✔ Pine is softer than oak, and cedar is harder than oak.

   When the second clause has the same subject as the first, you have the option of omitting both the second subject *and* the comma:

   ✔ Rebuilding costs more at the outset, but it helps avoid expensive maintenance later.

   ✔ Rebuilding costs more at the outset but helps avoid expensive maintenance later.

   If you mistakenly punctuate two sentences as if they were one, the result will be a run-on sentence (see pp. 187–9). If you use a comma but forget the coordinating conjunction, the result will be a comma splice:

   ✘ The Weil reaction of the capacitor is small, its impact is negligible.

   ✔ The Weil reaction of the capacitor is small, so its impact is negligible.

   Remember that words such as *however, therefore,* and *thus* are transitional adverbs, not conjunctions. If you use one of them to join two independent clauses, the result will again be a comma splice:

   ✘ Enantiometers have the same molecular structures and physical properties, however they cannot be superimposed.

   ✔ Enantiometers have the same molecular structures and physical properties; however, they cannot be superimposed.

Transitional adverbs are often confused with conjunctions. You can distinguish between the two if you remember that a transitional adverb's position in a sentence can be changed:

✔ Enantiometers have the same molecular structures and physical properties; they cannot, <u>however</u>, be superimposed.

The position of a conjunction, on the other hand, is invariable; it must be placed between the two clauses:

✔ Enantiometers have the same molecular structures and physical properties, <u>but</u> they cannot be superimposed.

A good rule of thumb, then, is to use a comma when the linking word can't be moved.

2. **Use a comma between items in a series.** Place a comma and a coordinating conjunction before the last item:

✔ Coding is a procedure that makes communication faster, cheaper, more reliable, and more private.

✔ Software reengineering redesigns a system to improve its quality, understandability, and maintainability.

The comma before the conjunction is optional for single items in a series. Decide whether you'll include it or leave it out consistently:

✔ Fractals are found in vegetables, leaves(,) or snowflakes.

For phrases in a series, however, use the final comma to help prevent confusion:

✘ Linseed is a superior material because it is made from natural products (linseed oil, flax, jute and wood fibres).

Here a comma prevents the reader from thinking that *linseed oil* is made from *jute fibres* as well as *wood fibres*:

✔ Linseed is a superior material because it is made from natural products (linseed oil, flax, jute, and wood fibres).

This is the reason many writers always add a comma before the conjunction as soon as there are three or more items in a series. One rule is certain—remember not to put a comma at the end of the series if the series begins the sentence:

✖ Heat distribution, electric charge diffusion, wave propagation, and even chemical reactions, have mostly a natural exponential form.

✔ Heat distribution, electric charge diffusion, wave propagation, and even chemical reactions have mostly a natural exponential form.

3. **Use a comma to separate adjectives preceding a noun when they modify the same element and when you can substitute the coordinator *and* for the comma while retaining the same meaning.**

✖ It is a pretty clever design. [The design is quite clever.]

✔ It is a pretty, clever design. [The design is both clever and pretty.]

However, when the adjectives do not modify the same element, you should not use a comma:

✖ It is a familiar, domestic task.

Here *domestic* modifies *task*, but *familiar* modifies the whole phrase *domestic task*. A good way of checking whether you need a comma is to see if you can reverse the order of the adjectives. If you can (*pretty, clever device* or *clever, pretty device*), use a comma; if you can't, omit the comma:

✖ It is a domestic familiar task.

✔ It is a familiar domestic task.

4. **Use commas to set off an interruption (i.e., "parenthetical element"):**

✔ The results, as expected, were inconclusive.

✔ It is important, however, that results be consistent.

Remember to put commas on both sides of the interruption:

✖ It is important however, that results be consistent.

✖ The build-up of these fumes, along with mold, bacteria, and dust can lead to "sick-building syndrome."

✔ The build-up of these fumes, along with mold, bacteria, and dust, can lead to "sick building syndrome."

5. **Use commas, like parentheses, to set off words or phrases that provide additional but non-essential information:**

✔ Our TA, Chandra Elliot, gives clear explanations.

✔ The video clip, a documentary on recycling, was popular among students.

In these examples, *Chandra Elliot* and *a documentary on recycling* give additional information about the nouns they refer to (*TA* and *video clip*), but the sentences would make sense without them. Here's another example:

✔ Polymers involve macromolecules, which have high molecular weights.

The phrase *which have high molecular weights* is a *non-restrictive modifier* because it doesn't limit the meaning of the word it modifies (*macromolecules*). Without that modifying clause, the sentence would still make sense. Because the information the clause provides is not necessary to the meaning of the sentence, you use a comma to set it off.

In contrast, a *restrictive modifier* is one that provides essential information. It must not be set apart from the element it modifies, and commas should not be used:

✔ Many people who are legally blind can read using a closed circuit TV.

Without the clause *who are legally blind*, the reader would not know which specific people are being referred to. More importantly, the addition of commas suggests that many people are legally blind—an error not to make.

To avoid confusion, be sure to distinguish carefully between essential and additional information. The difference can be important:

✘ Students, who are unwilling to work, should not receive grants.

✔ Students who are unwilling to work should not receive grants.

The first example makes an unacceptable generalization about all students, which you understand if you imagine parentheses in place of the commas.

The issue is never simple, as you can see above. In the example that follows, adding or omitting a comma changes the meaning just as significantly:

✘ There is really only one problem which calls for immediate action.

To avoid misinterpretation in such cases, it makes sense to follow the practice of using *which*, following the comma, only with non-restrictive (i.e., non-essential) modifiers; use *that* (without the comma) to introduce restrictive modifiers:

✔ There is really only one problem that calls for immediate action. (*restrictive*)

✔ There is really only one problem, which calls for immediate action. (*non-restrictive*)

6. **Use a comma after an introductory phrase, especially when omitting it would cause confusion:**

✘ After extensive planning tests were performed with real data.

✔ After extensive planning, tests were performed with real data.

✘ If the samples are random calculations need adjusting.

✔ If the samples are random, calculations need adjusting.

7. **Use a comma to separate elements in titles, dates, and addresses:**

David Gunn, President

February 2, 2019 (Commas are generally omitted if the day comes first: 2 February 2019)

117 Hudson Drive, Edmonton, Alberta

They lived in Dartmouth, Nova Scotia.

8. **Use a comma before a quotation in a sentence:**

Einstein said, "God is subtle, but he is not malicious."

For more formality, if the quotation is preceded by a grammatically complete sentence, use a colon (see p. 222).

9. **Do not use a comma between a subject and its verb:**

✘ The metals and other ions in the contaminated groundwater, increase the water's conductivity.

✔ The metals and other ions in the contaminated groundwater increase the water's conductivity.

10. **Do not use a comma between a verb and its object:**

   ✖ The second section explains, what solutions are possible.

   ✔ The second section explains what solutions are possible.

11. **Do not use a comma before "and" or "or" when linking pairs of words, phrases, or dependent clauses:**

   ✖ In the simulation, two robots think independently, and cooperate to achieve a common goal.

   ✔ In the simulation, two robots think independently and cooperate to achieve a common goal.

12. **Do not use a comma in place of the colon to introduce a list:**

   ✖ Two AI tools were considered as possible components, natural language processors and neural networks.

   ✔ Two AI tools were considered as possible components: natural language processors and neural networks.

Dash [—]

A dash abruptly and dramatically draws attention to the words that follow. Never use dashes as casual substitutes for other punctuation. Overuse can detract from the calm, well-reasoned effect you want to create.

1. **Use a dash to stress a word or phrase:**

   Pressure is a physics concept crucial to medicine—especially in lung physiology.

   Their solution was well received—at first.

2. **Use a pair of dashes to set off an important interruption:**

   Hawking postulates that if the universe has no boundary—no beginning and no end—then it is self-contained.

   Note the effect of parentheses in the same context. Dashes emphasize; parentheses add an aside:

   Hawking postulates that if the universe has no boundary (no beginning and no end) then it is self-contained.

Be careful to distinguish between hyphens and dashes. Two hyphens typed together with no spaces on their side represent a dash. This is the most space-efficient way of showing the feature, and word processors automatically convert this to a dash (called an *em-dash* because of its length) as you continue typing. Another method is to use an *en-dash*, one which is slightly longer than a hyphen, with single spaces left on either side.

Ellipsis [. . .]

1. **Use ellipsis points (three spaced dots) to show an omission from a quotation:**

   She reported that "to many farming families in the West, the drought in the Thirties [. . .] resembled a biblical plague, even to the locusts."

   You can use brackets around the ellipsis to indicate that you, not the original author, have left out the words. If the omission comes before or after the words quoted, ellipsis points are not used:

   She reported that the drought "resembled a biblical plague, even to the locusts."

   She reported that the drought "resembled a biblical plague."

2. **Use ellipsis points to show that a series of numbers continues indefinitely:**

   $y = 1, 3, 5, 7, 9, \ldots$

   In mathematical copy, put commas or operational signs after each term and after the ellipsis points (without an intervening space) if followed by a final term:

   $x_1, x_2, \ldots, x_n$

Exclamation Mark [!]

An exclamation mark helps to show emotion or feeling, usually in informal writing such as e-mails. Use it only in those rare cases, in non-scientific writing, when you want to give a point emotional and dramatic emphasis:

Prof. Furness predicted that the dollar would rise against the euro. Some forecast!

Hyphen [-]

1. **Use a hyphen if you are forced to divide a word at the end of a line.** Although it's generally best to start a new line if a word is too long, there are instances—for example, when you're formatting text in narrow columns—when hyphenation might be preferred. The hyphenation feature in word processors has taken the guesswork out of dividing words at the end of the line, but if you must use manual hyphenation, here are a few guidelines:

    - Divide between syllables.
    - Never divide a one-syllable word.
    - Never leave one letter by itself.
    - Divide double consonants except when they come before a suffix, in which case divide before the suffix:

        col-lect
        fall-ing
        pass-able

    When the second consonant has been added to form the suffix, keep it with the suffix:

        refer-ral
        begin-ning

    - Do not, however, divide a hyphenated compound word except at the hyphen:

        ✖ co-op-erative

2. **Use a hyphen to separate the parts of certain compound words:**

    - compound nouns:

        kilowatt-hour; brother-in-law

    - compound verbs:

        test-drive; mass-produce

    - compound modifiers:

        matrix-based consideration; first-aid kits

Do not, however, hyphenate a compound modifier that includes an adverb ending in *-ly*:

✖ a highly-developed prototype

✔ a highly developed prototype

Spell-checking features today will help you determine which compounds to hyphenate, but there is no clear consensus, even from one dictionary to another. As always, the solution for your writing style is for you to be consistent.

3. **Use a hyphen with certain prefixes (*all-*, *self-*, *ex-*, *e-*) and with prefixes preceding a proper name.** Practices do vary, so consult a dictionary when in doubt.

   all-inclusive; self-imposed; ex-president; e-commerce

   Use *former* rather than *ex-* in formal situations:

   Dr. Ling is the former chair of this department.

4. **Use a hyphen to emphasize contrasting prefixes:**

   The technician assessed both pre- and post-test findings.

5. **Use a hyphen to separate written-out compound fractions and compound numbers from one to ninety-nine:**

   seven-tenths full; two-thirds of a cup; twenty-two participants

6. **Use a hyphen to join a cardinal number and the unit of measurement when they precede what they modify:**

   a five-step process; 16-point type; a six-legged robot

7. **Use an en-dash rather than a hyphen (see p. 227) to separate parts of inclusive numbers or dates:**

   the years 1890–1914; pages 3–10

Parentheses [( )]

1. **Use parentheses to enclose an explanation, an example, or a qualification.** Parentheses show that the enclosed material is of incidental importance to the main idea. They make an interruption that

is more subtle than one marked off by dashes but more pronounced than one set off by commas:

✔ The frequency domain brings out the dynamic (non-random) characteristics of a signal.

✔ Only clusters with a population of greater than 3,000 (30% of the entire image) are processed.

Remember that punctuation should not precede parentheses but may follow them if required by the sense of the sentence:

✔ In cases that require special formatting (smoothed edges, shad-ing, or shadowing), the characters must be modified.

If the parenthetical statement comes between two complete sentences, it should be punctuated as a sentence, with the period, question mark, or exclamation mark *inside* the parentheses:

✔ The process requires substantial execution time. (Turnaround can take as much as 24 hours.) Nevertheless, the savings outweigh the costs.

2. **Use parentheses to translate acronyms the first time you use them**:

✔ There are different types of FACTS (Flexible AC Transmission Systems) controllers.

✔ The concept explains how the central nervous system (CNS) operates.

3. **Use parentheses for in-text author or year references**. See Appendix A for details.

Period [.]

1. **Use a period at the end of a sentence.** A period indicates a full stop, not just a pause.

2. **Use a period with abbreviations.** Canada's adoption of the metric system contributed to a trend away from the use of periods in many abbreviations. It is still common to use periods in abbreviated names and titles (Mr. M. J. Hunt, Rev. M. Collings-Moore, etc.) and

expressions of time (6:30 p.m.). Convention no longer requires them in academic degrees (MSc, PhD, etc.), and abbreviated names of states and provinces or territories (BC, PEI, NY, DC). In addition, most acronyms for organizations do not use periods (CIDA, CBC, UNESCO, WTO), nor do general acronyms (RPM, GST, EMF, STP).

3. **Use a period at the end of an indirect question.** Do not use a question mark:

   ✘ Users were asked if they found the manual useful?

   ✔ Users were asked if they found the manual useful.

4. **Use a period for questions that are really polite statements:**

   ✔ Would you please send him the report by Friday.

   ✔ May I congratulate you on your promotion.

Quotation Marks [" " or ' ']

American and British methods of punctuating quotations differ. American practice generally favours double quotation marks, while British practice generally favours single quotation marks. Sometimes the decision is based on space constraints (as happens with newspaper headlines, which use only single quotation marks). In Canada, either style is accepted as long as you are consistent. The guidelines outlined below are based on the American conventions, which are more common in Canada than the British ones.

1. **Use quotation marks to signify direct discourse (the actual words taken from a speaker or a text):**

   In 1912, Einstein wrote the following to a friend: "Compared with this problem [formulating the general theory of relativity], the original theory is child's play."

2. **Use quotation marks to show that words themselves are the issue:**

   The tennis term "love" comes from the French word for "egg."

   Alternatively, you may italicize the terms in question.

Only in informal writing are quotation marks occasionally used to show that the writer is aware of the difficulty with a slang word or inappropriate usage. You mark text this way only if you would use your fingers to make imaginary quotation marks when you are face to face with someone:

> Several of the "experts" did not seem to know anything about the topic.

In general, it's best to avoid sarcasm in any professional context. Remember the expectation of a professional attitude, however you may feel.

3. **Use quotation marks to enclose the titles of chapters, poems, short stories, songs, presentations, and articles in books or journals.** (In contrast, titles of books, films, paintings, and music are italicized.)

> The most interesting article in the June 2014 issue of IEEE Potentials is "What's behind your smartphone icons?"

4. **Use single quotation marks to enclose quotations within quotations**:

> He said, "Several of the 'experts' did not know anything about the topic."

Note that British style reverses this pattern so that double quotation marks enclose quotations within quotations.

Placement of Punctuation with Quotation Marks

The following guidelines for punctuating quotations are based on American rather than British conventions:

- A comma or period always goes <u>inside</u> the quotation marks:

  > The method involves identifying the "core business," the "extended enterprise," and the "business ecosystem."

- A semicolon or colon always goes <u>outside</u> the quotation marks:

  > Cybernetics relates to the developing "sciences of complexity": AI, neural networks, and complex adoptive systems.

- A question mark, a dash, or an exclamation mark goes inside quotation marks if it is part of the quotation but outside if it is not:

  One of the more important development questions is this: "How much investment money can be raised?"

  Did Prof. Hagen actually describe the Casuistic Theory of Value as "passing the buck"?

- If a reference is given parenthetically (in round brackets) at the end of a quotation, the quotation marks precede the parentheses, and the sentence punctuation follows them:

  Lipsey suggested that we should "abandon the Foreign Investment Review Agency" (Paisley 94).

Remember that questions, exclamation marks, and dashes are rare in scientific writing, but they have their place in informal communications.

Semicolon [;]

1. **Use a semicolon to join independent clauses (complete sentences) that are closely related:**

    Some samples contained sediment; others were clear.

    A semicolon is especially useful when the second independent clause begins with a transitional adverb, such as *however, moreover, consequently, nevertheless, in addition,* or *therefore* (usually followed by a comma):

    Daylight is the most efficient source of building lighting; however, its full potential has yet to be demonstrated.

    Some editors disagree, but it's usually acceptable to follow a semicolon with a coordinating conjunction if one or both clauses are complicated by other commas:

    On July 14, 2015, staff participated in a teambuilding exercise; but the effects were, unfortunately, short-lived.

2. **Use a semicolon to mark the divisions in a complicated series when individual items themselves need commas.** Using a comma to mark

the subdivisions and a semicolon to mark the main divisions will help
to prevent mix-ups:

✖ He invited Professor Ludvik, the vice-principal, Christine Li, and
Dr. Hector Jimenez.

Is the vice-principal a separate person?

✔ He invited Professor Ludvik, the vice-principal; Christine Li; and
Dr. Hector Jimenez.

A simpler alternative is to retain the commas and use parentheses around
the secondary material:

✔ He invited Professor Ludvik (the vice-principal), Christine Li, and
Dr. Hector Jimenez.

Slash [/]

1. **Use the slash to offer alternatives when either of a pair of words is
to be selected. There is no spacing on either side of the slash:**

   Addresses should include name, street, city, province/territory,
   country, and postal code.

   While *he/she* and *s/he* are gaining in popularity as gender-neutral pronoun pairs (see p. 245), be wary of using them in any formal writing.
   Unless space is an issue, write these out in full: *he or she*.
       Do not confuse the slash [/] with the backslash [\]. The backslash
   is generally only used in computing and should never be used to distinguish between alternatives.

2. **Use a slash to separate parts of a URL:**

   http://www.oupcanada.com/higher_education.html

The conventions of punctuation may not seem logical, but the rules
are easy to follow once you know them. Take the time to become familiar
with expectations, and then apply the rules consistently throughout your
writing.

Part 3 Misused Words and Phrases

Introduction

This section offers an alphabetical overview of words and phrases that are often confused or misused. A periodic read-through will refresh your memory and help you avoid mistakes.

a, an. When you want to generalize about a single item, these are alternatives to the word *one*. Use **a** before a consonant sound and **an** before a vowel sound (*a, e, i, o, u*) or silent *h*:

> This product has a history of recalls.

> It will take an hour to repair.

accept, except. Accept is a verb meaning *to receive affirmatively*; **except**, when used as a verb, means *to exclude*:

> She accepted the scholarship.

> The course was designed for upper-year students, non-majors excepted.

acoustics. This word is singular as it refers to the science, but plural with respect to the acoustic properties of a building:

> Acoustics looks at how a building's acoustics are planned.

advice, advise. Advice is a noun; **advise**, a verb:

> He was advised to ignore the advice of others.

affect, effect. Affect is a verb meaning *to influence*. **Effect** can be either a noun meaning *result* or a verb meaning *to bring something about*, usually with reference to change:

> The eye drops affect his vision.

> The effect of higher government spending is higher inflation.

> One job of the production engineer is to effect improvements.

all ready, already. To be **all ready** is simply to be ready for something; **already** means *beforehand* or *earlier*:

> The students were all ready for the test.
>
> Three days later, the test had already been marked.

all right. Write as two separate words: *all right*. (The single word *alright* is for informal writing only.) **All right** can mean *safe and sound, in good condition, okay, correct,* or *satisfactory*:

> Is everyone all right?
>
> The student's answers were all right.

(Does this second example mean that the answers were all correct or simply acceptable? Use a clear synonym instead.)

all together, altogether. All together means in a group; **altogether** is an adverb meaning *entirely*:

> He was altogether insistent on keeping the papers all together.

allusion, delusion, illusion. An **allusion** is an indirect reference; a **delusion** is a belief or perception that is distorted; an **illusion** is a false perception of reality:

> Her joke about relatives was an allusion to Einstein.
>
> He had delusions that he could pass the exam without studying.
>
> What looks like water on the road is often an optical illusion.

a lot. Write as two separate words: *a lot.*

alternate, alternative. Alternate means *every other* or *every second* thing in a series; **alternative** refers to a *choice* between options:

> The two sections of the class attended labs on alternate weeks.
>
> The students could do a research paper as an alternative to writing the exam.

among, between. The general rule is to use **among** for three or more persons or objects considered collectively and **between** for two (or more when used individually):

> Between you and me, there's trouble among the committee members.

amount, number. Note the difference between what's countable and not countable when choosing between these two words. **Amount** indicates quantity when units are not discrete and not absolute (i.e., uncountable); **number** indicates quantity when units are discrete and absolute (i.e., countable):

> A large amount of electricity was consumed.
>
> A large number of students were registered.

See also *less, fewer.*

analysis. The plural is **analyses.**

ante-, anti-. Distinguish the spellings here. **Ante-** means *before,* as in *antecedent* or *antedate.* **Anti-** means *opposite* or *against,* as in *antidote* or *antimatter.*

anyone, any one. Write the two words to give numerical emphasis on **one**; otherwise, **anyone** (and its informal synonym anybody) is written as one word:

> Any one of the proposals is reasonable.
>
> Anyone can write a reasonable proposal.

anyways, anywheres. Non-standard informal English. Use **anyway** or **anywhere** instead.

as, because. As a synonym of *because,* **as** should be avoided because it may be confused with *while* or *when*:

> ✘ As he was working, he ate at his desk.
>
> ✔ Because he was working, he ate at his desk.
>
> ✘ She arrived as he was leaving.
>
> ✔ She arrived when he was leaving.

aspect, respect. Distinguish carefully between these two nouns when **aspect** means *angle* and **respect** means *point*:

> This aspect of the problem needs expansion in two respects.

bad, badly. Bad is an adjective meaning *not good*:

> The weather turned bad.

> He felt bad about turning in his assignment late.

Badly is an adverb meaning *not well*. When used with the verbs **want** or **need**, it means *very much*:

> The results were recorded badly.

> The results badly needed corroboration.

basis, bases. Basis is singular; **bases** is plural.

beside, besides. Beside is a preposition meaning *next to*:

> She worked beside her assistant.

Besides has two uses: as a preposition it means *in addition to*; as a transitional adverb it means *moreover*:

> Besides her assistant, there was no one in the lab.

> She left because she was tired. Besides, there was no more work to do.

between. See **among**.

bring, take. Use **bring** for action coming closer to the speaker (*here*) and **take** for action going away (*there*):

> Bring me your resumé the next time you come.

> Take your resumé when you go to your interview.

centrifugal, centripetal. A **centrifugal** force is directed away from the axis of rotation, where a **centripetal** force is directed toward the axis of rotation.

cite, sight, site. To **cite** something is to *quote* or *mention* it as an example or authority; **sight** relates to vision or to views; **site** refers to a specific *setting* or *location*, as in *website*.

> The tourists hopped on a bus to see the sights.

> Visitors must put on work boots and hard hats before touring the work sites.

classic, classical. Use **classic** to mean *memorable* or *standard of excellence*. **Classical** is normally the choice in scientific writing (as well as music):

> Gaussian distribution predicts the classic bell curve.

> Classical physics does not account for black holes.

climactic, climatic. **Climactic** describes a *climax*; **climatic** refers to *climate*.

complement, compliment. As verbs, **complement** means *to complete* or *enhance*, while **compliment** means *to praise*. Make this distinction clear, especially when you use adjective endings (**-ary**):

> The two experiments produced complementary results.

> The professor's comments on the report were complimentary.

> New subscribers were promised complimentary apps.

compose, comprise. Both words mean *to constitute or make up*, but **compose** is preferred. **Comprise** is correctly used to mean *include, consist of*, or *be composed of*. Using **comprise** in the passive ("are comprised of")—as is tempting in the second example below—is frowned on in formal writing, especially because it uses three words where one will do:

> Four students compose the group representing the faculty.

> All systems comprise rules that govern them.

continual, continuous. Continual means *repeated over a period of time*; **continuous** means *constant* or *without interruption*:

> The strikes caused continual delays in building the road.
>
> Five days of continuous rain delayed the project further.

council, counsel. Council is a noun meaning *an advisory or deliberative assembly.* **Counsel** as a noun means *advice* or *lawyer*; as a verb it means *to give advice.*

> The college council meets on Tuesdays.
>
> A camp counsellor may need to counsel parents as well as children.

criterion, criteria. A **criterion** is *a standard for judging something.* **Criteria** is the plural of *criterion* and thus requires a plural verb:

> These are the criteria for evaluating the new product.

data. The plural of **datum. Data** refers to the set of information, usually in numerical form, that is used for analysis as the basis for a study. Informally, **data** is often used as a singular noun, but in formal scientific contexts, treat it as a plural:

> These data were gathered in random fashion. Therefore they are inconclusive.

deduce, deduct. To **deduce** something is *to work it out by reasoning*; to **deduct** means *to subtract or take away* from something. The noun form of both words is **deduction.**

defence, defense. Both spellings are correct: **defence** is standard in Britain and is somewhat more common in Canada; **defense** is standard in the United States.

defuse, diffuse. Although they sound similar, these words have quite different meanings. It is a bomb that you **defuse** and information that you **diffuse** (or send out).

delusion. See **allusion.**

dependent, dependant. Dependent is an adjective meaning *contingent on* or *subject to*; **dependant** is a noun.

> Suriya's graduation is dependent upon her passing algebra.

> Chedley is a dependant for income tax purposes.

device, devise. The word ending in **-ice** is the noun; the word ending in **-ise** is the verb.

> Once he had devised the new fastener, he patented the device.

different from, different than. Although **different than** is common in informal contexts, use **different from** in writing:

> The results were different from the predictions.

diminish, minimize. To **diminish** means *to make or become smaller*; to **minimize** means *to reduce* something to the smallest possible amount or size.

discreet, discrete. Discreet means *tactful* or *prudent*; **discrete** means *separate and distinct*, generally the meaning applicable in scientific writing:

> The interviewer was discreet in asking about previous jobs.

> Discrete samples were collected.

disinterested, uninterested. Disinterested implies impartiality or neutrality; **uninterested** implies a lack of interest:

> As a disinterested observer, she was able to judge the issue fairly.

> Uninterested in the proceedings, he yawned repeatedly.

dominant, dominate. Dominant is an adjective meaning *exerting control over* or *ranking above* something. **Dominate** is a verb meaning *to rule*:

> The dominant values are reported in Fig. 1.

> Safety should dominate all construction decisions.

due to. Although increasingly used to mean *because of*, **due** is an adjective and therefore needs to modify something:

> ✖ Due to his impatience, we lost the contract. [*Due is dangling.*]
>
> ✔ Because of his impatience, we lost the contract.
>
> ✔ The loss was due to his impatience.

economic, economical. Use **economic** in reference to *the economy* and **economical** in reference to *savings*.

e.g., i.e. E.g. means *for example*; **i.e.** means *that is*. It is considered incorrect to use them interchangeably.

eminent, imminent. Eminent means *prominent* or *distinguished*; **imminent** refers to time and means *soon*.

entomology, etymology. Entomology is the study of insects; **etymology** is the study of the derivation and history of words.

especially, specially. Especially means *particularly* where **specially** means *for a special purpose*:

> The device was specially designed for wheelchair users.
>
> Cost price is an especially important consideration in manufacturing.

etc. Avoid **etc.** (*et cetera*) in formal writing. End a list with two or three examples introduced by *such as*:

> ✖ The project leaders discussed risk, interest rates, etc.
>
> ✔ The project leaders discussed such variables as risk and interest rates.

everyday, every day. Both words mean *daily*, but **everyday** is an adjective (like *regular*), and **every day** is an adverb (like *regularly*):

> Sneakers are now appropriate for everyday wear.
>
> He wears sneakers every day.

exceptional, exceptionable. **Exceptional** means *unusual* or *outstanding*, whereas **exceptionable** means *open to objection* and is generally used in negative contexts:

> His accomplishments are exceptional.

> There is nothing exceptionable in his behaviour.

farther, further. Where **farther** generally refers to distance, **further** suggests extent:

> The aquifer lies farther south than expected.

> She explained the proposal further.

firstly. Use **first** or **first of all** to avoid annoying readers who consider **firstly** old-fashioned or pretentious.

flaunt, flout. Although they sound similar, these verbs have opposite meanings. **Flaunt** means *to show* something *off*, where **flout** means *to treat* something *with contempt or defiance.*

> The starlet flouted good taste by flaunting her diamonds.

focus. The plural of the noun may be either **focuses** (also spelled *focusses*) or **foci**.

foreword, forward. A **foreword** (or *preface*) refers to front matter in a book or dissertation; **forward** describes a direction:

> In his foreword, the author praised his team for continually moving the project forward.

good, well. **Good** is an adjective that modifies a noun; **well** is an adverb that modifies a verb. In medical contexts, however, **well** is an adjective meaning *healthy.*

> He is a good rugby player.

> The experiment went well.

> The patient reported feeling well.

hardy, hearty. To distinguish these sound-alike words, reserve the sense of *durable* for **hardy** and *substantial* or *energetic* for **hearty**:

> Corn is a hardy crop.

> Corn chowder makes a hearty meal.

he/she, his/her. In formal writing, do not resort to these abbreviations. If it is impossible to avoid generalizing in the singular, write out **he or she**, or the equivalent pronoun forms, in full.

> ✘ A co-op student should make sure his/her resumé is always up to date.

> ✔ A co-op student should make sure his or her resumé is always up to date.

> ✔ Co-op students should make sure their resumés are always up to date.

hopefully. In formal writing, do not use **hopefully** at the beginning of a sentence as a substitute for *it is to be hoped that*.

> ✘ Hopefully the results will be published.

> ✔ The investigators hope to publish the results.

i.e. This is not the same as **e.g.** See **e.g.**

illusion. See **allusion.**

incite, insight. Incite is a verb meaning *to stir up*; **insight** is a noun meaning (often sudden) *understanding*.

infer, imply. To **infer** means *to deduce or conclude by reasoning*. It is often confused with **imply**, which means *to suggest* or *insinuate*. Note the give-and-take in these words (we **infer** X from Y, where Y **implies** X to us):

> We infer from the data that there will be cost overruns.

> The data imply that there will be cost overruns.

inflammable, flammable, non-flammable. Despite its **in-** prefix, **inflammable** is not the opposite of **flammable**: both words describe things that are *easily set on fire*. The opposite of **flammable** is **non-flammable**. To prevent any possibility of confusion, most people have stopped using **inflammable** altogether.

inset, insert. Something that is **inset** is literally "set in," as a picture within a picture. Don't confuse this word with **insert**, a noun referring to something added separately:

> The histogram appears as an inset on the map of Cape Breton.

> A weekly regional paper comes as an insert in the *Saturday Record*.

intense, intensive. While both words refer to heavy concentrations, **intense** is a more subjective word, reflecting one's response to or impression of something; **intensive** is used as a more objective description:

> He found the course intense and had difficulty keeping up with the workload.

> It was an intensive course, designed to cover a lot of material in a short period of time.

irregardless. Irregardless may be found in dictionaries, but it is considered non-standard English. It is also redundant. Use **regardless** instead.

its, it's. Its is a possessive pronoun; **it's** is a contraction of *it is* or *it has*. It is an error to put an apostrophe anywhere in *its* to show possession:

✖ Every problem has its' solution.

✖ Every problem has it's solution.

✔ Every problem has its solution.

✔ It's time to leave.

lead, led. Lead (the metal) sounds like **led** (the past form of the verb **to lead**). Be careful to distinguish the spellings.

✖ The investigation lead to a public inquiry in 2013.

✔ The investigation led to a public inquiry in 2013.

✔ The investigation will lead to a public inquiry later this year.

less, fewer. Less is normally used with singular and uncountable units (as in "less information"). **Fewer** is the word to use with plurals (as in "fewer details"). However, **less** is also regularly used as a pronoun measuring statistics, distances, sums of money, or units of time, which are often thought of as amounts:

> Abstracts should be kept to 150 words or <u>less</u>.

lie, lay. To lie, an intransitive verb, means *to assume a horizontal position*; to **lay**, a transitive verb, means *to put [something] down*. The changes of tense often cause confusion:

Present	Past	Past participle
lie (recline)	lay	lain
lay (put)	laid	laid

✖   The doctor told the patient to <u>lay</u> down.

✔   The doctor told the patient to <u>lie</u> down.

✔   The patient <u>lay</u> down as requested.

like, as. Like is a preposition, but it is often used casually as a conjunction. To join two independent clauses, use the conjunction **as, as if**, or **as though** instead:

✖   The transformer looked <u>like</u> it was overloaded.

✔   The transformer looked <u>as though</u> it was overloaded.

✔   The residue looked <u>like</u> sand.

loose, lose. Loose, as an adjective, means the opposite of tight. Its verb form is **loosen. Lose** as a verb, means misplace or be defeated. Watch the spelling.

✖   The battery was <u>loosing</u> its charge.

✔   The battery was <u>losing</u> its charge.

media, medium. Use **media** as the plural of the singular word **medium**:

> The <u>media</u> have reported the increasing popularity of polyurethane foam as an insulation <u>medium</u>.

minimize. See **diminish**.

mitigate, militate. To **mitigate** means *to reduce the severity of* something; to **militate against** something means *to oppose* it.

myself, me. Myself is an intensifier of (not a substitute for) *I* or *me*. If you use it, include *I* or *me* in your sentence first:

  ✖   Please contact John or <u>myself</u> if you have questions.

  ✔   Please contact John or <u>me</u>.

  ✖   Jane and <u>myself</u> are presenting our findings.

  ✔   Jane and <u>I</u> are presenting our findings

  ✔   I completed the research <u>myself</u>.

number, amount. See **amount, number.**

off of. Drop the redundant **of:**

  ✖   The fence kept children <u>off of</u> the premises.

  ✔   The fence kept children <u>off</u> the premises.

orient, orientate. As a verb, **orient** means *to position something properly, to determine its bearings.* Although **orientate** is used with the same meaning, the shorter word is preferred.

passed, past. Passed is the past form of the verb **pass. Past** refers either to time or to one place farther than another:

     <u>Past</u> the bridge, they <u>passed</u> a sports car.

people, persons. Legal contexts (for example, elevator licences) use **persons** as the plural of **person** in case of liability. For all other purposes, use **people:**

  ✖   The media reported ten <u>persons</u> missing after the ferry sank.

  ✔   Twenty <u>people</u> registered for the first-aid class.

per cent, percentage. Per cent (from the Latin *per cent*) is used for numbers written as words (*four per cent*); with digits, use the symbol instead (*4.0%*). **Percentage** means proportion or amount and is used in generalizing about measurements:

What percentage of students graduate with honours?

Twenty-five per cent of students graduate with averages over 80underline{%}.

phenomenon. **Phenomenon** is a singular noun; the plural is **phenomena.** Not to be used as a synonym for *occurrence*, **phenomenon** refers to an exceptional circumstance.

practice, practise. **Practice** can be a noun or a modifier; **practise** is always a verb. (Note, however, that the standard American spelling is **practice** for both.)

In a practice game, players practise their skills.

precede, proceed. To **precede** is *to go before* (earlier) *or in front of* others; to **proceed** is *to go on* or *to go ahead*:

The dean's welcome preceded the awarding of certificates.

The presentation proceeded without interruption.

prescribe, proscribe. These words have quite different meanings. **Prescribe** means *to advise the use of* or *to impose authoritatively*. **Proscribe** means *to reject, denounce,* or *ban*:

The professor prescribed the conditions for the experiment.

The student government proscribed the publication of unsigned editorials on its blog.

preventive, preventative. Although both are used to describe measures of prevention, the shorter word, **preventive**, is preferred.

principle, principal. **Principle** is a noun meaning *a general truth or law*; **principal** can be used as either a noun or an adjective, meaning *chief*.

Her principal error lay in not understanding the principle.

rational, rationale. **Rational** is an adjective meaning *logical* or *able to reason*. **Rationale** is a noun meaning *explanation*:

That was not a rational decision.

The president's memo explained the rationale for the decision.

real, really. Real, an adjective, means *true* or *genuine*; **really**, an adverb, means *actually, truly, very,* or *extremely*:

> The nugget was of <u>real</u> gold.

> The gold nugget was <u>really</u> valuable.

remanent, remnant. Remanent is an adjective for describing residual magnetization (or *remanence*). **Remnant** is a noun naming something left over or remaining.

sceptic, septic. British and Canadian spelling prefers **sceptic** for a person who doubts or disbelieves (the American spelling is *skeptic*). Be careful not to confuse it with the lookalike **septic**, which is used with ulcers and sewers.

seasonable, seasonal. Seasonable means usual or suitable for the season; **seasonal** means of, depending on, or varying with the season:

> Meteorologists predict the return of <u>seasonable</u> temperatures later in the week.

> In the summer, employment figures are adjusted to account for <u>seasonal</u> employment increases.

simple, simplistic. Both words refer to something that is *easy* or *basic*. **Simplistic**, however, has the negative connotation of *oversimplification*, so it should not be used as a synonym.

> The solution was <u>simple</u>.

> His <u>simplistic</u> answer annoyed the examiners.

stimulant, stimulus. A **stimulant** temporarily increases some vital process in an organ or organism, where a **stimulus** incites the organism to act in the first place.

than, then. Than is a conjunction linking unequal comparisons; **then** is an adverb of time or sequence:

> A is shorter <u>than</u> B.

> Shorten A first <u>then</u> B.

that, which. **That** can introduce a restrictive clause, and **which** can introduce a clause that is either restrictive or non-restrictive (see pp. 220–1, 267).

> They studied cybernetics, which is a modern academic domain that touches all traditional disciplines.

Grammar-checkers point to an error when there is no comma before **which**, so it is safe to make the distinction:

> He followed the format that his company requires.

> He followed IEEE format, which his company requires.

their, there. **Their** shows possession for the third-person plural pronoun. **There** is usually an adverb, meaning *at that place* or *at that point*:

> They parked their bikes there.

> There is no point arguing.

tortuous, torturous. The adjective **tortuous** means *full of twists and turns* or *circuitous*. **Torturous**, derived from *torture*, means *involving torture* or *excruciating*:

> The graph presented a tortuous curve.

> The interview was a torturous experience for the applicant.

translucent, transparent. A **translucent** substance permits light to pass through, but not enough for a person to see through it; a **transparent** substance permits light to pass unobstructed, so that objects can be seen clearly.

try and. This is a feature of conversational English. Use **try to** instead.

> ✖ They were going to try and visit the exhibition.

> ✔ They were going to try to visit the exhibition.

turbid, turgid. **Turbid**, with respect to a liquid or colour, means *muddy, not clear*, or (with respect to writing style) *confused*. **Turgid** means *swollen, inflated*, or *enlarged*, or (again with reference to style) *pompous* or *bombastic*.

unique. This word, which literally means *of which there is only one*, is both overused and misused. As a synonym of *unparalleled* or *unequalled*, it should not be used in comparisons such as *more unique* or *very unique*.

use, usage. Distinguish between these seeming synonyms by employing **usage** only when you mean *usual practice* or *proper* **use**:

> Consult the manual about the usage of this device.

> Use of this device will save time.

Note that many caution against the wordiness of *the use of*. Often, you can save words by omitting the phrase:

> [The use of] calculators will not be permitted during the exam.

while. To prevent misreading, use **while** only when you mean *at the same time that*. Avoid using **while** as a substitute for *although*, *whereas*, or *but*:

- ✘ While she's getting fair marks, she'd like to do better.
- ✔ He headed for home, while she decided to stay.
- ✔ He fell asleep while he was reading.

-wise. Avoid using **-wise** as a suffix to form new words that mean *with regard to*, for the tone is too casual for formal writing.

- ✘ Saleswise, the company did better last year.
- ✔ The company's sales have decreased this year.

your, you're. **Your** is a possessive pronoun; **you're** is a contraction of *you are*:

> You're likely to miss your train.

Appendix C
Weights, Measures, and Notation

1. IMPERIAL AND AMERICAN, WITH METRIC EQUIVALENTS

Linear measure

1 inch	= 25.4 millimetres
1 foot = 12 inches	= 0.3048 metre
1 yard = 3 feet	= 0.9144 metre
1 (statute) mile = 1,760 yards	= 1.609 kilometres (km)
1 int. nautical mile = 1.150779 miles	= 1.852 km

Square measure

1 square inch	= 6.45 sq. centimetres
1 square foot = 144 sq. in.	= 9.29 sq. decimetres
1 square yard = 9 sq. ft.	= 0.836 sq. metre
1 acre = 4,840 sq. yd.	= 0.405 hectare
1 square mile = 640 acres	= 259 hectares

Cubic measure

1 cubic inch	= 16.4 cu. centimetres
1 cubic foot = 1,728 cu. in.	= 0.0283 cu. metre
1 cubic yard = 27 cu. ft.	= 0.765 cu. metre

Capacity measure

Name	System	Equal to	Metric
fluid oz.	imperial	1/20 imp. pint	28.41 ml
	US (liquid)	1/16 US pint	29.57 ml
gill	imperial	1/4 pint	142.07 ml
	US (liquid)	1/4 pint	118.29 ml
pint	imperial	20 fl.oz. (imp.)	568.26 ml
	US (liquid)	16 fl.oz. (US)	473.18 ml
	US (dry)	1/2 quart	550.61 ml
quart	imperial	2 pints	1.1365 litres
	US (liquid)	2 pints	0.9464 litre
	US (dry)	2 pints	1.1012 litres
gallon	imperial	4 quarts	4.546 litres
	US (liquid)	4 quarts	3.785 litres
peck	imperial	2 gallons	9.092 litres
	US (dry)	8 quarts	8.810 litres
bushel	imperial	4 pecks	36.369 litres
	US (dry)	4 pecks	35.239 litres

Avoirdupois weight

1 grain	= 0.065 gram
1 dram	= 1.772 grams
1 ounce = 16 drams	= 28.35 grams
1 pound = 16 ounces = 7,000 grains	= 0.45359237 kilogram
1 stone = 14 pounds	= 6.35 kilograms
1 quarter = 2 stones	= 12.70 kilograms
1 hundredweight = 4 quarters = 112 lb.	= 50.80 kilograms
1 (long) ton = 20 cwt. = 2,240 lb.	= 1.016 tonnes
1 short ton = 2,000 pounds	= 0.907 tonne

2. METRIC, WITH IMPERIAL EQUIVALENTS

Linear measure

1 millimetre	= 0.039 inch
1 centimetre = 10 mm	= 0.394 inch
1 decimetre = 10 cm	= 3.94 inches
1 metre = 100 cm	= 1.094 yards
1 decametre = 10 m	= 10.94 yards
1 hectometre = 100 m	= 109.4 yards
1 kilometre = 1,000 m	= 0.6214 mile

Square measure

1 square centimetre	= 0.155 sq. inch
1 square metre = 10,000 sq. cm	= 1.196 sq. yards
1 are = 100 sq. metres	= 119.6 sq. yards
1 hectare = 100 ares	= 2.471 acres
1 square kilometre = 100 ha	= 0.386 sq. mile

Cubic measure

1 cubic centimetre	= 0.061 cu. inch
1 cubic metre = one million cu. cm	= 1.308 cu. yards

Capacity measure

1 millilitre	= 0.002 pint (imperial)
1 centilitre = 10 ml	= 0.018 pint
1 decilitre = 100 ml	= 0.176 pint
1 litre = 1,000 ml	= 1.76 pints
1 decalitre = 10 l	= 2.20 gallons (imperial)
1 hectolitre = 100 l	= 2.75 bushels (imperial)

Weight

1 milligram	= 0.015 grain
1 centigram = 10 mg	= 0.154 grain
1 decigram = 100 mg	= 1.543 grain
1 gram = 1,000 mg	= 15.43 grain
1 decagram = 10 g	= 5.64 drams
1 hectogram = 100 g	= 3.527 ounces
1 kilogram = 1,000 g	= 2.205 pounds
1 tonne (metric ton) = 1,000 kg	= 0.984 (long) ton

3. SI UNITS

Base units

Physical quantity	Name	Abbr. or symbol
length	metre	m
mass	kilogram	kg
time	second	s
electric current	ampere	A
temperature	kelvin	K
amount of substance	mole	mol
luminous intensity	candela	cd

Supplementary units

Physical quantity	Name	Abbr. or symbol
plane angle	radian	rad
solid angle	steradian	sr

Derived units with special names

Physical quantity	Name	Abbr. or symbol
frequency	hertz	Hz
energy	joule	J
force	newton	N
power	watt	W
pressure	pascal	Pa
electric charge	coulomb	C
electromotive force	volt	V
electric resistance	ohm	Ω
electric conductance	siemens	S
electric capacitance	farad	F
magnetic flux	weber	Wb
inductance	henry	H
magnetic flux density	tesla	T
luminous flux	lumen	lm
illumination	lux	lx

4. TEMPERATURE

Celsius (or Centigrade): Water boils (under standard conditions) at 100°C and freezes at 0°C

Fahrenheit: Water boils at 212°F and freezes at 32°F

Kelvin: Water boils at 373.15 kelvins and freezes at 273.15 kelvins

Celsius	Fahrenheit
−17.8°	0°
−10°	14°
0°	32°
10°	50°
20°	68°
30°	86°
40°	104°
50°	122°
60°	140°

Celsius	Fahrenheit
70°	158°
80°	176°
90°	194°
100°	212°

To convert Celsius into Fahrenheit: multiply by 9, divide by 5, and add 32.

To convert Fahrenheit to Celsius: subtract 32, multiply by 5, and divide by 9.

5. METRIC PREFIXES

	Abbr. or symbol	Factor
deca-	da	10^1
hecto-	h	10^2
kilo-	k	10^3
mega-	M	10^6
giga-	G	10^9
tera-	T	10^{12}
peta-	P	10^{15}
exa-	E	10^{18}
deci-	d	10^{-1}
centi-	c	10^{-2}
milli-	m	10^{-3}
micro-	μ	10^{-6}
nano-	n	10^{-9}
pico-	p	10^{-12}
femto-	f	10^{-15}
atto-	a	10^{-18}

These prefixes may be applied to any units of the metric system: hectogram (abbr. hg) = 100 grams; kilowatt (abbr. kW) = 1,000 watts; megahertz (MHz) = 1 million hertz; centimetre (cm) = 1/100 metre; microvolt (μV) = one-millionth of a volt; picofarad (pF) = 10^{-12} farad, and are sometimes applied to other units (megabit).

6. POWER NOTATION

This expresses concisely any power of ten (any number that is composed of factors of 10). 10^2 or ten squared = $10 \times 10 = 100$; 10^3 or ten cubed = $10 \times 10 \times 10 = 1,000$. Similarly, 10^4 = 10,000 and 10^{10} = 1 followed by ten zeros = 10,000,000,000. Proceeding in the opposite direction, dividing by ten and subtracting one from the index, we have $10^2 = 100$, $10^1 = 10$, $10^0 = 1$, $10^{-1} = 1/10$, $10^{-2} = 1/100$, and so on; $10^{-10} = 1/10,000,000,000$.

7. BINARY SYSTEM

Only two units (0 and 1) are used, and the position of each unit indicates a power of two. One to ten written in binary form:

	Eights (2^3)	fours (2^2)	twos (2^1)	one
1				1
2			1	0
3			1	1
4	1	0	0	
5		1	0	1
6		1	1	0
7		1	1	0
8	1	0	0	0
9	1	0	0	1
10	1	0	1	0

For example, ten is written as 1010 ($2^3 + 0 + 2^1 + 0$); one hundred is written as 1100100 ($2^6 + 2^5 + 0 + 0 + 2^2 + 0 + 0$).

Appendix D

Example Documents

Sample example documents can be found online on the Companion Website for *Making Sense in Engineering*. The table below outlines the examples available online for students and instructors.

Lab Report 1   This example shows a report on a semester-long laboratory activity in a third-year engineering course. There is an informative abstract at the start of the report, which helps the reader appreciate what was covered. The author takes care to explain the background for the experiments in terms that reflect their knowledge, not drawing only from research sources. They have included a list of materials used in the lab, and a comprehensive procedure that explains the work that went on in the lab in a complete way, not breaking into a set of rigid steps. This is more reflective of what went on in the lab, and the reader gets a sense of the real work, including things that worked and ones that did not. Results are presented in graphical form using a format that successfully communicates the message; however, it would be more correct for the author to also describe the data and figures in text so the reader can appreciate the meaning of each graph and table. The discussion and conclusion do a good job of wrapping up the work. The references are appropriate for a third-year engineering report that is primarily covering hands-on work done in the lab.

Lab Report 2   Example 2 shows another example of a student's approach to reporting on a semester-long lab testing course. In this case, the student chose to include a table of contents but did not write a summary or abstract. The introduction is brief, but the student obviously intended the work to be read by colleagues who were familiar with the lab work already. This shows an example of writing with the intended reader in mind. The figures presented in the Procedure section are of high quality and are original work by the author so do not require citation. The figures are referred to in the text, so they are good explanations of the lab activity and background. While the student has put this content in the procedure section, some of it could equally have gone in the introduction, but this was a perfectly valid choice by the author. The measurements and results section very clearly present the lab data, including calculations that went into the interpretations. The discussion of this lab is dense but does an excellent job of explaining and reflecting for the reader. It could benefit by more clear division into paragraphs to make the reading easier. Conclusions and references are excellent and reflect a very appropriate level for a third-year engineering report.

Lab Report 3   This example shows a progress report on a semester-long design-build project in a second-year engineering course. Because this was an interim report, the author chose not to provide a lengthy introduction or background, assuming the reader was already familiar with the project underway. However, the author did an excellent job filling in the explanation that might not be commonly known by the reader, which was the student's particular motivation in their design. The illustrations are excellent, showing high quality hand-drawn sketches. It might have been easier to follow the text had the author used figure numbers and captions, but for a brief report there wasn't any confusion. They chose to use report headings that were specific to the task but that certainly fill the role of introduction ("Design Overview"), procedure ("Analysis"), and Results ("Data & Results"). The Results section is augmented with "Competition," which was appropriate in this context since the lab assignment was ultimately tested through an in-class snowball throwing competition. Finally, the author provides a thoughtful discussion of improvements that could have been made in light of the results described.

Lab Report 4   This example shows a different approach to the same report as the previous example. In this case, the student has chosen to provide more detailed calculations. Because this was intended to be an internal report, it was appropriate to include those calculations in the body of the report, and the fact that they are very neat and orderly makes it acceptable that they were done by hand. There is a discussion section that culminates in a "What I learned" discussion, which certainly shows that the student was thinking about the big picture and the purpose of the lab activity.

Lab Report 5   A brief lab report by a student for a single experiment done as part of a third-year engineering course. The addition of an abstract at the start of the report, similar to Lab Report 1, would have helped to orient the reader. The report shows minimal context and background information to reflect the fact that the experiment was a stand-alone test of simple principles and the report is to be read only by the professor and teaching assistants who are completely familiar with the context. The authors have done a terrific job in reporting the results, integrating graphics, and explaining the results at the level where a knowledgeable colleague can follow the work. The figures are properly labelled and are all correctly described in the text. As a student report, it was allowable in the class to use hand-drawn sketches and calculations, but the example of Figure 3 might have been more clearly reproduced. The discussion is genuine, even reflecting on difficulties in the lab when finding suitable workspace and asking for advice for the future.

Lab Report 6   This example shows a report on the same lab experiments as some of the previous examples, but with a different approach by the author. The abstract is a suitable length and provides sufficient detail to know what was covered in the lab. The Introduction and Background provide an excellent level of detail in giving the reader the information needed to understand the lab work presented, including citing the sources for the theoretical content. The student provided an excellent set of references for their work, and the report was generally very readable and accurately presented their lab work, including the successes and difficulties.

Design Report 1	More and more, engineers and scientists work in design companies that expect non-traditional presentations of creative and analytical work. This example shows a report from a semester-long design project that is structured along the lines of a creative project, presenting a great deal of graphical information. The Introduction is served by an "Idea Generation" and "Design Manifesto" section, the procedure is supported by the "Checkpoints" section where the student showed the feedback instructions from the professor and how/when they were addressed through the term. By quoting the instructor's actual feedback comments, it was not needed to explain the context to the reader (instructor and teaching assistant). The remainder of the report shows the successive rounds of design iteration, finishing with a section on conclusions reached from the design activity and successive prototypes.
Design Report 2	This example shows a brief report on a specific design/analysis task. The author does not offer a standard report structure, but, similar to Design Report 1, presents a custom format that is tailored to the purpose of the report. Because this was internal to a fourth-year elective course, the student wrote a report that was intended only for the instructor and minimized background information. There is jargon that is not defined, but in the context of an internal technical memo, this was appropriate. The literature citations are also appropriate for an internal memo which keeps the content tightly to that included in the course assignment.
Design Report 3	A fourth-year capstone design project report shows a very detailed analysis of several aspects of the design of a novel device. The report covers the basic concept, design modelling and simulation, prototype construction and tests, as well as design project outcomes. The report includes an excellent cover letter signed by all members of the design team. One addition that would improve the work would be a one-page executive summary. Clearly the level of effort and detail, and the technical sophistication of this example reflect the expectation of fourth year students completing a two-semester-long capstone design course.
Research Paper 1	This example presents a literature research report written by a first-year engineering student. The topic chosen was highly technical, including a level of jargon not familiar to most readers. The author did a good job trying to provide the extensive background required to follow the story. A glossary of terms in this example might have helped a great deal. The level of detail in the discussion and the bibliography were excellent. In-text citations to specific concepts and their sources would improve the scholarship of this example.
Research Paper 2	This report shows a brief paper to review the current state of art in a particular area of science. The author shows a good bibliography of sources, and they have shown a thoughtful comparison of different technologies without appearing to be biased. The references that are cited are very detailed and show that the student was able to collect technical papers at a suitable level for a first-year review of technology.

Research Paper 3	This report shows another example of a student report from literature research. This report was intended for team colleagues to know the field of technology as background for a future design project. The content emphasizes design challenges in the field, which was intended to show teammates what might be future areas for design. The references that are cited are excellent for a first-year review of technology. A senior student may have reduced some of the broad discussion in the introduction and focused more on the problem at hand. As it is, the writing is clear and very detailed, which suits the purpose of the report and the audience needs.
Resumé 1	This is a standard example of a topic-focused resumé in chronologic order with the student's academic level shown first, and skills shown last. In this example, the student has put the skills section at the very end of the resumé so that it is the last thing the hiring manager will see. The bullet points for the student work experience are brief and accurately summarize the skills. They could be improved by relating each of the skills to the experiences.
Resumé 2	The second example shows a more skill-based approach to a resumé than the standard format. While some employers might not like the use of colour, it was the candidate's attempt to visually stand out from the pile. The format was also interesting by very briefly breaking skills into categories that they thought the reader would value, in "Technical" versus "Digital." It's important that such definitions used are ones that are understood in the industry where this author was searching for a position. The experience section clearly focuses on supporting the skills by briefly giving examples of what the author has done while working on other roles. Finally, the author chose to provide a simple QR code link to a portfolio online that could be a place to present more detail and examples of the actual results of work done.
Team Charter 1	This example of a team charter for a group of engineers outlines the goals of the project as well as the responsibilities each member must be accountable for. It also provides instructions on how the group will assess group members' performance and how they will dismiss a group member from the project.
Letter of Reference 1	This letter of reference was intended to assist a student in an application for a summer job. The letter refers to specific skills and examples that the author recalls, which always helps the reader to appreciate the strength of the recommendation. Letters of recommendation that only give vague praise are far less important than ones which are clearly personal and cite specific qualities that the author believes relate to the specific job.
Letter of Reference 2	This letter of reference was intended to assist a student in an application for a scholarship. The letter relates a specific example to highlight the qualities of the student. Just as with the previous example, the letter is best received if it is clearly detailed and specific.

Glossary

abbreviation. A short form of a word, often consisting of the word's initial letters and a period; *eng.* is a typical abbreviation of *engineering*.

abstract. A comprehensive summary (50–250 words) accompanying a formal report, proposal, or paper and outlining its contents. As an adjective, **abstract** describes something theoretical or intangible rather than concrete.

acronym. A pronounceable word made up of the first letters of the words in a phrase or name: e.g., *SAW* (*surface acoustic wave*). A group of initial letters that are pronounced separately is an initialism: e.g., *GPS, UHF*.

active voice. See **voice**.

adjective. A word that modifies or describes a noun or pronoun: e.g., *cloudy, new, legal*. An adjective phrase or clause is a group of words modifying a noun or pronoun: e.g., *the results that are expected*.

adverb. A word that modifies or qualifies a verb, adjective, or adverb, often answering a question such as *how? why? when?* or *where?*: e.g., *slowly, absolutely, soon, there*. An adverb phrase or clause is a group of words functioning like an adverb: e.g., *in the lab, if X is valid*. (See also **transitional adverb**.)

agreement. Consistency in tense, number, or person between related parts in a sentence: e.g., between subject and verb, or noun and related pronouns.

ambiguity. Vague or equivocal language with meaning that can be taken two or more ways.

analysis. A structured approach to thinking, or the results of thinking in a structured way.

annotation. A note added to a graphic or to a text to provide further details. An **annotated bibliography** is a type of bibliography that includes a few sentences or a paragraph beneath the citation to explain the main arguments of the source, as well as its relevance to the current work.

antecedent (or **referent**). The noun for which a following pronoun stands: e.g., *engineers* in *Engineers are experts in their fields*.

antonym. A word with the opposite dictionary meaning as another word: e.g., *sad* and *happy*. (See also **synonym**.)

appendix. A section added at the end of a work to include material not essential to the main discussion but complementary to it.

archival material. Information, records, or data that is useful in orienting the reader or providing them additional information. This material is not included in the main body of the proposal or report but in the front matter, end matter, or appendix sections.

article. A word introducing a noun that identifies whether the noun is general or specific, singular or plural. *A* and *an* are called **indefinite articles**; *the* is a **definite article**. (See also **determiner**.)

backgrounder. A brief article, report, or memo that provides detailed context of an issue or project, or that summarizes a report or proposal for someone unable to read the full work.

bias. Showing a strong feeling or prejudice towards one person, group, or thing in comparison to another, often not based on fair judgement or appropriate data.

bibliography. A list of works used or referred to in writing a paper or report.

caption. A short, descriptive text that provides explanation for a graphic.

case. Any of the inflected forms of a personal pronoun

    Subjective case: *I, we, you, he, she, it, they, who*.
    Objective case: me, us, you, him, her, it, them, whom.

Possessive adjective case: my, our, your, his, her, its, their, whose.

Possessive noun case: mine, ours, yours, his, hers, its, theirs, whose.

chromatography. A laboratory technique for separating components of mixtures. The mixture is passed through a material that causes the components to travel through it at different rates.

chronology. A list of events in the order they occurred.

clause. A group of words containing a subject and a predicate. An **independent clause** can stand by itself as a complete sentence: e.g., *The solution remained stable*. A **subordinate** (or **dependent**) **clause** cannot stand by itself but must be connected to an **independent clause**: e.g., *Unless the temperature rises, the solution remains stable*. (App B)

cliché. A phrase or idea that has lost its impact through overuse: e.g., *beyond the shadow of a doubt; window of opportunity*.

collective noun. A noun that is singular in form but refers to a group: e.g., *family; team; staff*. It will take a verb that is either singular or plural, depending on whether it refers to the group as a whole or its individual members.

comma splice. See **run-on sentence**.

Computer Aided Design (CAD) rendering. A drawing created using a **CAD** program that converts three-dimensional models into two-dimensional images. Renderings show details like colour, material finish, and texture that are not visible in line drawings.

conclusion. The part of a paper or report in which the findings are pulled together or the implications revealed so that the reader has a sense of closure or completion.

concrete. Specific language that provides descriptive details: e.g., *grey crystalline deposits, rusted barbed wire, toxic waste*.

conjunction. A word used to link words, phrases, or clauses. A **coordinating conjunction** (*and, nor, but, or, yet*) links two equal (parallel) parts of a sentence (see **correlative conjunctions**). A **subordinating conjunction**, placed at the beginning of a subordinate clause, shows the logical dependence of that clause on another: e.g., (1) *Although the work is complete, it is unsatisfactory*. (2) *They ran several tests after they installed the software*. Do not confuse conjunctions with transitional (conjunctive) adverbs.

connotation. The range of ideas or meanings suggested by a certain word in addition to its literal meaning. Apparent synonyms, such as *artificial* and *imitation* and *synthetic*, even *counterfeit*, have differing connotations. (See **denotation**.)

context. The setting, background, or foundation for an investigation that helps establish its place in the larger scheme of things.

contraction. A word formed by combining and shortening two or more words: e.g., *isn't* from *is not; they'll* from *they will*. Contractions are appropriate in letters and casual messages, not in formal reports or academic writing.

coordinate axes or Cartesian axes. Two lines that intersect at the **origin** in a geometrical plane. These lines are fixed and perpendicular. Each axis represents a specific dimension.

coordinate systems. A method of specifying the location of points in space. The points are designated by their distance along a horizontal (x) axis and a vertical (y) axis from a reference point (**origin**). Coordinate systems form the basis of analytic geometry.

coordinating conjunction. See **conjunction**.

Cornell method. A note-taking system developed by Professor Walter Pauk of Cornell University that uses two columns and a bottom section to separate main notes, keywords or comments, and summary for easy review at a later date.

correlative conjunctions. Pairs of coordinating conjunctions that call for **parallel wording**: e.g., *either/or; neither/nor; not/but; not only/but (also)*.

cover letter. A letter that accompanies a job application that explains a candidate's credentials, skills, and interest in a position.

CubeSat. A miniature satellite used for space research that conforms to a standard size (1U or 10 × 10 × 10 cm). They can be extendable to larger sizes.

culture. The values and beliefs shared by a group of people, e.g., members of a profession, an organization, or a company.

Curriculum Vitae (CV). A detailed account of a person's education, previous experience, and qualifications that is often sent with an application for a job or other position. CVs can differ from a **resumé** in length and focus, with CVs providing a comprehensive list of credentials, research experience, publications, memberships, etc. rather than a focus on skills. CVs are not limited to one or two pages.

dangling modifier. A modifying word or phrase (often including a participle) that is not grammatically connected to any part of the sentence: e.g., *Examining the results, several discrepancies were noted.*

database. A collection of data and information that is organized so that it is easily accessible and searchable.

denotation. The literal or dictionary meaning of a word. (See **connotation**.)

derivation. The origin or development of something, usually a theory. In mathematics, the steps that show a conclusion follows from the initial assumptions.

design report. A report that provides details about the design and the design process of a project. Necessary sections include the problem definition, the design description, and the design analysis.

determiner. A word introducing a noun that identifies whether the noun is general or specific, countable or uncountable, singular or plural. All singular countable nouns must be introduced by a determiner. (See also **article**.)

diction. The choice of words with respect to their tone, degree of formality, or register. Formal diction is the language of research papers, reports, and legal contracts. Public presentations and business correspondence call for less

formal diction, but they are not as informal as the diction of everyday speech or conversational writing, which often includes slang.

digital object modifier (DOI). A unique alphanumeric string, assigned to works found online, that contains a prefix and a suffix separated by a slash (for example, 10.1037/0096-3445). Every article with a DOI is registered and can be easily identified and retrieved electronically, no matter whether the website where you found the article continues to exist.

discourse. Talk, either oral or written. **Direct discourse** (or **direct speech**) cites an actual quotation in its context: e.g., *Edison said, "There is no substitute for hard work."* In writing, direct discourse is put in quotation marks. **Indirect discourse** (or indirect speech) gives the gist of the quotation rather than a word-for-word citation. Quotation marks are not used, although the reference is documented: e.g., *Edison said that nothing could replace hard work.*

dynamics. The mechanics of motion and balance of bodies under force.

ellipsis points. Three spaced dots indicating an omission from a quoted passage [. . .].

endnote. A citation or note appearing at the end of a paper or a chapter in a book.

essay. A composition on any subject. Some essays are descriptive or narrative; in an academic setting, most are expository (explanatory) or persuasive.

executive summary. A short document that summarizes a longer report or proposal, clarifying key findings and conclusions. It allows the reader to understand what is in the report or proposal without having to read it all.

explanatory prose. Writing that explains or elaborates on a subject.

footnote. A citation or note appearing at the bottom of the page in a paper or an article.

Gantt chart. A system of coordinating multiple tasks along a timeline that allows managers to visualize all related activities at once.

gerund. A **verbal** marked by its *-ing* ending and functioning as a noun in a sentence: e.g., *We look forward to interviewing the candidate.*

grammar. The study of the forms and relations of words and of the rules governing their use in speech and writing.

hyperbole. An exaggerated statement or way of speaking, usually to make something sound more exciting or dramatic than it really is.

hypothesis. A testable statement that indicates what an experimenter expects to find through his or her work.

idea map or mind map. A way of organizing thoughts and ideas graphically to show the connections between themes, topics, and sub topics. They begin with a main idea and then branch out to show the breakdown and intersection of sub-topics.

idiom. A phrase or style of writing that is particular to a group or culture; the meaning of the group of words does not necessarily correspond to the individual definitions of the words (e.g. *Don't cut corners*).

independent clause. See **clause**.

indirect discourse (or **indirect speech**). See **discourse**.

infinitive. A **verbal** made up of the root form of a verb usually introduced by the marker *to*: e.g., *to evaluate*. The base infinitive omits the *to*: e.g., *evaluate*.

initialization. Applying the necessary processes for the start of an operation; the starting configuration.

intellectual property. A work or an invention (including ideas, designs, projects, etc.) that is the result of someone's creativity and intellect. These works are protected by law to prevent others from copying them or claiming them as their own.

intensifier (or qualifier). A word that modifies and adds emphasis to another word or phrase: e.g., *very slowly*; *quite important*. Avoid adding such words to absolutes like *major* or *empty* or *complete*.

interrogative. Question words used in direct queries or in noun clauses: e.g., *what, who, how*.

intransitive verb. A verb that does not take a direct object: e.g., *fall, sleep, happen*.

introduction. A section at the start of a report or paper that tells the reader what will be discussed—and why.

ISBN number. An International Standard Book Number (ISBN) is a 10- or 13-digit numeric code that identifies the origin, language, title, edition, volume number, and publisher of a book.

italics. Slanting type represented in handwriting or typescript by underlining.

jargon. Technical terms when used unnecessarily or inappropriately: e.g., *resource recovery facility* for *incinerator*.

lab report. A report that describes and analyzes a laboratory experiment. Necessary sections include materials, hypothesis, procedure, and results.

learning management system. A software application used by a post-secondary institution to store and deliver educational content. Common ones include D2L, Canvas, Blackboard, and Moodle.

literature. In science, the articles, books, reports, research data, etc., that is created by professionals, academics, and business and government organizations that form the basis of future research and designs.

matrix. The mathematical representation in which data and equations are organized into rectangular arrays of numbers and variables.

meeting minutes. An official record of a meeting; detailed notes of key issues and conclusions discussed in a meeting that help to inform both attendees and non-attendees of the content of the meeting, decisions made, and action items still to be resolved after the meeting.

memo or memorandum. An official note sent to internal members of an organization. They are usually brief and are used to inform employees and co-workers of policies and procedures.

milestone. In proposals, a pre-set goal to achieve during a project. A collection of milestones makes a **phase**. Milestones are composed of **tasks**.

mnemonic. A pattern of letters, words, or ideas that act as a memory device; a technique for remembering.

modifier. A word or group of words that describes or limits the context of another element in the sentence.

morphology table. A table that shows the range of alternative design ideas attached to a particular function visually.

multi-variable plots. A graph that uses various dots to represent multiple variables to show the relationship among them simultaneously.

nomenclature. The system of naming of things; the name applied to something.

non-restrictive modifier. See **restrictive modifier.**

noun. An inflected part of speech naming a person, a place, a thing, an idea, or a feeling—and usually serving as subject, object, or complement. A common noun is a general term: e.g., *day, school, automobile*. A proper noun is a specific name signalled by an introductory capital letter: e.g., *Wednesday, Queen's University, Toyota*.

object. 1. A noun or pronoun (called the direct object) that completes the action of the verb: e.g., *He asked a question*. An indirect object is the person or thing receiving the direct object: e.g., *He asked her* [indirect object] *a question* [direct object]. 2. The noun or pronoun in a group of words beginning with a preposition: e.g., *between them; in the corner*.

objectivity. A position or stance taken without bias or prejudice. (Compare **subjectivity**.)

origin. The point where the *x*- and *y*-axis intersect (0,0).

outline. With regard to a paper, presentation, or report, a brief sketch of the main parts, to help in organizing them; a written plan.

paragraph. A set of sentences arranged logically to explain or describe an idea, event, or object; the start of a paragraph is marked either by an indentation or by double spacing.

parallel wording. Wording in which a series of items has a similar grammatical form: e.g., *The Egyptians, the Babylonians, and the Sumerians all had types of calendars*.

parameters. Constants whose values characterize aspects of a system when the system's behaviour is represented as a set of equations.

paraphrase. A restatement of a sentence or passage using different words from the original.

parentheses. Curved lines enclosing and setting off a passage ( ); not to be confused with square brackets [].

parenthetical element. A word or phrase inserted as an explanation or afterthought into a passage that is grammatically complete without it: e.g., *Fuzzy logic, in more than one sense, resembles human decision making*.

participle. A verbal that functions as a modifier. Participles can be either present, marked by an *-ing* ending (e.g., *being* or *having* or *taking*), or **past** (e.g., *taken*); they also exist in the passive: e.g., *being taken* or *having been taken*.

part of speech. Each of the major categories into which words are sorted according to grammatical function. Some grammarians consider only inflected words (nouns, verbs, adjectives, and adverbs); others include prepositions, pronouns, conjunctions, and interjections.

passive voice. See **voice**.

past participle. See **participle**.

patent. A legal mechanism by which a person or company who owns a patent can sue others who make, use, or sell the product or process without the permission of the patent owner.

person. In grammar, the three classes of personal pronouns referring to the person speaking (**first person:** *I, we*), the person(s) spoken to (**second person:** *you*), and the distant person(s) spoken about (**third person:** *he, she, it, they*).

personal pronouns. See **pronoun**.

phase. In proposals, a section of the overall plan that represents a stage in the project's development. A phase is composed of **milestones** and **tasks**. Projects will have multiple phases.

phrase. A set of words lacking a subject–predicate combination, typically forming part of a clause. The most common type is the **prepositional phrase**—a unit consisting of a preposition and an object: e.g., *Experiments were divided into three stages*.

physical principles. The theories, rules, or laws that govern why something works or happens.

physical sketch. A quick, rough representation that helps to visualize a design or concept. Often hand-drawn but can be computer-generated. It tries to capture physical dimensions and attributes.

plagiarism. The deliberate use of someone else's work or ideas without acknowledgement.

plural. Indicating two or more, specifically with numbers. Nouns, pronouns, and verbs all have plural forms. (Compare **singular**.)

possessive case. See **case**.

prefix. An element placed in front of the root form of a word to make a new word: e.g., *pro-, in-, sub-, anti-*. (Compare **suffix**.)

preposition. A short word or phrase heading a group of words representing an object; together, a preposition and its object make up a **prepositional phrase**: e.g., *under the time limit; because of the constraints*.

primary source. Direct or first-hand evidence or documentation, for example lab experiment results, statistical data, video recording, and speeches (See also **secondary source**).

process pathways. Other directions or routes that can be taken to reach a different state or result.

process. A series of actions or operations leading to a particular and usually desirable result.

project log or logbook. A record of a project that includes design ideas, notes, research, sketches, and results.

project proposal. A document used to put forward an idea for a project with a current or potential business partner. Necessary sections include timeline, equipment, and team members.

project report. A document that provides details on the status or the likelihood of success of a project. Necessary sections include executive summary or abstract and recommendations.

pronoun. A word that stands in as a noun. A **personal pronoun** stands for the name of a person: *I, you, she, he, it, we, they*. (See **person**.)

proof of authenticity. Evidence that supports a claim of **intellectual property** ownership.

proposal. A document that outlines a plan for a project. There are two types of proposals: solicited an unsolicited. A **solicited proposal** is a proposal that was submitted to reviewers because they asked for one (see **Request for Proposal (RFP)**). An **unsolicited proposal** is one submitted to reviewers unasked, usually because it's an innovative project.

public domain. A term applied to work that lacks copyright protection; permission for copying is not required, although everything should still be documented.

punctuation. A conventional system of signs and symbols (e.g., comma, period, semicolon) used to indicate stops or divisions in a sentence.

qualitative. Non-numerical data, i.e. appearance.

quotation. The recording or repeating of something someone has said or written, also a bid or an estimate of the cost of a project.

random error. Variations observed in a data set but not explicable in a study.

raw data. Data or information that has yet to be interpreted; primary source data.

redundancy. Unnecessary or ineffectual repetition: e.g., *join together; first and foremost*.

references. Sources consulted when preparing a paper or report.

referent. See **antecedent**.

reflexive pronoun. A pronoun ending with -*self* or -*selves* to echo or emphasize a preceding noun or pronoun: e.g., *The researchers congratulated themselves*.

relative clause. A clause introduced by a relative pronoun: e.g., *The approach that was taken was the most cost effective*.

relative pronoun. *Who, which, that, whose*, or *whom*, used to introduce an adjective clause: e.g., *the approach that was taken*.

relative scale. Dimensions that are determined based on a comparison with something else.

request for proposal (**RFP**). A formal invitation describing project requirements. The appropriate response to an RFP is a formal proposal outlining both how the respondent plans to meet the project requirements and the expected compensation for completing the project.

restrictive modifier. A phrase or clause that identifies or is essential to the meaning of a term: e.g., *They read the article that their professor had recommended*. It should not be set off by commas. A **non-restrictive modifier** is not needed for identification and is usually set off parenthetically with commas: e.g., *They read Jennings's article, which their professor had recommended*.

resumé. A document that showcases a person's skills, qualifications, education, and experience, usually submitted as part of a job application. It is usually 1 to 2 pages in length. (See also **Curriculum Vitae (CV)**)

run-on sentence. A sentence that goes beyond the point where it should have stopped. The term covers both the **comma splice** (two sentences incorrectly joined by a comma) and the fused sentence (two sentences incorrectly joined without any punctuation).

schematic or "process sketch." A graphical representation of elements used to show the relationship between components.

secondary source. An interpretation of an original source, for example review articles, books. (See also **primary source**).

sentence. A grammatical unit that includes both a subject and a predicate. The end of a sentence is marked by a period.

sentence fragment. A group of words lacking either a subject or a complete predicate; an incomplete sentence punctuated as a sentence.

simplification. What was done to make a task or process easier to do or accomplish that could affect the results if tested under different circumstances.

singular. Indicating only one, specifically with numbers. Nouns, pronouns, and verbs all have singular forms. (Compare **plural**.)

sketch. A simple graphical or visual representation, often drawn quickly, usually by hand.

slang. Colloquial speech inappropriate for academic or professional writing, often used in a special sense by a limited group: e.g., *clicks* for *kilometres per hour; loonie* for *$1 coin*.

spectrogram. A visual representation of a spectrum of frequencies that shows variations across time.

squinting modifier. A kind of misplaced modifier that could be connected to elements on either side, producing ambiguity: e.g., *Students who study often do well on exams*.

stacked spectra. A graphical representation that shows spectrum results under varying conditions.

state. The condition of something at a specified time.

statistically significant. The likelihood of a result being caused by something other than chance.

storyboard. A series of visual images that outline a project or plan; a division of a project into blocked parts to get a better visual sense of the whole.

subjectivity. A personal stance that is based on feelings or opinions and is not impartial or disinterested. (Compare **objectivity**.)

subordinate clause. See **clause**.

subordinating conjunction. See **conjunction**.

subordination. Making one clause dependent upon another. (See **clause.**)

suffix. An element added to the end of a word to form a derivative: e.g., *-tion, -ify, -ment, -ize, -ful.* (Compare **prefix.**)

suppressed zero. Changing the 0,0 origin in favour of a higher variable to condense information.

syllabus. A document outlining the schedule, topic coverage, resources needed, and important policies for a post-secondary course.

synonym. A word with the same dictionary meaning as another word: e.g., *begin* and *start.*

task. In proposals, a job or work that is needed to accomplish a goal or milestone. A milestone will be composed of multiple tasks. (See **phase** and **milestone.**)

team charter. A document created by a group of individuals working on a project that indicates goals, values, and policies that will govern the group for the duration of the project.

technical drawing. A detailed and exact drawing of an object, used most often in architecture or engineering. An example of a technical drawing is a blueprint. (Compare **sketch.**)

technical report. A report that outlines the process and results of technical or scientific research. Important sections include Observations and Analysis.

tense. A set of forms, often inflected, that are taken by a verb to indicate past, present, or future time (i.e., they *went,* it *goes,* we *will go*).

theme. A recurring or dominant idea.

theory. A set of general statements or abstract principles created to explain a set of facts or phenomena.

thesaurus. A dictionary grouping words with their synonyms and antonyms, used for locating a word with the most appropriate connotation.

transitional adverb. A word or phrase that shows the logical relation between sentences or parts of a sentence and thus helps to signal the change from one idea to another: e.g., *therefore, however, for example.*

transitive verb. A verb that takes an object: e.g., *heat, bring, finalize.* (Compare **intransitive verb.**)

treatise. A formal piece of writing that deals seriously with a subject.

trendline. A line on a graph that indicates the general direction the variables appear to follow.

uncertainty. A measurement used to represent the variability within data.

underlying assumption. The laws and theories that underpin an experiment or a design.

usage. The way in which a word or phrase is normally and correctly used; accepted practice.

variable. An element that can represent any one of a set of values. In an experiment, the **independent variable** is the one manipulated by the experimenter; the **dependent variable** is what the experimenter predicts will be affected by manipulations of the independent variable.

verb. That part of the predicate expressing an action, a process, a state, or a condition, telling what the subject is or does. Verbs are inflected to show **tense** (time). The principal parts of a verb are the basic forms from which all **tenses** are made: the **infinitive**, the present tense, the past tense, the present **participle** and the past participle.

verbal. A word that resembles a verb in form but does not function as one: a **participle**, a **gerund**, or an **infinitive**.

voice. The form of a verb that shows whether the subject acted (**active voice**) or was acted upon (**passive voice**): e.g., *They presented the award* (active). *The award was presented by them* (passive). Only **transitive** verbs (verbs taking objects) can be made passive.

waterfall plots. A graph that visualizes the way an initial value is affected by changing positive or negative values. The initial value is shown in a full column while the transitional values are shown as floating columns.

X–Y graph. A basic line graph that uses a vertical (*y*-axis) and horizontal (*x*-axis) to show the relationship between two factors.

Index